PRAISE FOR *LEADERSHIP PAIN*

Given the many leaders who are imploding right before our eyes, this is a timely discussion from a capable resource! I pray you'll give Dr. Chand's thoughts deep contemplation whether you are a leader or serve one!

—BISHOP T. D. JAKES, SR., *NEW YORK TIMES* BEST-SELLING AUTHOR, PASTOR, THE POTTER'S HOUSE OF DALLAS, INC., DALLAS, TEXAS

Leadership and pain are often inseparable. And every time my pain level rises I have to remind myself (this is what leaders do) to lead in and through pain. My friend Sam Chand helps us understand how to embrace—and more importantly, grow—during and through our pain.

—JOHN C. MAXWELL, *NEW YORK TIMES* BEST-SELLING AUTHOR AND SPEAKER

Every leadership journey is filled with ups and downs, both triumphs and pain. However, we waste our mistakes and disappointments when we fail to learn from them. When we lose sight of our goals and vision, we will miss the opportunity to change, grow and move forward into an increased leadership capacity and capability. Dr. Sam Chand has personally dealt with the highs and lows of leadership, and he has enabled countless others to do the same with equal measures of godly wisdom, humor, and intention. *Leadership Pain: The Classroom for Growth* will help you turn the pain of your past into the strength of your future.

—BRIAN HOUSTON, SENIOR PASTOR, HILLSONG CHURCH

Dr. Chand is one of the best teachers on leadership I've ever heard. His new book, *Leadership Pain,* brilliantly addresses one of the least talked about but most important qualities of the best leaders: the ability to endure pain. Dr. Chand's insight is both practical and inspirational. Every leader who wants to grow should read this book and apply what he teaches.

—CRAIG GROESCHEL, SENIOR PASTOR OF LIFECHURCH.TV., AUTHOR OF *FROM THIS DAY FORWARD: FIVE COMMITMENTS TO FAIL-PROOF YOUR MARRIAGE*

In *Leadership Pain: The Classroom for Growth,* Sam Chand pulls back the curtain to give a behind-the-scenes look at the process of navigating through the pain of leadership. His insights will help any leader successfully face the inevitable challenges that all leaders must face. Sam is a brilliant communicator, and this book is a must-read for anyone who wants to become a stronger, wiser, more compassionate leader.

—JENTEZEN FRANKLIN, SENIOR PASTOR, FREE CHAPEL, AUTHOR OF *NEW YORK TIMES* BEST-SELLER, *FASTING*

Read Sam Chand's work, *Leadership Pain*, and listen as he strikes chords that resonate to the depths of our souls. His books are not so much "success handbooks" as "reality checks." The finest leaders are those of us who learn to identify the various ways we seek to minimize, run from, or deny our pain. However, the experience of pain is the path to becoming truly real about our vulnerability, mortality, frailty, fallibility, vanity, and folly. Honesty is the only way to "grow through it." Dr. Chand helps us take steps toward the "victory" we will win—steps we especially need to take when we feel like failures. Thanks again, Sam!

—Pastor Jack Hayford, Chancellor, The King's University, Dallas/Los Angeles

It seems everyone writes about the "how to" of leadership, but finally, someone has written about the pain. Sam Chand's new book, *Leadership Pain,* is about the raw and painful reality of leading people and organizations. Every leader needs to read this book. In today's distracted and disrupted age, the stakes are too high for "feel good" leadership. We need leaders who know how to navigate difficult decisions, challenging situations, and complex issues. Buy this book, because you can't afford to miss this opportunity to learn from the best.

—Phil Cooke, Filmmaker, Media Consultant, and Author of *Unique: Telling Your Story in the Age of Brands and Social Media*

Dr. Chand has walked with us through grief, death of loved ones, and church leadership transitions. Through it all he consistently brought hope in the midst of pain, reminding us that there is purpose in pain. The pain made us better leaders. This book will give you hope and purpose in your journey as well!

—Judah and Chelsea Smith, Lead Pastors, The City Church, Seattle, Washington

Pain is unavoidable for anyone in leadership. When pressures and pain arrive, I have to remind myself that this is simply part of the call. It's never a reason for quitting. I don't know of anything worthwhile that is achieved without paying a price—the greater the price, the greater the prize. Pain has an amazing way of drawing out motivations that we would never have tapped otherwise, and this in turn catapults us further than we would ever have gone without the pain. Thanks to my friend Sam Chand for bringing us insight so we can grow through our pain.

—Pastor Phil Pringle, OAM, Founder and President of C3 Church Global, Pastor C3 Church, Oxford Falls, President Oxford Falls Grammar, Author and Artist

Every leader experiences pain, but suffering seems to be the unexplored dimension of leadership. Samuel Chand, a superb leadership coach, has produced a book that offers a practical understanding of the *whats* and *whys* of pain so leaders can grasp its significance and learn the lessons God wants to teach from it. I have admired

Chand as a leader; now I appreciate this major contribution he has made to the understanding of leadership anguish.

—MARK L. WILLIAMS, GENERAL OVERSEER, CHURCH OF GOD, CLEVELAND, TENNESSEE

Every leader faces heartbreaking challenges. These difficulties can cause us either to give up or to press on and grow! This magnificent book by my friend Dr. Sam Chand will give you a practical understanding of pain, pressure, and your potential. Read this book to have your perspective forever transformed.

—JOHN BEVERE, AUTHOR / MINISTER, MESSENGER INTERNATIONAL

Leadership is a topic that many people talk about but few understand with the depth, insight, and biblical wisdom of Dr. Samuel Chand. In *Leadership Pain*, Dr. Chand explores the important role that pain plays in the life of any leader, especially those of us in ministry, and how it can become a catalyst for growth. This book comforts and consoles as it inspires and empowers leaders to view life's inevitable struggles as divine growing pains.

—CHRIS HODGES, SENIOR PASTOR, CHURCH OF THE HIGHLANDS, AUTHOR OF *FRESH AIR* AND *FOUR CUPS*

Any world-class athlete will tell you that growth and endurance come through a lifelong experience of discipline and pain. As leaders we can learn from the habits of our athletic counterparts. In *Leadership Pain*, Sam Chand breaks down a daunting element of leadership—teaching us how to embrace and manage pain for our benefit and for the benefit of those around us. This is certainly a great book to put in the hands of your team!

—WAYNE ALCORN: NATIONAL PRESIDENT OF AUSTRALIAN CHRISTIAN CHURCHES: SENIOR PASTOR OF HOPE CENTRE INTERNATIONAL

Burnout is a symptom of disillusionment, and it can hit pastors just as hard as CEOs. Dr. Chand has a great reputation for helping some of the most respected leaders in the world push past discouragement and deal with change. *Leadership Pain* tells some of these stories and shows how to let God use our painful situations to take us to new levels in our leadership.

—STEVEN FURTICK; LEAD PASTOR, ELEVATION CHURCH AND NEW YORK TIMES BEST-SELLING AUTHOR OF *CRASH THE CHATTERBOX*, *GREATER*, AND *SUN STAND STILL*

All too often, Christian leaders see pain as the enemy and do everything they can to avoid it. According to Dr. Sam Chand, however, this is exactly the wrong approach. In this insightful new book, he shows that we need to see pain as our friend and embrace it, because we and the organizations we lead will only grow to the threshold of our pain.

—Dr. George O. Wood, General Superintendent, The General Council of the Assemblies of God

Having been in leadership for over thirty-five years and as Senior Pastor for well over twenty years, I cannot say enough about Sam Chand's book *Leadership Pain*. I wish I'd had this kind of insight years ago. In those years we seldom received insightful teaching on the reality of the pain of leading people. Jesus understood and taught the upside down nature of leadership more than 2000 years ago: the first will be last; and to gain power, we have to become the lowest servants. In the same way, to build God's kingdom and grow personally, we have to experience pain. That's God's design. Thank you, Sam, for telling it as it is and for giving us all the insight we need to use our pain and allow the change it brings so we can hold our promises with both hands, within the call and within the challenge.

—Paul de Jong, Senior Pastor, LIFE, Auckland, New Zealand

I don't think there is a more powerful and challenging leadership statement than this: "You'll only grow to the threshold of your pain." If you want to increase your leadership capacity, you must increase your pain tolerance. Stretching and growing are painful processes, but the results are always worth it.

—Christine Caine, Founder of The A21 Campaign

Leading in a time of rapid, unprecedented change in the 21st Century often produces a sense of loss. Like it or not, there is pain in the journey. My dear friend, Dr. Sam Chand, has once again brilliantly addressed this vital leadership issue with clarity, consistency, and conviction. Happy reading!

—Dr. Mark Chironna, Church on the Living Edge, Orlando, Florida

My longtime friend, Sam Chand, has accurately diagnosed the pain of leadership, and he has written a prescription and a hopeful prognosis! By sharing the diverse stories of other leaders who have endured pain and survived, his message will help overcome the feelings of isolation and futility, and it will bring comfort to hurting leaders. I am thrilled that Sam has provided such a relevant resource to leaders! This is an answer to prayer!

—Bishop Dale C. Bronner, D. Min., Author/Senior Pastor Word of Faith Family Worship Cathedral, Atlanta, Georgia

Dr. Chand has written possibly the most important book right now for Pastors and Leaders. All of us will go through pain as we lead our organizations. *Leadership Pain* will help you do it well and come out stronger than before.

—BENNY PEREZ, LEAD PASTOR OF THE CHURCH, LAS VEGAS, NEVADA

Sam Chand's book, *Leadership Pain: The Classroom for Growth*, is essential for every leader! We only wish we had read it 25 years ago when we pioneered our church. If you want to stop the bleeding, experience God's healing and relight your love for leading, this is the book you've been praying for—it could quite possibly add decades to your leadership!

—JEFF AND BETH JONES, SENIOR PASTORS, VALLEY FAMILY CHURCH, KALAMAZOO, MICHIGAN

Dr. Sam Chand observes that leaders can only rise to the level of their pain threshold. Pain affects everyone differently, though all experience it. In his book Dr. Chand expertly, systematically, thoughtfully, and caringly addresses the anguish of pain and the lessons we learn from it. Read this book, and you will be a better leader.

—BISHOP MICHAEL S. PITTS, FOUNDING PASTOR, CORNERSTONE CHURCH, OVERSEER, CORNERSTONE GLOBAL NETWORK

Dr. Chand is one of the most astute minds I know. With profound yet simple wisdom, he unpacks the complex issues of life and empowers you with the tools to succeed. This book is loaded with wisdom and personal experiences of some of the most powerful people. It lets the reader know: "You're not alone, and there's actually life after this." My greatest lesson from this book is that this undeniable pain is my indicator of growth. This is an *awesome book*, and at my church it will certainly be a *required read*!

—SMOKIE NORFUL, SENIOR PASTOR, VICTORY CATHEDRAL WORSHIP CENTER, GRAMMY AWARD WINNING SINGER AND SONGWRITER, CHICAGO, ILLINOIS

Life is joyful and life hurts. Although we delight in the times of wonder, our growth comes from the chapters of pain. My friend and fellow coach, Dr. Sam Chand, has spent a lifetime gathering intimate knowledge and developing personal insights from both suffering and winning. He has learned the value of pain and how to use its anguish to create transformation in daily life and ministry. Sam shares that wisdom in his extraordinary book, *Leadership Pain: The Classroom for Growth*. I recommend you read this book carefully. Examine it thoroughly, and learn from it. Don't suffer the pain and miss the message.

—DR. DAVE MARTIN, AMERICA'S #1 CHRISTIAN SUCCESS COACH AND AUTHOR OF TWELVE TRAITS OF THE GREATS

I have always said that different leaders should read different books. I was wrong. Every leader needs this book. Pain will come to every leader, and when it does, this book will be a sure and true help. Sam Chand is a sage voice of wisdom in a noisy world of buzz, and his wisdom here will sustain you during the hard times.

—WILLIAM VANDERBLOEMEN, PRESIDENT, THE VANDERBLOEMEN SEARCH GROUP, AUTHOR OF *NEXT: PASTORAL SUCCESSION THAT WORKS*

This book packs a punch. It speaks truth. Behind the humor and witty aphorisms lies a vein of inescapable truth that those who have been in leadership know all too well—leadership is painful. Pain is the leader's rite of passage. Every level of leadership growth comes with pain. Dr. Sam Chand challenges me. He is my sharpening iron. His genuineness. His questions. His intellect. His spirit. His testimony. He inspires me both in and out of the pulpit, to become a better person and leader. Allow him to inspire you too. *Leadership Pain* is a book for the journey. It is good medicine for every leader who's felt isolated, misunderstood, or betrayed. Here you'll find wisdom and strength as you pursue leadership growth and effectiveness. Read it before there's any pain. Rehearse it when there's pain. Recommend it after the pain.

—MENSA OTABIL, CHANCELLOR, CENTRAL UNIVERSITY, ACCRA, GHANA

Sam Chand has again touched the core of what leaders face in their daily lives. His insightful books always accurately address the core issues leaders face. In this book Sam describes the fact that pain is the companion of any leader who is initiating change and being a true influence. The commitment to solve problems and initiate change inevitably produces pain. The insights in this book, however, aren't just academic; Sam understands the emotional life of a leader. He guides leaders through the challenge of pain as part of their growth in leadership. He also explains the privilege of leadership and the fact that great destiny is always accompanied by great adversity. This book is an excellent tool for leaders who need to know how to navigate the challenges of their leadership world.

—ANDRE OLIVIER, SENIOR PASTOR, RIVERS CHURCH, SOUTH AFRICA AND AUTHOR OF *PAIN IS INEVITABLE, MISERY IS OPTIONAL* AND *PRINCIPLES FOR BUSINESS SUCCESS*

In over twenty-four years of ministry leadership, we have never read a book that so clearly communicates the need to identify and work through the pain of leadership. Having known Dr. Chand for fourteen years as a consultant for our ministry, we know firsthand that the wisdom he shares can catapult leaders into their next levels of greatness. We are so excited to be able to share this book with our church leadership and business owners connected to our ministry.

—BISHOP KIM W. BROWN AND ELDER VALERIE K. BROWN, MOUNT LEBANON BAPTIST CHURCH "THE MOUNT," K.W. BROWN INTERNATIONAL MINISTRIES, INC., CHESAPEAKE, VIRGINIA

LEADERSHIP
PAIN

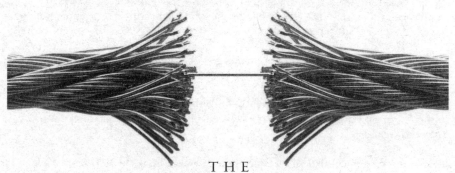

THE
CLASSROOM
FOR
GROWTH

Samuel R. Chand

THOMAS NELSON
Since 1798

NASHVILLE   MEXICO CITY   RIO DE JANEIRO

Published in Nashville, Tennessee, by Thomas Nelson. Thomas Nelson is a registered trademark of Thomas Nelson, Inc.

Thomas Nelson, Inc., titles may be purchased in bulk for educational, business, fund-raising, or sales promotional use. For information, please e-mail *SpecialMarkets@ ThomasNelson.com*.

Unless otherwise noted, all Scripture quotations are taken from The Holy Bible, New International Version®, NIV® Copyright © 1973, 1978, 1984, 2011 by Biblica, Inc.® Used by permission. All rights reserved worldwide.

Scripture quotations marked MSG are from *The Message*. Copyright © 1993, 1994, 1995, 1996, 2000, 2001, 2002. Used by permission of NavPress Publishing Group. All rights reserved.

Note: Some of the names and details in the stories in this book have been changed to protect anonymity.

Library of Congress Control Number: 2014952899

Hardcover: 978-0718-0315-9-6

e-Book: 978-0718-0316-1-9

Printed in the United States of America

20 21 LSCH 15 14

I couldn't possibly write a book on leadership pain without honoring Brenda, my wife and "pain partner" since 1979 and my best friend since 1973. Together we have been through the darkest times—leadership failures, poverty, deaths, marriage challenges, parenting, failed business ventures, people disappointment, betrayal, plans gone awry, and so many more.

Brenda is my bride, my best friend, the best mother and grandmother, and the wisest person I know.

All that I am has to be credited to the Lord and His gracious gift of Brenda. She has sat next to me every day in pain's classroom for growth.

About Leadership ❋ Network

Leadership Network fosters innovation movements that activate the church to greater impact. We help shape the conversations and practices of pacesetter churches in North America and around the world. The Leadership Network mind-set identifies church leaders with forward-thinking ideas—and helps them to catalyze those ideas resulting in movements that shape the church.

Together with HarperCollins Christian Publishing, the biggest name in Christian books, the NEXT imprint of Leadership Network moves ideas to implementation for leaders to take their ideas to form, substance, and reality. Placed in the hands of other church leaders, that reality begins spreading from one leader to the next . . . and to the next . . . and to the next, where that idea begins to flourish into a full-grown movement that creates a real, tangible impact in the world around it.

NEXT: A Leadership Network Resource committed to helping you grow your next idea.

leadnet.org/NEXT

CONTENTS

ACKNOWLEDGMENTS

Even though my name is on this book as the author, I couldn't have written it without the contribution of many teachers in my *classroom for growth*. I am indebted to each one.

My wife, Brenda, my daughters, Rachel and Debbie, Zack, my son-in-law, and my granddaughters, Adeline and Rose, are sources of great joy and comfort as I face the pains of life.

Many friends in ministry and the marketplace have confided their pains to me—teaching me that pain is every leader's classroom.

My writer, Pat Springle, eases my pain by taking my raw thoughts, piles of notes, and hours of recordings to create something cogent for me . . . and now, for you.

A number of gifted, wise, and tenacious mentors throughout the years have encouraged me to embrace my pains, persevere, and keep moving forward.

From all of them, I've learned—and I keep learning—that you will grow only to the threshold of your pain.

A LOOK INSIDE

Over the years, I've had the distinct privilege of working with some of the finest leaders in our nation and around the world. Many of them contacted me when they were at their lowest level, their wit's end, the end of their rope. I've watched these remarkable men and women encounter some of life's most difficult problems, and I've seen them learn life's most valuable lessons from their experiences with all kinds of pain.

I've asked a number of these people to write their stories, and I've included them at the beginning of each chapter. They offer a rare look inside the minds and hearts of some of the finest leaders on the planet. Don't skip over these stories. Read them carefully. You'll be amazed and inspired, and you might borrow some of their courage to face your painful situations.

1

LEADERSHIP LEPROSY

We must embrace pain and burn it as fuel for our journey.
—Kenji Miyazawa

Craig Groeschel, Founder and Senior Pastor of LifeChurch.tv, Edmond, Oklahoma

Before we started LifeChurch.tv back in 1996, one of my ministry role models told me that he had one and only one promise for me. I remember thinking that he was going to promise something encouraging like, "God would do more through me than I thought possible." Hanging on his every word, I waited eagerly for his promise of good news. Pausing, as if for dramatic effect, my mentor said slowly and soberly, "The only thing I can guarantee is that God is going to . . . break you."

Great.

That's not what I wanted to hear. But his words could not have been any more true.

Over the course of the next dozen or so months, God started to do a deep work in my soul. It wasn't a work resulting from time in his word or time in prayer. It was a work stemming from pain, heartache, disappointment, and betrayal.

So much of the pain we experienced as a church could have been spared if I had been a better leader. But at the young age of 28, I specialized in making easy things more difficult. For starters, I panicked and hired staff members I shouldn't have hired. Within a year, I had to replace almost every staff member I brought on, along with most of our key volunteers. If you have ever fired anyone, you know the pain of looking into the eyes of someone you care about and telling them that they can no longer be employed. I can't even remember how many tears I shed and how often I couldn't hold my dinner down because of the agony involved with removing people I loved from their ministry roles.

Another great blow came right after we launched our new small group ministry. With just over 100 people coming to our church, we were thrilled to start some groups to help people grow spiritually and develop deeper relationships with one another. One particular group exploded with growth to 30 or more people each week. The leader was a close friend of mine, but our theology differed in one important area. I asked him not to teach on that subject, but he continued to teach on that very topic week after week. Because I believed what he was teaching was dangerous, I pleaded with him to stop. He shocked me by saying he'd just take his group and start his own church. We weren't even one year old and experienced what resembled a church spilt. People chose sides. Many people got caught in the crossfire. And our small startup church hit an unexpected landmine that left me reeling. Losing the people that helped us start the church was a big blow. Losing the friendship was even more difficult.

But nothing compares to losing my mentor in ministry. To respect the family, I won't go into the details. There are parts of this story that no one knows but my friend, my wife, and me. And we will keep it that way as long as we live. My mentor and best friend was one of the most amazing men of God I knew. Unfortunately he struggled with depression, and he was tormented by the sins from his past. When I had to confront my hero over something he needed to deal with, the encounter went sour. After exploding at me, he charged out of the room and said things I'm sure he wished he hadn't said.

I assumed we'd have a chance to iron things out. But that chance never came. His wife called me days later in sheer panic explaining that she found her husband dead, hanging from a rope tied around a beam in his garage. A few days later, burdened by things I could never reveal about his struggles, I officiated the funeral of my best friend and mentor.

That event changed my life forever.

The promise that God would break me was true. I started out confident, bold, and full of faith. One year into our church plant I wondered how much longer I could continue. If leading a church was always going to be this difficult, I didn't know if I had what it took to be a pastor.

Some time later, I was at a pastor's conference, still spiritually bleeding from the recent wounds. Sitting on the second row, I cried all the way through a talk given by Dr. Sam Chand. He explained that the best leaders had to endure more pain. And many people could never have more influence because they didn't have a big enough leadership pain threshold. Dr. Chand explained, "If you are not hurting, you are not leading."

And that's when I started to learn the lessons I believe God wanted to teach me.

Here are a few of the things I believe God has shown me about pain.

- The longer I avoid a problem, the bigger it generally becomes. If I summon the courage to endure small amounts of pain and do what's right early, I will avoid larger doses of pain later.
- Pain is a part of progress. Anything that grows experiences some pain. If I avoid all pain, I'm avoiding growth.
- Often the difference between where I am and where God wants me to be is the pain I'm unwilling to endure. Doing what's right, no matter how difficult, is a rare trait in ministry. Most choose easy. We must choose right over easy.
- God is always faithful. Even when life is hard, God is always working for our good. Pain teaches us to depend on Him. It purifies our motives. It keeps us humble and moves us to pray.

Looking back at all the hard decisions, misunderstandings, false accusations, relationships gone sour, and heartbreaking losses, I'd never want to endure any of it again. And I know there's even more pain coming around the corner. But I'd never change what God does in me through these hard times. Because of what He's done in me, He can now do more through me. Today, I find myself thanking God for breaking me. Even though it's painful, the pain is worth the progress. And it's an honor to suffer in a very small way for the One who suffered and gave it all for us.

It's inevitable, inescapable. By its very nature, leadership produces change, and change—even wonderful growth and progress—always involves at least a measure of confusion, loss, and resistance. To put it the other way: leadership that doesn't produce pain is either in a short season of unusual blessing or it isn't really making a difference. So,

Growth = Change
Change = Loss
Loss = Pain

Thus,

Growth = Pain

When leaders in any field take the risk of moving individuals and organizations from one stage to another—from stagnation to effectiveness or from success to significance—they inevitably encounter confusion, passivity, and outright resistance from those they're trying to lead. It's entirely predictable. Any study of business leaders shows this pattern in the responses of team members. Pastors' teams and congregations are no exception. The long history of the church shows that God's people are, if anything, even *more* confused, *more* passive, and *more* resistant when their leaders point the way to fulfill God's purposes. Organizational guru Peter Drucker observed that the four most difficult jobs in America are, in no particular order: president of the United States, university president, hospital CEO, and pastor. (I've been in two of these roles: pastor and university president.) If you're a church leader and struggling in your role, you're in good company!

The public image of church leaders may be of gentle people who read most of the time when they aren't visiting people in the hospital. Certainly, reading and caring for the hurting and needy are important parts of spiritual leadership, but the public doesn't see the incredible complexity and persistent strains happening behind the scenes.

It Shouldn't Be a Surprise

The principles and practices in this book are addressed primarily to people who are in positions of leadership in ministries and nonprofit organizations. This includes pastors, staff members, and volunteer leaders. The stories and insights here, however, aren't limited to the realm of ministry. They apply to leaders in businesses and every other kind of organization. Every leader feels pain.

In fact, leadership—all leadership—is a magnet for pain, which comes in many forms. We catch flak for bad decisions because people blame us, and we get criticism even for good decisions because we've changed the beloved status quo. When people suffer a crisis, we care deeply for them instead of giving them simplistic answers (or blowing them off). We "carry their burden," which means at least some of the weight of their loss and heartache falls on us. We suffer when our plans don't materialize or our efforts fail, and we face unexpected new challenges when our plans succeed and we experience a spurt of growth. Along the way, we aren't immune to the ravages of betrayal by those we trusted, the envy of our friends, and burnout because we're simply exhausted from all the struggles of leading people—especially God's people.

> I am not a theologian or a scholar, but I am very aware of the fact that pain is necessary to all of us. In my own life, I think I can honestly say that out of the deepest pain has come the strongest conviction of the presence of God and the love of God.
>
> —Elisabeth Elliott

Some leaders feel shackled by past failures or past pains. Others look into an uncertain future and feel paralyzed. I've consulted with leaders whose churches and nonprofits have grown from a few hundred to several thousand, but they feel overwhelmed because they have no idea how to manage an organization of that size. A few of these leaders have difficulty articulating the vision God has put on their hearts. They can almost taste the future, but all they get are blank stares when they try to explain the direction God has given them. For most, the crush of financial worries is an almost constant strain. Merging new staff and volunteers with an existing team can make everyone feel confused. And sometimes a leader has to dig deep to find the courage to fire a friend. Misunderstanding, conflict, and all other types of stress come into our personal lives from our families, our staff and leadership teams, our church, and our communities. Sometimes, like Moses, we want to scream, "God, why have you given me these obstinate people?"

At a retreat for pastors who were considering leaving the ministry because they were burned out, the director asked, "Why did you enter the ministry years ago? What were your hopes, your aspirations, and your expectations?"

Of the dozen or so deeply discouraged pastors in the room, all but one remarked that they had an idealized view of ministry when they began. During the conversation it gradually dawned on one or two of them that their idealism had set them up for shattering disappointment. They had been surprised—shocked!—when they encountered difficulties in ministry and when God didn't resolve them neatly and quickly. One commented, "I was sure 'God's blessings' meant things would go smoothly and growth would happen naturally. Maybe if I'd realized difficulties are part of God's curriculum, I wouldn't have been so devastated." His eyes widened as the insight hit him. "And the heartaches that have shattered me would have been God's tools to shape me and my church. Oh, man, I missed it. I really missed it."

At conferences, round tables, and consultations, I've talked to many Christian leaders who were not idealistic at the beginning of their ministries, but they certainly didn't expect the level of conflict, discouragement, and struggle they endured as they were "doing God's work in God's way." They were blindsided by the pain, and many of them assumed something was terribly wrong with God or with them because the pain didn't quickly go away. Their solution was to do anything and everything to stop the pain.

They didn't realize this was exactly the wrong response. Numbness isn't a viable answer. In fact, it always compounds the problems. It's what I call "leadership leprosy."

Nerve Endings

In her book *On Death and Dying*, Elisabeth Kübler-Ross observed the progression of dying patients as they faced the ravages of their disease. She noted they went through definable stages of grief: denial, anger, bargaining, grief (or sadness), and acceptance.[1] Others observed that people pass through these stages in any kind of significant loss. Leaders experience them too.

When the reality of pain strikes, the first response is often, "This can't be happening!" That's denial.

Then, when the leader can't ignore the painful truth, anger surfaces—at the cause, at himself, at God, or at anyone else who comes to mind.

A natural and normal reaction to blunt the pain is bargaining. The person instinctively tries to make a deal. "What can I do to get rid of the pain and go back to normal?" It seems like a perfectly valid question, but it is more of an escape than the courage to face the hard facts.

Slowly, gradually, the person gives up on making some kind of deal to get out of the pain. The loss takes shape. It's almost palpable. And profound sadness fills the heart. This stage may look and feel a lot like depression, but there's a light at the end of the tunnel.

Sooner or later the person experiences renewed hope. New insights—ones that couldn't have been learned any other way—become treasures found in the darkness. The person now has more compassion, deeper joy, and more love to share with others.

The stages of grief aren't linear. People can go forward and backward in deeper cycles of pain realization. It's messy and ugly, but it's essential if people are to make peace with their pain.

The normal human response to pain is to do anything except face it. We *minimize* the problem ("Oh, it's not really that bad"), *excuse* those who have hurt us ("She didn't really mean it"), or *deny* it even happened ("What conflict? What betrayal? What hurt? I don't know what you're talking about!").

> Pain is no evil, unless it conquers us.
>
> —Charles Kingsley

But pain isn't the enemy. The inability or unwillingness to face pain is a far greater danger. I grew up in India where I saw thousands of lepers. They are often missing noses, ears, fingers, and toes—but not because their flesh rots away. (That's a common misconception.) Various body parts become severely damaged because they don't sense the warning signs of pain to stay away from dangers. Dr. Paul Brand worked with lepers in India and the United States. In *The Gift of Pain*, coauthored by Philip Yancey, Brand tells the story of four-year-old Tanya. When her mother brought Tanya to the national leprosy hospital in Carville, Louisiana, Dr. Brand immediately noticed the little girl appeared totally calm as he removed her bloodstained bandages and examined her dislocated ankle. As the doctor gently moved her foot to assess the extent of the damage, Tanya appeared bored. She felt no pain at all.

Her mother explained that she first realized Tanya's problem when she was only eighteen months old. She had left her daughter in a playpen for a few minutes. When she returned, she saw Tanya finger painting with large red swirls on the sheet. She hadn't remembered giving her daughter any paint. When she got closer, she screamed in horror. Tanya had bitten off the end of her finger and was using her blood as paint! When her mother screamed, the little girl looked up with "streaks of blood on her teeth."

Tanya suffered from a rare genetic malady called congenital indifference to pain, a condition very similar to leprosy. In every other way, she was a healthy little girl, but she felt no pain at all. Seven years later, Tanya's mother called Dr. Brand to tell him that the little girl had lost both legs to amputation as well as most of her fingers. Her elbows were constantly dislocated, and she suffered sepsis from ulcers on her hands and leg stumps. She had chewed her tongue so badly that it was swollen and lacerated.

Years earlier, Tanya's father left because he couldn't handle the stress of raising her—he had called her "a monster." Dr. Brand observed, "Tanya was no monster, only an extreme example—a human metaphor, really—of life without pain."[2]

Leprosy can be contagious, but Dr. Brand assured his colleagues at the hospital they were in no danger. Then, one night after a flight from America to London, Dr. Brand went to his hotel and began to undress for bed. When he took off one of his shoes, he realized he had no sensation in his foot. The numbness terrified him! He found a pin and stuck it into the skin below his ankle. Nothing. He pushed it deeper into his flesh. This time some blood appeared, but still he felt no pain.

All night Dr. Brand lay in bed with his mind racing to imagine his new life as a leper. How would it affect his personal life? Would he have to leave his family and live in a colony so they didn't catch it? What assurance could he now give his staff that they, too, wouldn't contract the disease?

The next morning, as the day dawned, Dr. Brand picked up a pin and stuck it into his ankle. This time he yelled. *It hurt!* From that day forward, whenever he felt discomfort from a cut, nausea, or anything else, he responded with genuine gratitude, "Thank God for pain!"[3]

Fresh Eyes, Open Hearts

Tanya and millions of others without the capacity to feel pain endure a severe, involuntary handicap, but the rest of us often *choose* to be numb and suffer the consequences. Many leaders think they have to put on a happy face (or at least a stoic face) for the people in their organizations, so they refuse to admit their discouragement, disappointment, and disillusionment— even to themselves—or they try to delay their pain. They tell their worried (and maybe angry) spouse, "As soon as the building campaign is over, the new music program is in place, the new staff member is hired, or some other benchmark is achieved, I can slow down and the stress will subside." For pastors and all other leaders, ignoring pain is leadership leprosy. It may promise the short-term gain of avoiding discomfort, but it has devastating long-term consequences.

> Pain is meant to wake us up. People try to hide their pain. But they're wrong. Pain is something to carry, like a radio. You feel your strength in the experience of pain. It's all in how you carry it. That's what matters. Pain is a feeling. Your feelings are a part of you. Your own reality. If you feel ashamed of them, and hide them, you're letting society destroy your reality. You should stand up for your right to feel your pain.
>
> —Jim Morrison, *Nobody Gets Out of Here Alive*

Paradoxically, Christians often have more difficulty handling personal pain than unbelievers. They look at the promises of God and conclude that God should fill their lives with joy, love, support, and success. That's reading the Bible selectively. The Scriptures state—clearly and often—that enduring pain is one of the ways, perhaps the main way, God works his grace deeply into our lives.

For church leaders, pain is pervasive and persistent. People who are involved in any form of church leadership, and especially pastors, see more of the underbelly of life than members of any other profession. Insurance agents see those who come to them for protection against loss; bankers and mortgage brokers see people who have financial needs; doctors treat physical problems; and mechanics look under the car hood—none of them look into people's heart like a pastor does. None of these people see people at the apogee and perigee of their lives—times of greatest celebrations, like weddings and births, and times of deepest loss, like divorce, disease, and death.

Pastors are exposed to the highest hopes and the deepest wounds of those in their care. And it's not temporary; it's from the womb to the tomb.

One of my friends laughed as he told me that pastors are present in the three most critical events of a person's life: hatch, match, and dispatch. The pastor is there when a baby is born and a mother dies. The pastor celebrates with a couple when they move into a new home, and he comforts them when the mortgage company forecloses on that home. The pastor rejoices when people are promoted at work, and he grieves with them when they're unemployed. The pastor is thrilled with parents when their children win awards and scholarships, and he goes to jail with them when they have to post bail for wayward kids. He's full of hope as people stand at the altar and say, "I do," and he weeps with them when they growl, "I quit." Pastors are exposed to the dreams and dreads of people at every stage of life. In the span of an hour, a pastor may receive several glowing reports and as many messages about tragedies. This role in the lives of families is an incredible honor, but it produces tremendous pressure and often excruciating vicarious pain. If they aren't careful, the cumulative pain can crush the life out of them—figuratively and literally.

Making Friends with Pain

We need a fresh perspective. We need to make friends with our pain. In a recent op-ed article for the *New York Times*, columnist David Brooks offered a surprisingly biblical view of the power of pain. He observeed that Americans are obsessed with the pursuit of happiness, but they often feel empty, alone, and without meaning. He noted, "People shoot for happiness but feel formed through suffering. . . . Happiness wants you to think about maximizing your benefits. Difficulty and suffering send you on a different course." Brooks shares this insight: "The right response to this sort of pain is not pleasure. It's holiness . . . placing the hard experiences in a moral context and trying to redeem something bad by turning it into something sacred." In the process, we may not come out healed; we come out different.[4]

Church leaders can look to those outside the family of faith for good examples of those who have been transformed by the experience of pain. When Lou Gerstner became the chairman and CEO of IBM in 1993, the company was in trouble. During his first meeting, the leadership team discussed IBM's strategy. When that eight-hour meeting was over, Gerstner said he didn't understand a thing; it was as though the other leaders spoke a different language.

That meeting, as painful as it was, revealed to him exactly what he was up against in making the company profitable. Eventually, he had to transform IBM's powerful culture, a culture that made it both famous and successful in the 1960s and '70s. Imagine being a company outsider and having to transform an icon like IBM. How did he do it?

Gerstner made friends with his pain. He embraced the pain of transforming the entire IBM culture, the pain of centralizing what had become a very individualistic operation, and the pain of making hamburger out of the company's sacred cows—operational processes that were considered standard operating procedure before he arrived. By embracing these pains, he turned IBM around.

Athletes often play while they are hurting. They know they have to make friends with their pain. An NFL lineman says that playing football is like "being in a car wreck every day."[5] Why do they continue doing it? Because they love playing, and they understand that their aches and pains are the price they must pay to stay on a team and compete on the field.

Embracing your pain is never easy. All leaders must bear the pain of criticism. You can't be a leader and avoid being criticized. Everything the president of the United States says and does is intensely scrutinized by Republicans *and* Democrats. Every Sunday morning talk show dissects the chief executive's policies and actions. It takes thick skin to be the president.

A few years ago when Camilla Parker Bowles, the Duchess of Cornwall, visited America with Charles, the Prince of Wales, the media criticized her for what she wore and what she didn't wear. They wrote about how many changes of clothes she brought for an eight-day visit. Imagine being Camilla and reading an article that said she looked "frumpy." That's painful. But if you want to be a princess or a president—or hold any kind of leadership office—that's what you have to handle.

Making friends with your pain is part of leadership. Our pains tell us we're moving in the right direction. New pains will always be a part of your life as you continue climbing the ladder to your destiny.

There are, of course, many sources of pain. Some of these are self-inflicted and should be avoided or resolved as quickly as possible. But other kinds of heartache can't be avoided if we're committed to being strong, caring, visionary leaders who make a difference in the lives of individuals and communities. Pain isn't an intrusion into the lives of spiritual leaders; it's an essential element in shaping the leader's life. New Testament scholar N. T. Wright observed that God accomplishes his purposes through pain. In his explanation of how the early church faced pain, he noted:

> Early Christians understood their vocation as Jesus' followers to include . . .
> their own suffering, misunderstanding, and likely death. . . . The suffer-
> ing of Jesus' followers is . . . not just the inevitable accompaniment to the
> accomplishing of the divine purpose, but actually itself part of the *means*
> by which that purpose is fulfilled.[6]

In the early centuries of the Christian church, the church experienced explosive growth. But this wasn't an enlightened age for believers. They suffered incredible torture at the hands of the Roman Empire. Christians were drawn and quartered, put on stakes and set on fire, torn to pieces by wild animals, and tortured with holes bored into their heads in which hot lead was poured in—and then they experienced the devastating effects of two massive plagues. Through it all, people saw something they'd never seen before: hope, faith, and love. And millions were drawn to Christ.

In *Reaching for the Invisible God*, author Philip Yancey related his discovery that Basil of Caesarea's faith was called "ambidextrous" because he held God's blessings in his right hand and life's difficulties in his left, trusting God to use both to accomplish his divine purposes in and through him.[7] All of us need ambidextrous faith.

Your Call

Do you want to be a better leader? Raise the threshold of your pain. Do you want your church to grow? Do you want your business to reach higher goals? Reluctance to face pain is your greatest limitation. There is no growth without change, no change without loss, and no loss without pain.

You'll grow only to the threshold of your pain.

If you're not hurting, you're not leading. Your vision for the future has to be big enough to propel you to face the heartaches and struggles you'll find along the way.

But this book is not a theological treatise on pain. There are several excellent books I recommend to give people a biblical analysis of pain.[8] My purpose is to provide a concrete, practical understanding of the pain we experience so we interpret it more accurately and learn the lessons God has in it for us. If we see pain as only an unwelcome intruder, we'll fail to ask the right questions, and our heartache will be wasted. In these pages, we'll avoid (like the plague!) simplistic answers to life's hardest questions. This is a ruthlessly honest and very practical book. We'll examine the principles and practices that make our pain a means of fulfilling God's divine purposes for us, our churches, and our communities.

My father was a pastor, and I've been a pastor. I consult with pastors and CEOs every day, and I speak at leadership conferences. If you're a church leader, I'm one of you. I understand your hopes and hurts because I've been there, and I'm still there every day. When I began consulting with leaders, I asked God for two gifts: detached concern and favor. I get calls from some of the top leaders in the world. They are the CEOs/lead leaders/ senior pastors of their churches. They don't call me because they want to hear interesting stories or pass the time because they're bored. They call me because they're in pain and they want some answers. I have to convince them that the remedy will cause more pain before they sense any relief. To get stronger, they have to go deeper. Why? Because like a patient in surgery, you have to be willing to feel worse before you can feel better. This book is about what I've learned about the pain of leadership. And these lessons never come easily.

> Occasionally we talk about our Christianity as something that solves problems, and there is a sense in which it does. Long before it does so, however, it increases both the number and the intensity of the problems. Even our intellectual questions are increased by the acceptance of a strong religious faith. . . . If a man wishes to avoid the disturbing effect of paradoxes, the best advice is for him to leave the Christian faith alone.
>
> —Elton Trueblood, *The Incendiary Fellowship*

I came to the United States from India in 1973. I was twenty years old and looking for a better life. Bob and Vivian Steinbough lived in Pasadena, California, and they sponsored my college education at Beulah Heights Bible College[9] in Atlanta. They sent a check every month to the college to pay for my expenses: tuition, lodging, food, books, and some incidental expenses. One year later, the Organization of the Petroleum Exporting Countries (OPEC) severely reduced gas supplies to the United States. Lines at gas stations circled blocks, interest rates skyrocketed, inflation climbed to double digits, and the nation suffered a severe financial recession. During this difficult time, Bob Steinbough lost his job, and I lost the checks he and Vivian had been sending to the college.

The nation was in crisis, and *I* was in crisis. I had to find a way to make some money, so I knocked on doors up and down Berne Street, near the college. I asked people if they would let me mow yards, rake leaves, or sweep sidewalks. I was willing to do anything. Time after time, the residents must have thought a young man from India looked very out of place in southeast Atlanta. They shook their heads and told me to leave. But then I offered, "I'll do it for free."

This intrigued some of them. They invariably asked, "Then what do you want from me?"

I answered, "When I'm finished, you can make me a peanut butter and jelly sandwich. That's all."

A few of them took me up on my offer, but it wasn't enough to stave off hunger. About a half mile from the college was Simpson's Grocery Store. Desperate times call for creatively desperate measures. I went to the store and asked to speak to the manager. I asked him, "Do you ever throw food away?"

He looked a bit puzzled, but by then I was looking pretty thin, so my question wasn't too hard to understand. He nodded, "Yes, of course, almost every day. We can't sell any food past the expiration date."

I asked, "Have you heard about all the hungry children in India?"

"Yes," he looked at me with a curious smile.

"Well, a hungry Indian is here!"

For many months I went to the grocery store to see the manager. He couldn't actually give me the food he was going to throw out, but he packed it and carefully dropped it into the six-foot-high commercial Dumpster in the back of the store. I had to wait until he went back inside the store, and then I jumped into the Dumpster, picked out the food, threw it out, and then climbed out. He discovered I could use frozen foods, especially pizzas and bags of vegetables, but he also let me know when there were fruits—bananas, apples, and oranges—that were too ripe to sell but not too spoiled to eat.

For about a year, this grocery store manager was my lifeline for survival. Then a position opened for a janitor at the college. I applied and got the job. Soon they also needed a breakfast cook and a dishwasher, and they gave me those jobs too. I was glad to have three part-time jobs—and now I had access to food every day. It was marvelous! Of course, I didn't get a paycheck. It was a barter arrangement. For my campus work, the college gave me tuition, books, and room and board.

When I told this story to a group of people, someone asked, "Why didn't you just go back to India?"

That's easy to answer. If I didn't have enough money for food, I certainly didn't have enough for a plane ticket to the other side of the world! I was so poor I didn't even have money to talk to my parents during those years. Long distance calls were very expensive.

Once, a friend asked, "When was the last time you talked to your parents?"

I thought for a few seconds and answered, "I've been here four years. I haven't talked to them at all during that time."

He gave me fifteen dollars so I could call my parents and talk for a few minutes.

When I called, my father answered. I said, "Hello, this is Sam!"

After a pause, he replied, "Sam who?" It had been so long he didn't recognize my voice.

I told him, "Sam, your son."

The rest of the family got on the phone, even though it was the middle of the night in India. We had a wonderful though very short conversation to catch up with each other.

Experiences shape perceptions. This period of poverty created a deep groove in my psyche that insisted, "Money gives people options, but I'm poor, so I don't have any options. I'll always be poor. It's my lot in life." I firmly believed I could only afford frozen pizzas. I could live only in the cheapest places. I can't have friends because everybody is ashamed of my poverty. Who would listen if I tried to say anything?

The pain of being poor made a dent that seemed irreparable, but gradually I began to reinterpret those excruciating years. I began to see I had options—plenty of options. My past didn't dictate my future. I had to learn to think more broadly, to imagine possibilities not limited by my experiences. Even in the darkest circumstances, we can uncover creative options. I called it *blue sky thinking*. It's not idealistic and irrational. Instead, it's infused with a powerful hope.

My Hope for You

In the chapters ahead we'll identify the main causes of leadership pain—the people, situations, and processes that make us bleed—and I'll offer some effective solutions to help you respond with wisdom, strength, and grace.

Let me give you a taste of the principles I want to impart to you. When you're bleeding:

- Understand and interpret your pain.
- Clarify the lesson you're learning.
- Spend time with leaders who have high pain thresholds.
- Take care of yourself—mentally, physically, spiritually, relationally.
- Always be aware of your internal temperature.
- Listen to your spouse (or best friend).
- Don't ask God to raise your pain threshold. He might just answer that prayer!

I've known many leaders whose potential hit a ceiling and stopped when they refused to break through their pain threshold. Some completely bailed out, but most settled for something less—often far less—than the grand design God had for them. Their pain threshold became their ceiling. My hope for you is that you'll acquire the heart, perspective, and skills to continually raise your pain threshold. In the principles and stories in this book I hope you'll find the courage to do three things:

1. **See pain as your greatest teacher.** Don't avoid it. Don't minimize it. And don't numb yourself to it. Pain never just goes away. When it's not resolved, it sinks deep into our minds, creates anxiety in our hearts, causes resentment and depression, and creates tension in our relationships. As the old motor oil ad said, "Pay me now or pay me later." Face pain sooner and you'll learn important lessons about

God, about yourself, and how to help others grow as they encounter difficulties. Face it later with devastating results.

2. **Let your vision drive you.** Keep the vision fresh and strong. Don't let your mind be consumed by your immediate pain and obvious limitations. When you interpret your pain as bigger—more important, more threatening, more comprehensive—than your vision, you'll redefine your vision down to the threshold of your pain. Focus on the big picture and let your anticipated legacy give you the courage you need to face each day's troubles. Your vision will continually renew your hope, restore your courage, and refresh your perspective. It will enable you to pay the price to face the pain and take the next step forward.

3. **Have a rigorous personal development plan.** If you have a plan to grow spiritually, relationally, and professionally, you'll incorporate difficulties into the learning process. Don't coast. Read the best authors, spend time with courageous leaders, and craft a plan to sharpen your skills. At many points you'll bump up against various obstacles—internally and externally, real and perceived. As you face each of them with courage, you'll raise your pain threshold and you'll become a better leader. In the process, you'll see pain as your friend, not your enemy.

Without a fresh perspective about pain, a compelling vision, and a clear plan, every heartache has the potential to stop you in your tracks. A driving sense of destiny opens your eyes to the lessons you can learn from betrayal, crises, and failure.

In his book *The Healing Path*, psychologist Dan Allender described the spiritual perception we can have about painful events in our lives. He wrote:

If we fail to anticipate thoughtfully how we will respond to the harm of living in a fallen world, the pain may be for naught. It will either numb or destroy us rather than refine and even bless us. . . . Healing in this life is not the resolution of our past; it is the use of our past to draw us into deeper relationship with God and His purposes for our lives.[10]

To be a better leader, raise the pain threshold in your life. To accomplish this, you first need a firm grasp on the three kinds of difficulties you will encounter: external challenges, internal stresses, and growing pains. That's where we're going next.

At the end of each chapter, you'll find insights and exercises to help you apply the principles you've just encountered. Don't rush through these. There are no bonus points for speed. Take time to think, consider, remember, and pray. Trust God to speak to you and give you wisdom. If you use this book with a team or small group, use the questions for your discussions.

Know This

You'll grow only to the threshold of your pain. To grow more, raise your threshold.

Do This

Make a commitment to be ruthlessly honest with yourself, with God, and with at least one other person as you read this book.

Think About This

1. How would you define and describe leadership leprosy? What effects does it have on the leader and those who are following?
2. Do you agree or disagree with this statement: Leadership is a magnet for pain. Explain your answer.
3. What would it mean to you to have "ambidextrous faith"?
4. Can you think of a time when you let your pain reinterpret

(and lower) your vision? Describe the time when this happened? How do you wish you had responded?
5. Why are you reading this book? What do you hope to get out of it?

And remember: *you'll grow only to the threshold of your pain.*

2

EXTERNAL CHALLENGES

*Success is not measured by what you accomplish but by the
opposition you have encountered, and the courage with which
you have maintained the struggle against overwhelming odds.*
—Orison Swett Marden

Benny Perez, Lead Pastor of The
Church, Las Vegas, Nevada

Many cities in the country suffered a real estate crisis when the
recession began in 2008. Las Vegas was hit especially hard. Six
years before that time, we had begun our church with 27 people
in the living room of our house, and it had grown to 2500 every
weekend. We were so excited about what God was doing, and
we bought some land so we could build our church. When the
crisis hit and real estate valuations dropped, our bank asked for
a meeting. I knew it wasn't going to be a social call. The bank
officer told us that we had to come up with $900,000 to bring

our "loan to value" down to 75 percent. We took the money out of our savings for a new building, and we paid the bank. We were spared. At least, that's what we thought.

A year later, the real estate crisis in Las Vegas became a catastrophe. Property values fell off a cliff. The land we had purchased for $4.5 million was now worth only $800 thousand. On the land and building, we owed $8 million, but they were valued at only $2.4 million. We wanted to build because we were on a fast tract of growth. We posted it on our website that we were going to raise enough cash to build the Wendell E. Smith Auditorium. The bank called us and told us any money we raised we had to pay toward the debt. The bank had us backed into a corner—we couldn't grow the church. I was at a dead end.

I wondered how in the world all this could be happening. Such great things had happened at our church. God had poured out His blessings on us. Was it going to end here? I considered letting the bank have the land and the building, but I soon discovered they'd have a lien on any new facilities we might build. The bank turned our account over to a national "special assets division." I got a call from a bank officer in Florida who tried to intimidate me. Things had already gone from bad to worse; now it was nasty.

At the time, I didn't know anyone who could help me navigate these unknown waters. I felt helpless and alone, and to be honest, a wave of shame clouded my thinking. How could I have let this happen? I had trouble sleeping many nights, so I was exhausted during the day. My thoughts were preoccupied with our financial crisis 24/7. When I was at the church, I was thinking about it. When I was at home, I couldn't get my mind off it. When our family was on vacation, I thought about it constantly. I wanted to find someone to help me carry the burden, but there was no one. My staff, our church, and my family—as well as the bank—were looking to me for answers, but I had none.

We kept on worshipping and leading programs. That was our mission, and that was our joy, but behind the doors of our offices, I felt the crushing pressure of trying to hold the church together.

I often felt overwhelmed, but these heartaches turned into the most tender and intimate times with the Lord. The psalmists poured out their hearts to the Lord, and so did I. In the middle of the night when I couldn't sleep, I wept and prayed, "Why are you downcast, O my soul? Why so disturbed within me? Put your hope in God, for I will yet praise him, my Savior and my God" (Psalm 42:5).

Of course, all of this affected every part of my life, including my marriage. Wendy had always looked to me for answers, but now when she asked about the future, I had to admit, "I don't know." That was really hard. Wendy and I were already seeing a counselor. During this time, we started seeing her even more often. I may lose the land and the church, I concluded, but I wasn't going to lose my marriage.

A good friend came to town and asked to have lunch with me. He told me he had heard about our problems with the bank, and he gave me some excellent advice: "Hire the best attorney you can find." My friend referred me to a top law firm in his hometown, and after he made a couple of calls, I had a meeting with one of the best real estate lawyers in Las Vegas. When I explained our circumstances and the bank's demands, this Jewish attorney leaned back in his chair and said, "Pastor Perez, I just took my synagogue through the same situation. I know exactly what to do." It was like an angel had spoken to me! I finally found someone who understood.

The next conversation wasn't so positive. After he talked to the bank to try to come up with a solution, he called to tell me, "Pastor, I have bad news. They don't want to work out a deal, and it's worse: they're coming after you personally." I was heartbroken.

We had to declare Chapter 11 bankruptcy protection because the bank gave us no options. We endured months of depositions, audits, and endless conversations with attorneys. The bank hoped they'd find irregularities in our books, but all our finances were perfectly in order.

One day the attorney came to me and explained that the bank refused to budge, and they planned to sue me for any balance not covered by the sale of the church and land. He represented the church. He advised me to get another attorney to represent me personally.

Months later, the church's attorney came to meet with our executive team. He said, "It's over. We've lost. You need to stop paying me, and you need to move on."

I went home. I felt devastated. I couldn't even talk to Wendy except to say, "We lost." I cried and cried all night. The next morning, I told God, "Okay, God, I'm going to trust you. I don't know what that means, but I'm going to trust you."

Within 24 hours, the attorney called me again. He said, "Benny, you must believe in miracles, because it looks like you're going to get one. The bank is offering the church a deal." They offered to take an amount we would have gladly agreed to pay at any time during the long, grueling ordeal. We gladly accepted the deal.

We had 60 days to pay it off in full, but we only had about

a fourth of the money we needed. A few days later, I got a call from a total stranger in a foreign country. Somehow, he had heard about our situation. He asked for details, and I told him all about it. He said, "Let me talk to my wife. I'll call back in a few minutes." I could hardly wait for the phone to ring. When he called back, he offered to contribute a large sum of money and give an interest-free loan for the rest we needed to pay off the bank.

I shouted, screamed, and yelled praises to God. I was astonished, but the Lord whispered, "Son, I have people all over the world. I'm not limited by time, space, or culture." I trusted God a little, and He came through a lot. Amazing grace.

The most important lesson I learned through all this is the necessity of utter abandonment to the faithfulness, love, and purposes of God. I had talked about trusting God for many years, but now I had a new understanding of what it means to put everything into His hands.

I also learned to hire the very best professionals we can afford when we need them. Hiring the right attorney was very important. His expertise gave me a sense of peace. He was a gift from God.

During this painful season of testing, I reassured my staff and the people in our church that the mission of our church has never been about land or buildings, but about people. Hearts and souls matter more than any tangible thing. God was going to get us through it so that the people were protected and blessed—and He did.

My advice for pastors is to reach out to others who can help. The enemy tells you that you're alone, and shame can make you feel worthless and helpless. Find a friend or mentor or counselor who can walk with you through dark times. That person is worth more than gold. In fact, if your church is having financial troubles, call me. I'll be glad to help.

Mike Kai, Pastor, Inspire Church, Waipahu, Hawaii

Ministry is full of joy and sorrow, triumphs and heartaches. We love to see lives changed—thousands giving their lives to Jesus, many discovering their calling and becoming disciples of Jesus, lives restored, marriages healed, addictions overcome, and deliverance—but a very real enemy is also trying to thwart the work of God. The enemy of our souls, the adversary, would like nothing more than to bring discouragement and defeat into our lives.

My wife Lisa and I have learned that how we handle tough moments can determine important outcomes: will I become tender and stay tender, or could stress turn me into a tyrant? One of the core values that we share is an appropriate transparency with our church and our staff. The closer people are to us, the more transparent we become. We also expect others to be equally transparent with us.

Staff transitions can either be painful or pleasant. But even when we have the best intentions, the pain can still be intense. One of the most painful experiences I've had in the ministry was when a staff member who was very close to me began to turn on me. I didn't know it was happening at the time, but in retrospect, the signs were definitely there.

We were a smaller church then, about 500 to 700, and were still meeting in an elementary school cafeteria. We were making the big leap from the school to leasing something much larger and more expensive in a shopping center in Hawaii. We were neck deep in church expansion, fund raising, building renovation, and all the meetings and stresses that come with growth. It was an extremely busy time for me and the entire staff. We were all being stretched beyond our capacity.

I had been told that not everyone on our staff team would be able to make the adjustment and "cross over the Jordan River" into our new destiny. It made sense. Not everyone will stay with you on the journey, but I didn't know who would stay and who would go.

We had a very close staff team, but my responsibilities were changing. I couldn't show up at every celebration, every potluck, and every other event I had attended when we had a smaller congregation. Not only was the church changing; I was changing too. With added pressure and responsibility, my role expanded. I had to rearrange my priorities. I couldn't do all the things I'd done in the past, and this realization really hurt. It was *the pain of increased capacity.*

My new priorities really bothered a particular staff member. He began to share his frustration with three key members of my team. For months, I wasn't aware that they were complaining to one another about me. They went on night diving trips (that's big in Hawaii), but I was never invited. That hurt. I might have not been able to go, but I was never even asked. To make matters worse, these trips were the times when they complained about me. I was oblivious. They were going fishing, but they were having me for lunch!

Gradually, I noticed a change in demeanor by these three staff members. They were a little colder . . . a bit distant around me. I began to pick up on the changes. Then, after a staff hire I had made to help us manage the business side of things, one of the guys began to act in a peculiar way.

One day, I pulled him to the side to see what was going on with him. This conversation was the beginning of the Lord bringing things out into the light. It was a hard and frustrating conversation.

When our talk was over, I realized things were much worse than I could imagine. I dug a little deeper and realized that the ringleader of the discontented staff members had done all kinds of things (too many things to list) to sabotage my leadership. But the ringleader, the man I trusted most, was on vacation in California. I could've called him, confronted him, and fired him immediately, but I thought about his young kids. I didn't mind ruining his vacation, but I didn't want to ruin it for his children. The schedule, though, proved to be a problem. Before he was scheduled to come back, I was going to Australia for a conference. He would be back about four days before I returned. I decided to wait until I got back. In the meantime, I confronted the other two before I left for my trip.

My two weeks away in Australia were miserable. I hate to admit it, but I cried a few times, and Lisa consoled me. I had never experienced staff betrayal and a possible church split— the potential was there; he had won the hearts of a large part of the church.

I realized I had no option. I was going to fire him. That would be the first order of business when I got home. Toward the end of the trip, however, Lisa asked me a tough question: "Mike, have you done everything you could do to salvage him before you take the last step and fire him?"

I hated the question. I protested, "Of course there's more I could do, but does he truly deserve it?" Another week in Australia went by, and then we returned home.

As soon as I got back to the church, I had a meeting with the guy. Of course, by then he had heard that I uncovered the plot to undermine my leadership. The advanced warning gave him a few days to prepare for our conversation—and I knew he would be sweating it out until I returned.

Lisa's question prompted me to rethink my approach. "Doing everything" meant that I offered him two months to get his head together. Full pay, no strings attached. He graciously accepted. But within a few days, just a week before our opening of the new church, he had already began telling people, "I'm outa here and heading back to the mainland." Some of the leaders had heard him say this, and they came to me to tell me what they knew. I met with him once more, this time with some key elders, and released him.

By God's grace—and a lot of conversations to help everyone process the anatomy of what happened—we were able to save the relationship with the other two staff members.

This season was one of the hardest times I've ever experienced in ministry, but I learned to avoid reacting too quickly and to seek God's best at all times. The high road is often the road less traveled, but it becomes the pavement of God's grace and growth in our lives.

In the movie *Gladiator*, the noble Roman general Maximus Decimus Meridius leads his forces to victory over a barbaric Germanic tribe. Emperor Marcus Aurelius visits Maximus at the site of this victory and tells him that he plans to appoint the general as his successor and gives him the mission to lead the empire and delegate power to the senate. Aurelius's son, Commodus, discovers that his father plans to bypass him in the succession. In a fit of rage, he murders his father and declares himself emperor. Maximus becomes his adversary. To get rid of him, Commodus orders Maximus's execution and crucifies the general's family. Maximus, however, survives, but he becomes an outcast.

As a refugee, Maximus is captured by slave traders and sold to become a gladiator. Unlike any of the other fighters, he makes friends of those he may someday fight in the arena. Meanwhile, in Rome, Commodus sponsors gladiatorial games to, ironically, commemorate his father's death and celebrate his ascension to the throne. On one of the days of games, a group of gladiators is herded to the center of the arena as soldiers in chariots enter and encircle them as a reenactment of a great battle. But in a stunning reversal of expectations, Maximus orders those who will follow him to form ranks and defeat the charioteers. Maximus becomes the darling of the crowd . . . and even more hated by Commodus.

To get rid of his rival, Commodus orchestrates a one-sided fight. He pits Maximus against the undefeated Tigris of Gaul in an arena filled with tigers whose chains put their jaws and claws in reach of any misstep. During the fight, Maximus is severely wounded, but he keeps fighting. After a grueling duel, Maximus defeats Tigris. He turns to the crowd and the emperor for their decision to kill or spare his adversary. It is, as always, the emperor's decision. He turns his thumb down, but Maximus spares Tigris anyway. The crowds cheer and proclaim him to be Maximus the Merciful.

Commodus is infuriated. He decides to kill Maximus himself. The emperor lures him into personal combat, but before their public battle, he treacherously punctures the gladiator's lung. Maximus is weakened, but he fights and kills the emperor—with the emperor's own blade. Maximus the Merciful had to keep fighting even when he was wounded.

Truth is, everybody is going to hurt you; you just gotta find the ones worth suffering for.

—Bob Marley

Maximus is like many leaders I know: noble, misunderstood even when they have the best motives, attacked by those who should be applauding, deeply wounded, choosing mercy over revenge again and again, and staying in the fight until the end. Most of the leaders I know are regularly stabbed beneath their armor. They're cut, bleeding, and sore, but they don't give up.

As we lead organizations—businesses, nonprofits, and churches—size doesn't matter as much as another crucial factor. The biggest difference between leaders of large organizations and small organizations isn't their location, the size of their building, the scope of the vision, the number of staff members, or their talent. In fact, some of the best leaders I've ever met have small organizations. But in all my consulting and conferences, I've seen a single factor: leaders of larger organizations have proven they can handle more pain.

Devils All Around You!

There are many different external challenges for pastors, but resistance and personal animosity rank at the top. I was raised in a pastor's home, I've been a pastor, and I talk with pastors every day. The greatest heartache I hear from them is the pain inflicted by their friends. It doesn't take very many of these people to make our lives miserable. When I speak on this topic, I like to have a little fun. I tell the audience, "I know one thing about your church. I may have never set foot on your campus, but this one thing I know: at least 10 percent of your congregation are devils!"

It's not about going around trying to stir up trouble. As long as you're honest and you articulate what you believe to be true, somebody somewhere will become your enemy whether you like it or not.

—Criss Jami

They usually laugh at that point, but they understand exactly what I'm saying. Those 10 percent cause 90 percent of the headaches and heartaches. They not only resist change at all costs, they question the leader's integrity, wisdom, and authority. If they can't stop progress by open defiance, they go underground with vicious gossip campaigns. It doesn't take many of these people to spread the poison of doubt to every corner of a church!

After a pause to let this sink in, I ask, "So, if you have a church of one hundred people, how many devils are in your congregation?"

They yell, "Ten!"

"If you have a church of a thousand, how many devils are there?"

"A hundred!"

Sometimes I add, "If you have a church of ten thousand, how many devils are deeply committed to sabotaging everything you do?"

"A thousand!"

Now I can make my point:

If you can't handle ten devils, why would God trust you with a hundred or a thousand of them? If you and your church will grow only if you raise the threshold of your pain, the question is simple: How many devils can you handle? In other words, how many naysayers does it take to steal your joy, erode your enthusiasm, and consume your time so that you lose focus on your God-inspired vision? That number is the limit of your growth. Through Jeremiah the prophet, God asked his people, "If you have raced with men on foot and they have worn you out, how can you compete with horses?" (Jeremiah 12:5) Learn to run with the devils in your midst today, and God will reward you with many more to deal with!

I then tell them, "Remember: growth equals change; change equals loss; loss equals pain; so inevitably, growth equals pain. That's why leadership is both brutal and beautiful. It's *bleedership*! It's *brutiful*!"

If you're leading, you're bleeding.

Financial Strains

Some of the challenges pastors face come from public perceptions of their role. The vast majority of parishioners consider their pastors and staff members to be "on call" all day every day. This means pastors can never completely relax. One pastor was at a college football game with his wife and another couple when his cell phone rang. It was the wife of a man in his church. She explained that her husband had just died, and she expected the pastor to come to the hospital immediately. The stress of always being "on" puts pastors in the high-risk category for life insurance, similar to loggers but ahead of munitions workers.

Many people assume pastors spend most of their time playing golf and drinking coffee with friends in the church and the community. They don't have an accurate perception of the demanding administrative burdens coupled with the open-ended responsibilities to care for a troubled and needy group of people. According to a recent survey by the National Association of Church Business Administration, the average pastor in 2012 makes an annual salary of $28,000. One in five has to work a second job to support his family. The average teacher's salary is $42,000. These two professions, pastors and teachers, are the two lowest paid degreed professions in the country.

Of course the pastors who make the news are often megachurch pastors who make far more than this meager amount. In fact many church leaders struggle to make ends meet. Like teachers who bring home tests to grade and lessons to prepare, pastors spend untold time after hours preparing for meetings and messages, answering calls, and making visits. Many took out student loans to go to seminary, which is often one of the most expensive academic pursuits. After graduation, as a trained and degreed professional, they work long hours for meager pay. When the salary and actual hours are taken into account, many pastors make less per hour than those who work for lawn crews or at fast food restaurants.

We might assume the people who receive God's blessings from the pastor's teaching and compassionate care would want to provide adequate compensation, but that's often not the case. Many lay leaders, especially those from the older generations, assume the role of pastor necessarily involves suffering and sacrifice, including financial suffering and sacrifice.

Financial pressures don't always happen to the other guy. I know. I've been there. Not long after I took a position as pastor of a country church in Michigan, Brenda gave birth to Rachel, our firstborn. Soon, we discovered Rachel had a severe allergy to milk, so we had to buy a soy substitute—a very expensive substitute. My salary at the church in 1980 was $125 a week. (So don't complain about how little you make!) We were already living on the edge before Rachel was born. Now, the added expenses of a new baby and soy formula shot us over the cliff. We needed help. We decided to go to social services to apply for food stamps.

We lived in a small town. Distances weren't far, and everyone knew everyone else's business. The social services office was about three hundred yards from the church. We filled out the forms and soon we were called back for a meeting with a caseworker. When she walked in, she recognized me, smiled, and said, "How are you today, pastor?"

Suddenly she was embarrassed, and we were embarrassed. She looked at the forms we had filled out, and she asked a few more questions. Finally, she put the papers on the table and told us, "Pastor, you're making a little too much money to qualify for food stamps. I'm sorry."

I asked, "How much is too much?"

She winced, "Twenty-two dollars a month."

In those days, I didn't have a wise mentor to call. I could have asked the church to cut my pay by twenty-two dollars a month, and we could have gotten the soy formula, bread, cheese, and other groceries to live on.

I don't know how the word got out, but our little family's financial stress soon was combined with public humiliation as people whispered that the new pastor had applied for food stamps. Brenda and I had to buy the soy formula out of our meager income, which meant we had to decide *if* we would eat each meal daily, not *what* we would eat. A private and urgent need made us a public spectacle. The two were a one-two punch to the gut.

From the Outside Looking In

The Fuller, Barna, and Pastoral Care research groups published these conclusions about the external challenges for pastors:

- 40% report serious conflict with a parishioner at least once a month.
- 66% of church members expect a minister and family to live at a higher moral standard than themselves.
- The profession of "Pastor" is near the bottom of a survey of the most-respected professions, just above "car salesman."

Their research also showed that many pastors lived looking over their shoulders because they realize their jobs are tenuous:

- Over 4,000 churches closed in America last year.
- Over 1,700 pastors left the ministry every month last year.
- Over 1,300 pastors were terminated by the local church each month during the past year, many without cause.
- Over 3,500 people a day left the church last year.[1]

In another study of pastors, Richard Krejcir reported:

- 78% were forced to resign from a church at least once.
- 63% had been fired from their pastoral position at least twice.

In a more detailed analysis of the causes of termination, Krejcir found:

- 52% identified the primary reason was organizational and control issues, for example, conflict with an elder, a key lay person, or a faction in the church.
- 24% said the primary reason for dismissal was that the church was suffering from a significant degree of conflict when they arrived, and the pastor's approach failed to resolve it.
- 14% identified the primary reason was resistance to their leadership, vision, teaching, or to change, or their leadership was "too strong" or expected change "too fast."
- 8% said they failed to make a personal connection with the leaders and people of the church, sometimes because they were very loyal to the previous pastor and refused to accept anyone as a replacement.[2]

Common Causes

Some Christians can be sneaky, some might say devious. Everybody is smiling when they walk through the doors on Sunday morning, but behind the smiles occasionally lurk lethargy, suspicion, distrust, and sometimes devious plots to undermine the pastor's authority and destroy his reputation. In addition to personal conflicts, leaders face a wide range of organizational and cultural obstacles. Let's look at the most common ones.

Criticism

Jesus said, "For where two or three gather in my name, there am I with them" (Matthew 18:20). But it's also true that where two or three are gathered in his name, someone is finding fault with the others. It's human nature for people to try to build themselves up by putting others down, and ministry leaders are very visible, accessible, vulnerable targets. If they're visionaries, they're criticized for not being patient or valuing traditions or not caring for those who are hurting. If they're devoted to the sick and make many hospital calls, they're criticized for not being in the office enough to manage projects or failing to chart a bold path to the future. If their gifts are administrative, they're criticized for not being a great speaker.

The point is clear: no matter what your gifts and style may be, no matter how much you pour your heart into people, and no matter how much time you devote to your ministry, you'll face criticism.

Betrayal

If you lead long enough, you'll inevitably endure the deep wounds of betrayal. It's a paradox of leadership: our efforts to help people experience the love and power of Christ create envy in the hearts of some who are watching (and receiving our love). Most people are grateful, but a few—and it only takes a few—undermine us with open opposition, lies, and gossip. In *Leading with a Limp*, Dan Allender defined this wound and described how it further isolates the victim:

> Betrayal is a deep psychic wound that hardens the heart against grief and deadens its hunger for intimacy. Grief is meant to open our hearts and eventually move us to care for others. But what if we feel profound shame with our grief? Shame distances us from people and the comfort they could offer us in our grief; shame also causes a person to hate the innate desire to be connected to others.[3]

Allender observes that betrayal occurs primarily in two forms: abandonment or abuse. When those we trust turn their backs on us, refuse to support us in a time of need, and withhold love when we need it most, the impact is like a knife in the heart. Undoubtedly, that's how Jesus felt when all his closest followers (except John and the women) left him as he suffered torture and death on the cross. The other form of betrayal, abuse, is an active, brutal, direct wound. In this case, the hurt isn't caused by the absence of a kind smile when we need one; it's the presence of a scowling, bitter face when we need support.

To be fair, betrayal isn't always a one-sided affair. Certainly, Jesus was completely innocent, and his betrayal was completely unfair, but none of us is as pure. Leaders who are insecure often demand a level of loyalty that isn't healthy for the leader or the followers. When anyone questions him (too often or too loudly), he may react with feelings of betrayal that aren't based in reality. In times of intense criticism, factions, and betrayal, leaders need an objective, wise friend, coach, or consultant to help them navigate the turbulent and murky waters. They need to admit their part in the conflict, even if it's a small part. Assigning appropriate responsibility is important in any disagreement, and especially as the conflict threatens to escalate.

The Complexity of the Job

A major challenge for modern pastors is the sheer complexity of the job. A generation or two ago, the pastor's role was to prepare sermons each week, shepherd the flock, and keep things running smoothly. That wasn't too hard when there were only a few cogs in the machine. Today, even in small churches, the machine is very complicated. Every magazine, every conference, and every blog has new, innovative ideas. It's impossible to keep up. In an article called "Eight Reasons Why Pastors Fail," Joseph Mattera's first reason is that "churches are becoming complex enterprises which pastors are not equipped to lead." Some of the responsibilities that have added to the complexity include:

- Keeping up with real estate zoning laws, bank financing for new buildings and expansion, and relating to business leaders in the community about facility needs. Location is a key to growth, so pastors have to stay on top of the demography of their communities.
- As churches grow, pastors have to hire the right architect, decide on complex building plans, and conduct the always popular capital campaign. During particular seasons, fund-raising can easily become the pastor's obsession.

- Financial accounting becomes exponentially complex as the church grows and new staff and facilities are added.
- All of these skills aren't taught in seminary or college, and they aren't in the core competencies of most ministry leaders. Until they can hire an executive administrator, they have to juggle all these organizational balls themselves.
- In urban and some suburban communities, the needs of the poor quickly outstrip the church's resources, so pastors need to spend time building relationships and coordinating resources with local service organizations.
- Leaders who are over forty years old need to learn a new language and culture: postmodernity. Old-style apologetics don't connect with the minds and hearts of the younger audience. If these ministry leaders don't learn how to speak their language, they'll seem (or actually be) irrelevant. A part of this shift in culture resurfaces issues of gender identity, racism, ecology, and a host of other issues.
- With only a click or two, every person in the congregation can listen via the Internet to the best Bible teachers in the world. It was hard enough to be effective when pastors competed with the guy down the street at the other church, but now he competes with the very best anywhere. This puts added pressure on his ability to deliver outstanding sermons—and to use all his spare time to prepare.
- As churches grow, the selection of staff members becomes a critical element for the culture of the team, the effectiveness of each department, and the continued growth of the church. Good selections are crucial; poor ones will exact a heavy price.
- In addition, pastors also need to devote themselves to shepherding the flock, developing leaders, caring for the sick and grieving, and attending countless meetings.[4]

Inheriting a Toxic Culture

Jeremy had been a youth pastor for only a few months when the pastor was fired over a moral failure. For a couple of years before the pastor's sin was discovered, tension had built within the church. A number of people had suspected his dalliance, but they didn't have any hard evidence. The pastor's repeated denials kept him in his position. When the evidence was confirmed, a volcano of pent up anger blew! After the firing, the residue of resentment and betrayal didn't fade. The executive team asked Jeremy to be the new pastor, but now they had a deep-seated suspicion of pastors—including Jeremy. They may have chosen him because he was young and idealistic or maybe because they thought they could control him. Whatever the reason, Jeremy didn't realize he had stepped into a boiling cauldron of anger.

Whether it's wise or not to take a position like the one Jeremy took when his pastor was fired is a complicated question. In the decision-making process, we need to be ruthlessly realistic about the challenges of stepping into a position when the previous leader leaves under a cloud.

But the opposite situation may prove to be equally problematic. I've known churches that were so loyal to the previous, beloved pastor that they couldn't accept anyone taking his place. The football coaches who are hired to follow legends at the best programs seldom succeed. Expectations are simply too high. They try their best, but the culture is untenable.

Toxicity may come from a different source: the pews. Some people love the feeling of power, and they think the church is a good place to exercise it because they may assume the pastor, the staff, and other members are naive. These power-hungry people haven't learned the upside-down kingdom principles: to gain power, we have to give it away; to be honored, we give honor first to God and others; and true riches come from lavish generosity.

Masks, Lies, and Deceit

"Who can you trust?" a pastor asked when he learned one of his executive team members had been indicted for tax fraud. "I've worked with him for over a decade," he lamented. "I never imagined anything like this could happen." The pastor was immediately concerned for the man's wife and teenage children. He didn't anticipate the local news van pulling up to interview him about the arrest and impending trial. Suddenly the cause of Christ had a black eye in the community. It was another huge rock on the load the pastor had to carry, at least for a while. It would have been enough stress to care for the family.

Sometimes the sins of deception aren't directed toward the pastor, but he has to bear the load of helping people understand what happened, soothe fears, and restore the reputation of the church.

The Conflict Between Vision and Tradition

The debate between long-held, treasured traditions and new ideas isn't new. Every generation has to fight this battle and learn the skills of diplomacy. When change is suggested, some people feel their history and, in fact, their identity are threatened, so they resist even the most reasonable steps forward. Church members are notorious for fighting with each other over the most trivial things, but to them the style of music, the pastor's clothes, the times of the worship services, and a hundred other things are more important than peace and unity in the family of God.

Heartaches at Home

And speaking of family, stressed pastors can't leave their problems at the office. They take them home. They may try to shield their spouse and kids from the trouble they face at the church, but they can't. The hurt, anger, and sadness leak out into their lives too. All of the painful statistics we've identified under internal stress and external challenges affect the family too, maybe indirectly, but deeply. Over half of all pastors surveyed (58%) report that a spouse has to work outside the home to supplement the income earned from the church. Similarly, more than half of pastors' wives (56%) say they have no close friends. And like the rest of the population, half of all pastors' marriages end in divorce, but that painful number doesn't address the many others who choose to remain married but suffer under the constant strain and occasional crises of financial difficulties, misunderstandings, conflicting priorities, and resistant people.

Leading the Lethargic

Several surveys of church attendance show that fewer people are attending church, giving generously, and volunteering to serve.[5] Not long ago, people were considered to be regular attenders if they attended church twice a month. Now that figure may be less than two times a month.

Today, there are far more distractions than ever before that draw people away from church. Kids' soccer games are scheduled on Sunday mornings. Families have more disposable income, so they travel more. Cable television has great movies on Sunday morning. People can worship by tuning in to their favorite pastor on television or online.

In addition to immediate distractions, powerful forces in the culture have eroded the credibility of churches. In *Bad Religion: How We Became a Nation of Heretics*, Ross Douthat identified a number of ways Christianity positively influenced America up to the last decades of the twentieth century. Then five social catalysts combined to dampen the positive impact of the church:

- Political polarization drove mainline Christians to the left and evangelicals to the right, making the church look like a political pawn of one side or the other.
- The sexual revolution often made the biblical ethic of sex appear unrealistic and out of touch to many, mostly young, people.
- Globalization and modern communication has made it appear that Christianity is a Western religion and supportive of Europe's dark record of racism, colonialism, and anti-Semitism.
- Rising prosperity in the West has effectively insulated people from a sense of need for rescue and hope for the future.
- Finally, all of these factors have significantly influenced the educated and affluent people in each community, the ones who are the gatekeepers of communication and culture.[6]

What does all this have to do with the challenges of being a pastor today? Everything! It means many of the people Christian leaders are trying to reach in the community begin with a negative bias against God, against the church, and against the pastor. And those who come to church are often so distracted by other things that they do little more than show up a time or two a month to check "spirituality" or "church attendance" off their list of good things to do. Richard Krejcir's research shows that in the most conservative, Bible-believing churches, less than 25 percent of those attending are involved in any groups or studies beyond the Sunday morning services, and he suspects the numbers are actually lower.[7]

Today, pastors are speaking to people who attend less regularly, and when they show up, they aren't paying attention. It's very difficult to base a bold vision of the future on men and women who really aren't interested. They're glad to watch from a distance, but they don't want anything to get in the way of their comfort, pleasure, and ease.

Of course, there are some wonderful people who are radically committed to Christ and his cause. We celebrate them and value them as trusted partners in the adventure of restoring a broken world. But everyone isn't like them, not by a long shot.

Limited by Team Members

For years I've used the metaphor of a ladder to help leaders understand the influence of team members. In my book *Who's Holding Your Ladder?* I explain that the leader's vision is his ladder. As he tries to climb it, he doesn't need any help to go a few rungs up a twenty-foot extension ladder. It's stable and secure if he's only a few feet off the ground. But if he wants to go higher, he needs someone to hold the bottom so it doesn't come loose from its moorings. If the helper isn't paying attention, the ladder could slip and the pastor could fall and be injured. So even to climb a short distance farther up the ladder, the pastor needs someone attentive and sturdy.

If he wants to climb to the top of his ladder, the pastor will need two or three people who are just as strong and attentive as the first ladder holder. What if his vision reaches fifty feet? Or a hundred feet? The people holding his ladder determine how high he can go.

It doesn't matter how high the vision is; what matters is the quality of his ladder holders.

Many pastors have wonderful visions of how God can use the church to accomplish great things, but they haven't selected the right people to hold their ladder. They may have found someone who could hold it if they went up to twenty feet, but no farther. If they're unwilling to make changes in the people holding the ladder, they'll never climb higher. Never. Leaders can do one of three things with those who hold their ladders: *retain* them because they're effective, *release* them because they aren't, or *reassign and retrain* them to hold someone else's ladder.

Most ministry leaders are more committed to keep from hurting anyone's feelings than accomplishing the vision God has given them. I've never been to a church where someone didn't need to be fired. I'm not suggesting pastors and other leaders become brutal taskmasters. Far from it. They have to hold two goals in tension: vision and shepherding. They can't afford to let go of either one if they want to be the leaders God has called them to be. The reluctance to fire or reassign a friend has limited the ministry of countless pastors, and it has added immeasurably to their levels of stress because they're trying to get staff members to do something they can't or won't do.

Unreasonable Rules

Sometimes our culture is backward, stunted, and repressive. Prejudice inflicts enormous pain. In the early 1970s, when I was a janitor at Beulah Heights Bible College, one of my duties was to pick up the trash in every office. During my first week, when I went to the dean's office, I saw a lovely young lady who was his executive assistant. Oh, she looked nice. I introduced myself. She replied sweetly, "My name is Brenda." Like any other love-struck young man, I began to strategize how I could get to know her and take her out. But there was a problem: Brenda was Caucasian and I was Indian. Brenda and I met about ten years after President Lyndon B. Johnson signed the Civil Rights Act, but it appeared that some people in Georgia had never heard of racial equality.

I didn't have enough money to date Brenda, but the mere fact that I obviously liked her sent ripples of tension throughout the campus. In response, the college's board met in an urgent session and passed a policy to forbid people dating outside their ethnicity. But they soon realized that wasn't clear enough. They needed to define dating. So they defined it as having a conversation longer than five minutes, sitting at the same cafeteria table, riding in the same car, sitting next to each other in class, or sitting in the same church pew. In effect, the board members tried to establish an exclusion zone expressly designed to keep me away from Brenda.

Brenda and I respected the leadership of the college, but we also wanted to see each other. On three occasions, the dean, acting on behalf of the college board, called us into his office and threatened to expel us if we continued to talk to each other. Expulsion would be uncomfortable for Brenda but catastrophic for me. She could attend any other school in the country. The move would require some dislocation and interruption, but her life wouldn't be upset for very long. On the other hand, if I were expelled, I would lose my student visa and be deported. Under the immigration terms of the time, I would never be allowed to enter the United States again for the rest of my life.

Another dean on campus was the designated counselor for the students, and he occasionally called Brenda to see him. He told her that if she kept seeing me, she would go to hell. (I'm not kidding or exaggerating.) Brenda has great respect for authority, so she left these meetings crushed with guilt and confusion. After each one, she told me she had to break up with me because she didn't want to go to hell. After a while, she realized the dean was using these threats to manipulate her, and we got back together. That happened several times.

Brenda and I have boxes of notes we wrote to each other during our time at Beulah Heights Bible College. When we couldn't see each other, we wrote or called. The phones in our two dorms were only about twenty yards apart, but using them was safer than meeting face to face. Our dance of love and secrecy lasted for three years. We both took risks, but they were worth it.

One year on Secretary's Day, I was sure no one would acknowledge Brenda and thank her for her faithful and excellent service, so I used the little money I'd saved to buy a bouquet of flowers and have them delivered to her desk. Someone noticed the pretty flowers and asked her, "Who gave these to you? They're beautiful!"

Without thinking, she answered, "Sam did!" When word spread, we were both summoned by the dean.

I was brought up in a culture that deeply respects those who are in authority. India is a gracious land that gives the highest honor to parents, teachers, and other leaders. In every threatening conversation with the dean, I never barked back or stormed out. I sat quietly and listened, and when he was finished, I said, "Thank you, sir." Even as a young man in college, I understood that the fear and racism evident on the board didn't appear out of a vacuum. To a great degree, those men were the products of their culture. They had lived for decades under Jim Crow laws that allowed racial discrimination in the South for nearly a century after the Civil War; I hadn't. They had recently seen marches and police brutality; I hadn't. They had watched as Martin Luther King Jr. and Robert F. Kennedy had been assassinated; I had come to an America that was suffering enormous pain and fear.

During those awful years when I was a student, I believed the leadership and the school board were ignorant, not prejudiced. Somehow I sensed that the reaction of the board and the dean wasn't the true content of their hearts. I don't think the dean believed what he was doing was good, right, and fair. He was given the task to enforce the board's policy, and he tried to do it the best he knew how. I don't think the board was acting out of spite but out of fear. They didn't know any better. The board was filled with people from rural areas and small towns where racial equality was perceived as a grave threat to their way of life. They were suffering from the pressures of a repressive, racist culture, and they simply didn't know how to reconcile their faith in a gracious, welcoming God with the rampant racism found in their nation.

I went back to India in 1977, but I couldn't stop thinking about Brenda. Thankfully, pleasant thoughts about me filled her mind and heart. I came back two years later and asked her to marry me. She said, "Yes!" We planned to get married in the church next to the campus where both of us had been very involved. Brenda had tithed faithfully and led the nursing home ministry, among many other ways she had served the church. Before returning to India, I had been the worship leader and choir coordinator as well as occasional preacher whenever the pastor was away.

Brenda and I made an appointment to see the pastor. When we asked him to marry us, he flatly said, "No." I asked why, and he explained, "Because I don't think your marriage can work. She's white, and you're Indian." (As if we hadn't noticed.) I asked if we could rent the church for our wedding. He agreed to my suggestion, and we found another clergyman to perform the ceremony.

In this emotionally charged environment, we unwittingly put everyone we invited to the wedding on the horns of a dilemma. Should they come or not? Were they being faithful to their leaders by staying away, or did they have freedom of conscience to come and celebrate with us? Our friends made an array of different choices: some came to the wedding but not the reception, some came to the reception but not the wedding, some came to both, some didn't come to either. Our wedding intensified the divisions and suspicions in the Beulah Heights community. For Brenda and me, excruciating pain clouded our joyous moment.

We had to get away from there. A friend in Oregon had invited me to be his youth pastor. He said, "I can't pay you anything, but I can give you a place to live." Three days after Brenda and I were married, we packed our car and drove across the country to make a new start.

I served as youth pastor for over a year and then became a pastor in Michigan for about nine years. During that time, our church began supporting Beulah Heights Bible College, and we sent students there. We were happy to help them grow in their faith and learn the skills they'd need for a lifetime of success. The faculty asked me to come back to speak at workshops and symposiums at the school. After many trips back to Atlanta and a lot of time working with faculty, the board invited me to be a member of the board. Suddenly, I was sitting at the same table with those who had passed a policy to prevent me from spending time with Brenda.

To build bridges, I invited several board members to come to Michigan to speak at our church. Some of them stayed at our home. In their own way, all of them apologized for how they had treated us. Old wounds were healing. New understanding was developing. When the president took a role at another university, the board asked me to become president of Beulah Heights Bible College.

Ten years after Brenda and I left Beulah Heights with deep feelings of hurt and confusion, we returned, but this time, I was the college president. Amazingly, a radical healing transformation had occurred. Board members now welcomed me as the new leader of the institution.

The darkest chapters of my history occurred at Beulah Heights, but in God's amazing, redemptive grace, he used the same people and the same institution to bring new hope, creativity, and fruitfulness into my life. But, first, we needed to clear up a few things.

Soon after I took the new role, I went to the dean's office and said, "Years ago I sat in this chair in this office across from you, and you threatened to expel me. I was your janitor. Now I'm your president. I'm okay with you. The question is whether you're okay with me."

He assured me that the past was, indeed, past, and we would move together into the future. In my fifteen years as president at Beulah Heights, the dean became one of my most trusted and valued partners.

When I arrived as president of Beulah Heights in 1989, we had eighty-seven students; when I left fifteen years later, we had almost eight hundred. When I arrived, we weren't accredited; when I left, we had dual accreditation. No one cheered louder or was more helpful than the dean. His constant refrain was, "Sam, the best is yet to be. We haven't yet seen all that God is going to do here!"

Still . . .

Yes, being a leader is an incredibly stressful role. The hours are usually long, the pay is often short, and the people are sometimes contentious, but a study by the University of Chicago National Opinion Research Center reports that pastors are the happiest people on the planet, outranking even well-paid and highly respected professions like doctors and lawyers.

Yes, being a leader is an incredibly stressful role. The hours are usually long, the pay is often short, and the people are sometimes contentious. Even with these difficulties, many pastors and other church leaders find enormous fulfillment in their roles. They see lives changed, and they have the joy of knowing God has used them to communicate His tenderness and strength.

Being a Christian leader in any organization is one of the most difficult jobs in the world—full of risks, strains, and challenges for the leader and his family—but it's also the one that offers the greatest hope to make a difference both now and for eternity.

Know This

You'll only climb as high as the quality and capacity of those who hold your ladder.

Do This

On a scale of 0 (not at all) to 10 (maxed out), rate your current level of angst that comes from the external challenges of:

- Criticism
- Betrayal
- The complexity of the job
- Inheriting a toxic culture
- Masks, lies, and deceit
- The conflict between vision and tradition
- Heartaches at home
- Leading the lethargic
- Limited by team members
- Unreasonable rules

What does this quick evaluation tell you about the source of your external challenges?

Think About This

1. At this point, what is your capacity to deal with devils around you? How is this limiting the growth of your leadership and your church?
2. In the brief evaluation of challenges above, which two or three give you the most trouble? Who knows how much you struggle with these things? Who can help you find a way forward?
3. How would you advise someone who suffered from a recent betrayal? Have you taken your own advice to deal with yours? Why or why not?
4. Who's holding your ladder? How high can you climb with them holding it? Do you need to make any changes? If so, when and how will you make them?
5. Do you agree or disagree with the findings of the study about job satisfaction for ministry leaders? What is your level of satisfaction with your role? Explain your answer.
6. What lessons (about God, about you, and about your role) does God want to teach you from your external challenges?

And remember: *you'll grow only to the threshold of your pain*.

3

TOO MUCH TOO OFTEN

Never trust a leader who doesn't walk with a limp.
—Dr. J. Robert Clinton

**Bishop Mark J. Chironna, Church on the Living Edge
and Mark Chironna Ministries, Orlando, Florida**

Someone once said, "It is the nature of life to be stormy." When
I was 50, a number of factors in my ministry and my personal
life converged to make a perfect storm of horrific proportions.

On the ministry side, my schedule was hectic, and
demands to speak at conferences and other events required a
lot of travel. The continual wear and tear of travel, along with
the pressures of ministry, began to wear me down.

We were doing multiple services and in need of an adequate facility. In the process of selling our existing site, we
encountered a number of setbacks just prior to each scheduled closing. And we faced numerous challenges in finding

a new site. Every option seemed to require more time and money.

We had sold our building, but the new one had fallen through. This left us in a very precarious place. Eventually, we had to purchase a facility 30 minutes from the current site. Overnight, our mortgage soared $7000 to $70,000 a month. For those armchair quarterbacks that would accuse us of poor planning, please withhold your judgment. We had some of the finest minds in the church world, the legal world, and the accounting world advising us.

We hoped our numbers would grow when we opened our new building, but over 2000 people didn't want to make the drive. We had less than 700 adults in a facility whose overhead was 10 times the previous one.

I've been through many building programs, but this time the financial pressure was gargantuan. After a few months, we still weren't growing like the experts predicted, and the level of my anxiety was skyrocketing! Worry was my constant companion. "What if" thinking was affecting me consciously and unconsciously.

It is easy to quote Paul in Philippians: "Be anxious for nothing." It is just as easy to ignore his journey in 1 Corinthians where he speaks of being in "weakness, fear, and much trembling" at a season in his life. The financial pressure had a profound impact on my sleep patterns, my ability to relax, and my ability to function.

Prolonged anxiety also came with a friend: depression. If you had asked me earlier if I ever thought depression and anxiety would happen to me, I would have quoted you a number of Scripture verses about how they *couldn't* happen to me.

My body was feeling the wear and tear of stress. I was

becoming quite fatigued in spite of taking supplements and eating appropriately. I began to lose a great deal of weight, and eventually I lost my appetite altogether.

However, the knockout punch had not yet been delivered. It would send me into an almost four year long, seemingly unending battle with anxiety, despair, and warfare with the powers of darkness. The tunnel was long, and dark, and it felt like a life sentence.

The storm became perfectly horrendous when my younger son was a teenager. He and his brother are both adopted; attachment disorder is a fairly common problem for adopted children. He had been diagnosed with the disorder when he was a very young. Bonding was a major difficulty for him. The disorder, along with other neurological issues, caused him to "act out" in vengeance against the entire family during his teenage years. The consequences of his behavior had a tragic effect on all of us. The emotional heartache and pain we endured was beyond what we could imagine. Finding the grace to endure required constant vigilance. Chaos and uncertainty were the order of the season. False accusations lead to legal and social implications, with financial costs, which made my responsibility to provide even more difficult.

The strain was crushing me. I battled severe insomnia, which contributed to even more anxiety and the depression. I was on very strong medications, but the days and nights became endless. I had to make a moment-by-moment choice to keep moving forward, even when only sleeping perhaps one night out of five or six.

I honestly did not believe I would get through it all. What got me through was not simply the doctors or the therapists, but a friend who, like the Lord Himself, stuck closer than a brother. He is a pastor and a life-long friend who has known seasons of intense spiritual warfare and stress. During this time, he traveled with me, he sat up with me at night when I couldn't sleep, and he paced the floors with me as I prayed for a breakthrough, which never came.

I have graduate degrees in psychology and theology, so the "head knowledge" was always present, but the actual experience was almost unbearable. In life, you can't heal yourself; it takes relationships to heal you. I lost perspective, and I lost my identity. I needed close friends and close staff members to remind me of who I was.

That terrible season lasted almost four years. From my human perspective, it took the "best" of my decade of the fifties when I hoped to be in my "prime." I had to learn, as H. Beecher Hicks taught us years ago, to "Preach through the Storm." I didn't know I would have to preach through it for more than 185 Sundays and daily align my thoughts with the truth for 1278 days!

Liminal space is a concept in theology and psychology. It is the intermediate, in-between, transitional state where you cannot go back to where you were because a threshold has been crossed, and you have yet to arrive where you are going because it is not yet available to you. Essentially, it is the hallway between the past and the future. I can tell you quite candidly: it's hell in the hallway.

By God's grace I finally found the gate on the other side of the liminal space. It took far longer than I wished, and took far more effort and focus than I wanted to expend. What have I learned? I no longer flippantly quote Scriptures to those who are suffering. Now, I often weep when I hear about the heartaches of people. I no longer have pat answers for them. I have learned how to just be with them and sit where they sit, like Ezekiel sitting with the exiles by the River Chebar. I have also learned a number of things about anxiety and depression that enable me to come alongside my brothers and sisters, and by the power of the Holy Spirit, help them learn how to "be with" the anxiety, without it either defining them or governing them.

For those who want quick fixes, I have found there aren't any—and there never have been. Casting burdens on the Lord, depending on how heavy they are, takes time. The heart knows its own bitterness, and a stranger doesn't share its joy. Prayer and supplication are processes that require time. It takes time to reach down deep and bring hidden pains and fears to speech, especially when you believe it is a sin to admit you have hidden fear. For a long time, I didn't allow myself to be fully human.

In order to come to a new orientation, I had to experience disorientation. In that liminal space in both soul and circumstance, I went through the process of reorientation. In the end, it was all worth it. If you don't believe my testimony, ask Job about his season in liminal space, or Elijah, or Jeremiah, or Paul, or perhaps, Jesus Himself.

Bishop Dale C. Bronner, Word of Faith Family Worship Cathedral, Austell, Georgia

Nothing in Bible school or seminary prepares ministers for the pain of ministry. There is a pain to build and there is a pain to grow. Starting off young in ministry, I was under the assumption that if you served God faithfully, His blessings and favor would rest upon your life and ministry. I still believe that is true. However, where I made a grave error in judgment was in assuming that God's favor meant exemption from problems and pain in ministry!

In 2010, I was in the middle of a building project that began in 2007: a $33 million dollar multipurpose facility to serve our church family and our community. Before I began the project, I was already keenly aware that things generally cost more than you estimate and require more time than that you anticipate. With this in mind, I spent time planning and preparing. I'm a firm believer that faith is not a substitute for wisdom; and hope is not a strategy!

Although I had been pastoring for nearly 20 years, this was the first noticeable pain in ministry for me. Some pain screams, but this was a sneaky pain. In fact the only way that I knew I was experiencing the growing pains of ministry was because of insomnia that surfaced in my life for the first time. Sometimes a person can't sleep because of something that he's eating. Other times a person can't sleep because of what's eating him or her.

During the day, I didn't feel the pain of all the pressure I was under. But every night when I got ready to go to bed, I would doze off, sometimes for an hour or two, then awaken and not be able to get back to sleep. At first I thought the Lord was waking me up because He wanted to commune with me or share some revelation with me, but after several nights of insomnia, I began to feel weary. This wasn't like me.

When I went for my annual physical, the nurse took my blood pressure and told me that it was a bit high. She was a believer, so she said to me, "Whatever you're stressed about, just forget it, and let the Lord handle it." Well, that's easier said than done.

Although the nurse meant well, I knew she didn't understand my situation. I tried to explain, "I have great faith in God, but I'm building a big building, and this is just the result of the pressure I subconsciously feel." I went on to tell her, "It is just like a person who is lifting heavy weights, like 250 pounds, who then begins shaking after doing a few reps. It doesn't mean the person lacks faith just because he's shaking under the weight of the pressure. It just means the person is bearing a heavy load, and this is how their body is reacting to it."

Was building a $33 million dollar project intimidating for me? Absolutely! But was I building it anyway? Absolutely! I spent five years planning the project. In my counting the cost, however, I never imagined that it would cause the pain of insomnia. One sleepless night is tolerable, maybe even two. But when this condition stretches out for weeks, you have a problem!

I realize that in the same way that favor doesn't exempt us from pain, faith doesn't exempt us from fear. I was building a part of my dream. A dream is not merely what you see during sleep; a dream is that which keeps sleep from you! My dream is a part of my passion. Incidentally, the word "passion" literally means "pain." Passion is about suffering for what you love! When a musician is passionate about music, he or she suffers through hours of daily practice.

Passion was alive in me. It was as though I was pregnant, and the baby would kick and become active during the night! It has planning sessions at the most inconvenient times. But I learned that every dream requires sacrifice to come into existence. Sacrifice is simply giving up something good in order to get something better!

I believe the insomnia was a form of pain, perhaps even

the pain of fear—the fear of failure or not finishing well. But again, faith isn't doing something in the *absence* of fear but in the *presence* of fear. Faith has no contextual meaning if fear is not present! So I was building while I was scared. I was doing what I call "trusting and trembling." I was running scared, but I was moving!

Can you imagine what it feels like to be a faith teaching leader who appears as invincible as Superman in front of the people, but who turns into Clark Kent in private? Well, that's what I felt like. I would lie awake for extended periods of time. Time seems to stand still when you are awake during the night.

I tried everything to fall back to sleep. I tried counting my blessings. I was still wide awake. I tried reciting Scripture. Sleep was still escaping me. I tried counting sheep. That didn't work. I tried praying the insomnia away. It didn't work. I tried confessing it away. It still didn't work. I tried physically tiring myself out before bed. That didn't work. My last resort was to turn to a prescription sleep aid. I could only endure so much of the pain of sleeplessness before I had to anesthetize the pain so I could function the next day.

Never in a million years did I think I would take a sleeping pill, but long-term pain makes you desperate! Desperate people do desperate things. This whole insomnia episode lasted for about two years! Then suddenly God used my precious wife to pray for me and boldly declare, "You won't need those sleeping pills anymore." And since that day, I've slept like a baby and have not had another sleeping pill!

I am extremely grateful for God's supernatural intervention in my life, but I light-heartedly tell people, "God really missed a marvelous opportunity to surprise me by showing up early with His intervention!" Although I suffered many sleepless nights, my faith remained steadfast in God. In the middle of the night while I was wide awake, I was reading the words of the Apostle Paul describing some of his pain:

> Are they ministers of Christ?—I speak as a fool—I am more: in labors more abundant, in stripes above measure, in prisons more frequently, in deaths often. From the Jews five times I received forty stripes minus one. Three times I was beaten with rods; once I was stoned; three times I was shipwrecked; a night and a day I have been in the deep; in journeys often, in perils of waters, in perils of robbers, in perils of my own countrymen, in perils of the Gentiles, in perils in the city, in perils in the wilderness, in perils in the sea, in perils among false brethren; in weariness and toil, *in SLEEPLESSNESS* often, in hunger and thirst, in fastings often, in cold and nakedness—besides the other things, what comes upon me daily: my deep concern for all the churches. (2 Corinthians 11:23–28)

Reading all the painful circumstances Paul endured as a leader put my pain in perspective. It stood out to me that Paul suffered with insomnia, too—not because he lacked faith, but because of the pressure he was under managing all his daily responsibilities and his care for the churches. If the Apostle Paul dealt with these painful things, why should I expect to be exempt from pain? I learned that God doesn't abandon us in our pain. He is right there with us, comforting and strengthening us, and granting us the grace necessary to complete our assignment!

So the next time you find yourself dealing with a pain associated with leadership, don't consider it to be abnormal. You aren't the first, and you won't be the last to experience it.

Realize that there is a grace supplied by God Himself through Jesus for you to endure the pain. Think about this: God gave Jesus a crown of thorns, so why should you expect a crown of roses?

The Apostle Paul encouraged young Timothy to "be strong in the grace that is in Christ Jesus" (2 Timothy 2:1). So don't always look to get out of a situation until you get from the situation what God has hidden in it for you! That's why Paul reminded Timothy, "You therefore must endure hardship as a good soldier of Jesus Christ" (2 Timothy 2:3).

Sometimes God delivers you from the fiery furnace; other times He makes you fireproof! When He makes you fireproof, you must endure it! God is more concerned with your development than He is with your comfort. You will be set ablaze, but you will not be consumed! There is a story that you must tell for His glory that records your personal journey from pain to pleasure!

Steve had been a successful assistant pastor for several years, and when an offer came to be the senior pastor at a church in New Jersey, he felt he was ready for the challenge. He and his wife, Rachel, packed their two children, their dog, and all their belongings and set off on an adventure of faith. For three years Steve poured himself into his church and his community. He had to make some tough decisions: to diplomatically remove the youth pastor and find someone who fit the role, completely revamp the music, restructure the volunteer organization of the church, wade in to resolve some long-standing hurt feelings between families, and show up at every civic function as the face of the suddenly growing church.

Before he came to New Jersey, Steve regularly put in fifty hours a week at the church. Now, he regularly spent sixty or seventy hours and sometimes eighty to keep all the plates spinning. For two years he loved every minute of it. (Well, almost every minute. There's always plenty of drudgery in any job.) But during the third year, the grind was getting to him. He gained weight, missed more of his kids' games than before, and sometimes snapped at his wife—or his assistant or the youth pastor or the dog or anyone else who was around. Rachel and plenty of others asked, "Are you okay, Steve?"

He smiled and assured them, "Sure. No problem. Just a little tired, that's all."

After several months of good-hearted questions, Steve began to realize that the stress of being a pastor was getting the best of him. No matter how much he prayed, how hard he worked, or how much he tried to avoid the vision stealers and joy killers, he kept sliding deeper into an emotional and spiritual hole. Steve had no idea how to climb out.

Then, in October 2012, Hurricane Sandy hit the coast near the church. Within hours, the complexity of Steve's life multiplied a hundredfold! As the storm approached, Steve grabbed his family and the dog and drove inland about fifty miles. They spent the night wondering if the dire predictions would come true. All the networks carried images and on-site reporting 24/7. It was worse than anyone had imagined.

The next day Steve left Rachel and the kids at a hotel and drove back to his community. He first stopped at his house. The roof was leaking in two places, but there was no structural damage. The church had stood up pretty well, but debris from shattered homes and businesses littered the lawn and the parking lot. One look at the streets told him that his priority list had just been rewritten. Soon he discovered that at least half of the homes of people in the church had been destroyed or at least were temporarily unlivable. When cell service was restored, he called the youth pastor and some members of his leadership team to check on them. Their homes were damaged, but they were ready to help others in greater need.

For the next few days, Steve, his staff, lay leaders, and church members marshaled their efforts to gather resources—food, water, clothes, toys, and medical supplies—for church members and others in the community who had lost their homes. It was exhausting but exhilarating to know they were making a difference. The power finally was turned back on at his house, so Rachel and the children came back home.

For the next two months, Steve devoted himself to helping everyone in need. It was, in many ways, his finest hour. People deeply appreciated his hard work, hearty hugs, and kind words. Gradually, people either repaired their homes and moved back or found other places to live. Steve didn't know it at the time, but about a third of the people in his church never came back. They'd had enough of the sea and its threats. During all this time, most of the church's bills kept coming in, but the giving plummeted. Oh, people were giving, but they were giving to relief for their friends and neighbors, not the church's general fund.

A new normal settled over the church and the community, but not for Steve. He had been showing signs of stress before the hurricane slammed into the East Coast. Ironically, the additional demands had brought out the best in him, but they completely sucked the life out of him. Four months after the storm, Steve hit a wall. It was a classic case of burnout.

> No one can fully understand us. What hurts more is that few really want to understand us because such understanding would call them to join the world—and the pain—of the leader.
>
> —Dan Allender, *Healing Path*

Too Much

Contrary to the thinking of many people, stress isn't the problem. *Too much unrelieved* stress is the culprit. A little stress brings out the best in us. Our adrenaline flows, and we become more creative, more energetic, and more determined to reach higher than before. But many leaders live without safety valves. They are like pressure cookers with a blocked valve. Every difficult conversation, every hard decision, every failure, every challenging question, and every self-doubt adds to all the ones that have already filled the pot. With each new strain, the addition seems imperceptible, so the person doesn't do anything about it. As stress rises to the point of explosion or implosion, it seems completely, absolutely normal.

You can be sure of this: if you're a leader in a nonprofit, a church, or a business, problems will find you, and they come in many different packages: a disappointed spouse, an unreasonable delay in an important project, a sullen team member, an accident, an untimely death, an unexpected drop in production, a fussy child, a financial crisis, or a hundred other permutations of headaches and heartaches.

The *sources* of stress vary widely, and the *signs* of multiplied, unrelieved stress come in all shapes and sizes. People try to cope with intense pain in different ways: some become more driven and frenetically active in an attempt to control people and situations, others withdraw emotionally and physically to avoid conflict, and others blend the two—they're paralyzed on the outside but terribly anxious under the surface. The signs of stress include:

- Emotional symptoms: feeling overwhelmed, hopeless, isolated, irritable, or moody
- Behavioral symptoms: eating too much or too little, sleeping too much or too little, using medications or alcohol to relax, neglecting normal responsibilities, compulsive behaviors, low resistance to temptation, and not enjoying things that used to bring pleasure
- Cognitive symptoms: anxiety, scattered or racing thoughts, inability to concentrate, and lack of judgment
- Physical symptoms: stomach problems, tension headaches, odd aches and pains, or the loss of interest in sex

Leadership involves vision, drive, and godly ambition to advance God's kingdom or expand a business, but without safeguards, visionary leaders can suffer from exhaustion, loneliness, and burnout. And redoubling their efforts to control people usually backfires and creates more stress. Stress, though, isn't reserved for the hard-driving types. Other pastors and executives are sensitive, compassionate, and always available, which can lead to dependent, needy relationships, confusion, and emotional exhaustion. And redoubling their efforts to help people almost always makes the problem worse.

If a stressed-out leader has the courage to admit the struggle, well-meaning but uninformed friends may say, "Oh, don't let it bother you. Let it go, brother. Just let it go."

Most people have no idea what it's like to be a Christian leader. We care. We care deeply about the people God has entrusted to us. The Creator and King has called us to represent him to the people in our churches, businesses, and communities. When they have a need, we want to be the hands, feet, and voice of God to them. When those needs can't be met, it bothers us. It bothers us a lot.

Richard Swenson, a medical doctor, addresses this problem in *Margin: Restoring Emotional, Physical, Financial, and Time Reserves to Overloaded Lives*.[1] At a conference for ministry leaders, he held up a small tree branch, bent it a little, and then let go. It immediately snapped back to its former shape. He explained that a little stress that is soon resolved has no lasting effect. Then he bent the branch more severely and for about a minute. When he let go of one end of the branch, it recovered only partially, but stayed significantly bent. He explained that significant, unrelieved stress causes prolonged effects. Then he slowly pulled the branch until a slight cracking sound could be heard, and then it broke. He explained that when people experience severe, prolonged, unrelieved stress—namely, burnout—the result is lasting, devastating damage. In some ways, a person never fully recovers.

Some in the audience wanted to push back on the doctor's pessimistic prediction, but those who had friends who had suffered the devastation of burnout only nodded.

In the vast majority of cases, burnout is the result of a long series of disappointments, setbacks, and heartaches. Any one of them cannot cause irreparable damage on their own, but the cumulative effect of unrelieved tension, ungrieved losses, and unresolved conflict ultimately exacts a heavy toll.

Unrelieved personal pain creates a sense of desperation. People want relief, and they want it *now*! They look for any and every way to block the pain, if only for a few minutes. It's easy to get lost in meaningless television shows, sports, video games, and countless other diversions. Some of these are more than distractions; they are sources of destruction. Perhaps the most devastating are pornography and illicit sex. Statistics about Christians and porn are alarming but familiar to any Christian leader. Among parishioners, 50 percent of men and 20 percent of women admit they are addicted to pornography. It's worse in the pulpit. In *Men's Secret Wars*, Patrick Means reports that 63 percent of pastors surveyed confessed they struggle with compulsive sexual desires or sexual addictions, including pornography, masturbation, and a wide array of other sexual behaviors.[2] These behaviors gradually (or not so gradually) break down moral barriers and shatter spiritual convictions, making people more vulnerable to the temptation of adultery, with consequences that shatter individuals, families, churches, and the name of God in the community.

> It is easier to find men who will volunteer to die, than to find those who are willing to endure pain with patience.
>
> —Julius Caesar

Maybe You Don't Want to Know

Pastors face pressures that are similar to any CEO or top company executive but with the added dimension that he is expected to be an outstanding teacher and a compassionate friend in addition to being excellent at planning, delegation, and administration. They are expected to be "all things to all people" inside and outside the church. In other words, pastors are uniquely vulnerable to the stress of unrealistic expectations. A number of organizations have surveyed pastors in the past couple of decades. The most recent and comprehensive studies show alarming results.

A major study found:

- 90% of pastors work between 55 to 75 hours per week.
- 80% believe pastoral ministry has negatively affected their families. Many pastors' children do not attend church now because of what the church has done to their parents.
- 33% believe the ministry is a hazard to their families.
- 75% report they've experienced a significant stress-related crisis at least once in their ministry.
- 90% feel they are inadequately trained to cope with the ministry demands.
- 50% feel unable to meet the demands of the job.
- 70% say they have a lower self-image now than when they first started.
- 70% do not have someone they consider a close friend.
- 33% confess having been involved in inappropriate sexual behavior with someone in the church.
- 50% have considered leaving the ministry in the last months.
- 94% of their families feel the pressures of the pastor's ministry.

In addition, this study found:

- 1,500 pastors leave the ministry each month due to moral failure, burnout, or contention in their churches.
- 50% of the marriages of pastors end in divorce.
- 80% of those who enter the ministry will leave it within five years.
- 70% of pastors chronically struggle with depression.[3]

Dr. Richard J. Krejcir of the Francis A. Schaeffer Institute of Church Leadership Development conducted a study of 1,050 pastors attending two conferences. He discovered:

- 100% had a close associate or seminary friend who had left the ministry because of burnout, conflict in their church, or a moral failure.
- 90% stated they are frequently fatigued and worn out on a weekly and even daily basis.
- 71% stated they were burned out and battled depression beyond fatigue on a weekly and even a daily basis.
- 89% considered leaving the ministry at one time, and 57% said they would leave if they had a better place to go—including secular work.
- 77% felt they did not have a good marriage.
- 75% felt they were unqualified and/or poorly trained by their seminaries to lead and manage the church or to counsel others. This left them disheartened in their ability to pastor.
- 38% were divorced or currently in the divorce process.
- 30% had either been in an ongoing affair or a one-time sexual encounter with a parishioner.
- 23% said they felt happy and content on a regular basis with who they are in Christ, in their church, and in their home.[4]

Sadly, the trend line isn't encouraging. These studies show significant increases in the incidence of stress-related problems in the ministry.

A Closer Look

The causes of stress are as varied and complex as human nature, but we can easily identify a few common sources. These rarely occur in isolation or one at a time. They tend to happen in clusters, over time, and with multiplied effects.

Role Confusion

As we'll see in a chapter 5, leaders display a wide range of gifts, leadership styles, and interests. Some are talented speakers but can't organize their way out of a closet. Others excel in hospital visitation and in counseling, but they aren't very good at casting vision, planning, and delegating. Others are phenomenal visionaries but lack empathy for hurting people around them. The problem for all these pastors, of course, is that their people expect them to be outstanding in all these areas.

Leaders in every field feel drawn to the areas where they feel strong and effective, but they feel guilty—and they hear plenty of complaints—when other areas of ministry are neglected. Certainly, no job perfectly fits anyone, but when a person operates out of their strengths too long, their energies and enthusiasm are gradually depleted. They assure themselves they're serving and sacrificing, but they often don't realize they're running on fumes.

Compassion Fatigue

Loving others made Christ completely vulnerable to the point of death. For us, loving others makes us vulnerable to being misunderstood, unappreciated, and discarded. In his book *Can You Drink the Cup?* Henri Nouwen wrote,

> Every time we make the decision to love someone, we open ourselves to great suffering, because those we most love cause us not only great joy but also great pain. The greatest pain comes from leaving. When the child leaves home, when the husband or wife leaves for a long period of time or for good, when the beloved friend departs to another country or dies . . . the pain of the leaving can tear us apart. Still, if we want to avoid the suffering of leaving, we will never experience the joy of loving. And love is stronger than fear, life stronger than death, hope stronger than despair. We have to trust that the risk of loving is always worth taking.[5]

The exhaustion caused by constantly loving, giving, serving, and sacrificing—especially coupled with feeling alone, resentful, and hurt—erodes a Christian leader's ability to cope with life. Some call it *compassion fatigue* and compare it with combat fatigue. Beginning with the Civil War and then much more in World War I, doctors realized that the strain of battle seriously affected soldiers' competence. Many had to be taken to hospitals to recuperate even though they hadn't suffered a scratch. The condition was called shell shock in the early twentieth century. During World War II, doctors charted the condition and found that it was most predictable after a soldier had been on the line for ninety days. A new label was coined: *combat stress reaction*. After ninety days of constant exposure to fighting, a soldier "became steadily less valuable until he was completely useless."[6] One doctor treating soldiers suffering the stress of prolonged combat noted:

> Many have chronic dysentery or other disease, and almost all show chronic fatigue states. . . . They appear listless, unkempt, careless, and apathetic with almost masklike facial expression. Speech is slow, thought content is poor, they complain of chronic headaches, insomnia, memory defect, feel forgotten, worry about themselves, are afraid of new assignments, have no sense of responsibility, and are hopeless about the future.[7]

Compassion fatigue is a milder form of shell shock that is associated with doctors, nurses, and emergency personnel—especially those who work in trauma units. For pastors and church staff, caring for needy people is standard operating procedure—it's their calling, their responsibility, their privilege—but the unusual intensity of specific events or prolonged seasons of care can significantly downgrade a person's ability to function effectively.

Comparison and Competition

A pastor who attended a national conference for his denomination was disgusted by what he experienced. After the first day, he told a friend, "When I met people, the most common questions they asked were, 'How many people attend your church?' and 'What's your annual budget?' They were checking each other out to see where they are on the pecking order.

Size is power. Size is prestige. Size gives you an identity and authority—at least, that's what they obviously thought. It was nauseating."

There's nothing wrong with wanting a church to thrive and grow so that people experience God's grace, changed lives, and a transformed community. But we can want those same results for darker, more sinister motives. How can we tell if pride is driving us? It's not that hard to figure out. Do we feel threatened, or do we celebrate when another church is growing and another pastor receives applause? Do we feel superior to pastors whose churches are smaller and inferior to those whose are larger? Is there a sense of resentment when others are asked to speak at pastors conferences and we're overlooked? Do we secretly rejoice when a successful leader falls? All of these (and many others) are signs we're insecure, fearful, and driven by pride instead of a "sincere and pure devotion to Christ" (2 Corinthians 11:3).

> The difficulty we have in accepting responsibility for our behavior lies in the desire to avoid the pain of the consequences of that behavior.
>
> —M. Scott Peck, *The Road Not Taken*

Clouded Personal Vision

Like leaders in every field, pastors often enter the ministry with youthful idealism. That's not a bad thing, unless it isn't soon tempered by experience and deepened by rubbing shoulders with seasoned, wise leaders. For many, the problem isn't the church's vision. That's clear enough. The difficulty is that they feel they're in a boat without a paddle on a fast-flowing river. They're moving, but they have little sense of place in the scheme of things.

This problem is often the cousin of role confusion. They want to serve in their strengths, but they know all the other tasks need to be done too—and done well. They see the corporate executives who come to church who have far more money and far more authority (at least, that's the way it seems, and we know it's not true), and they feel twinges of self-pity, resentment, and a desire to escape. Over time these pressures completely obliterate the original idealism. It morphs into cynicism. They try hard each day just to keep up with all the demands, but they're slowly dying inside.

The Hole in the Donut

David had his mighty men, Paul had Barnabas, Timothy, and Silas, but many leaders have no one they can call on for encouragement and support. Maybe they've tried opening up to a person on their leadership team or another leader, but they were given simplistic answers like "Just trust God" or "Pray about it." Trust and prayer are essential, but sometimes we need another person we can trust who will listen without giving advice or criticism, who will pray with us and for us. Without a true friend, lonely leaders put their heads down and plod forward. Tenacity is laudable, but people, like cars, run out of fuel, need new tires, and sometimes need major repairs. Neglect only leads to bigger problems.

Leaders need someone who will listen—really listen—as they talk about struggles with their families, their leadership team, their finances, and all the other complex problems they face. As a leadership consultant, I've found that simply listening with empathy is as helpful as finding a solution to an immediate problem. In the right time and the right way, leaders also need someone who will give them sound feedback about their team, communication, growth, and other issues, including personal challenges. They also need a pat on the back. Past experiences of being misunderstood shouldn't prevent leaders from looking again to find someone they can trust. Without a friend or two, they'll wither.

Unresolved Pain from the Past

Leaders don't enter their roles (or marriage or any other relationship or role) as blank slates. We may think we're rugged individualists, but to a large extent we've been shaped by our past experiences, especially our relationships with our parents. If that relationship was supportive, we have a solid platform to take risks and excel. There are no guarantees—we can still make a mess of our lives no matter how wonderful our parents have been—but we have a head start on love and trust in relationships and making work meaningful.

Two stories from the National Football League show the impact of the past. The documentary *The Book of Manning* describes Archie Manning's very positive influence on his sons, Cooper, Peyton, and Eli, but especially Peyton. Archie was a football star at the University of Mississippi in the late 1960s. He had a career in the NFL, primarily with the New Orleans Saints. During those years, his sons were born and began to show prowess on the football field. Archie's father had committed suicide when Archie was a boy, so his dad wasn't around to share his victories and defeats.

As the Manning boys grew up, Archie was dedicated to changing the family script. He became a devoted, attentive father. The documentary focuses on the love, understanding, encouragement, and support Archie gave his three sons. Top programs recruited all three, but their careers weren't all successes and awards. Before his first game at Ole Miss, Cooper was diagnosed with a congenital spine disorder. The surgery wasn't a complete success, and for a while the family wondered if he'd ever walk again. Through the long days of pain and anguish, Archie was by his side. Peyton became a premier quarterback in college and in the NFL. His strong relationship with his father provided a firm foundation of love and trust so he could excel on the field. Eli showed remarkable promise as a quarterback at Ole Miss, but a drinking problem almost cost him his career. Again, Archie's support and direction helped a son steer to the right track for his life and his football career. By the end of the documentary, viewers are struck by the obvious love, humility, courage, and tenderness the family shares. Cooper, Peyton, and Eli stand on the shoulders of their dad, a great and good man.[10]

A second example shows the other side. Painful relationships can have a range of destructive effects. Some people react to hurt, fear, and anger by withdrawing into a shell of self-protection. Some try desperately to please others to win the approval they've missed. And still others are driven to prove themselves worthy of the respect denied them. Brett Favre was a driven man. He explained to *USA Today* that his father's message that he was never good enough drove him to become one of the best quarterbacks in NFL history and compelled him to keep playing far beyond the age most quarterbacks retired from the league.

His dad had also been his high school coach. He demanded excellence from Brett, and he didn't accept any excuses. When Irv Favre died at age fifty-eight from a heart attack, Brett "lost his biggest fan—and most vocal second-guesser." His father was tough on his son. Brett remembers, "If you grew up in a household with a football coach who looks like a drill sergeant, you would think you would be tough. Anytime I was hurt, or thought I was hurt, his advice was, 'Get your ass up.' Most of the time, I was probably milking it, like any kid who wants attention. He was having none of it. Never did he say he loved us. But we knew. And vice versa: We never said it to him."

Favre had two ways of coping with the pain of his childhood: he was driven to be the best, and he used alcohol and prescription drugs to numb the pain. One was considered by most fans to be a laudable character trait, but they didn't understand the source of his unquenchable ambition. And most people excused the abuse of prescription drugs as simply a result of the aches and pains of an NFL player. Favre's wife, Deanna, knew better. After he tried to get clean several times and failed (even when the league mandated treatment), she gave him an ultimatum: stop the drugs or she was going to leave him.

Throughout his career, Favre continued to hear the voice in the back of his mind, the critical voice of his father that drove him to be the best. In the year he came out of retirement to play again, he explained, "Part of my success always has been that I felt I had something to prove, even after I won three MVPs. That has not changed today. If I am going to play, I'm going to be the best and have this chip [on my shoulder]. You have to play with the mentality that you are about to lose your job, and that they're going to talk about 'The Other Guy' first. You have to think, 'I want my name mentioned first.'"[9]

To a significant degree, all of us are products of our past. We may have the blessing of wonderful parents who built a foundation of security, love, strength, and courage, and we want to pay it forward to our children and churches. But many of us didn't have parents like Archie Manning. We may not have been abused or abandoned, but to a degree we came into our marriages and careers with deficits—deficits we may not have ever recognized. Our natural and normal desire is to please others to win approval, dominate to control people and situations, or hide behind walls of self-protection—and probably a combination of these coping strategies. Each one promises short-term relief, control, power, and applause, but they don't resolve the underlying problem of genuine hurt. And that pain will eventually bite us.

> There is no coming to consciousness without pain.
>
> —Carl Jung

When the Pain Overwhelms Us

There is a common fallacy that Christians should be immune to pain, suffering, and heartache. The image presented by some high-profile leaders is that walking with God always enables us to fly on eagles' wings over our troubles. If this is the expectation for the average Christian, what is it for pastors and other leaders? Sadly, many of them expect, to use J. I. Packer's trenchant phrase, "more than God intends to deliver." This false expectation of always soaring over problems, Packer asserts, is cruel because it sets people up for crushing disappointment and even depression.[10]

Perfectionism is a fairly rare theological conviction among a handful of Christians, but functionally it is an epidemic among leaders and pastors of all theological stripes. Tenderhearted and often insecure leaders absorb criticism from others, and they compound it with negative self-talk. After a while, they don't need any help coming up with self-condemning accusations. They're self-contained soul destroyers. After a very good sermon, they tell themselves, "That part wasn't clear. I should have looked at one more commentary. The lady in the third row was sleeping. Was it really that bad? I forgot a key line in that illustration. What's the matter with me? Will I ever get it right?"

And that's after a good sermon.

After meetings with the leadership team, the messages are much the same: "Bob disagreed with me. I wonder if he'll talk to others to get them on his side. I didn't explain my plans very well. No wonder they're against me. I've listened to Patrick Lencioni talk about leading teams. Won't I ever learn how to do it?"

Perfectionism creates unrealistic expectations, which inevitably produce either nagging self-condemnation or crushing self-doubt. But this isn't the only thing that can overwhelm leaders. A strained marriage, kids out of control, debt, health problems, unresolved tension, taking care of elderly parents, moral failure, secretiveness, and a hundred other problems can take them beyond discouragement into depression.

Depression comes in many different forms and from several different causes. Some forms have physiological causes, such as illness, cancer, or a chemical imbalance caused by disease. Most cases of depression, however, are caused by circumstances outside the body; in other words, unrelieved stress and unresolved anger. One of the classic ways to describe this kind of depression is anger turned inward. This common depression can range from mild to severe. According to the Mayo Clinic, dysthymia is

> a mild but long-term (chronic) form of depression. Symptoms usually last for at least two years, and often for much longer than that. Dysthymia interferes with your ability to function and enjoy life.
>
> With dysthymia, you may lose interest in normal daily activities, feel hopeless, lack productivity, and have low self-esteem and an overall feeling of inadequacy. People with dysthymia are often thought of as being overly critical, constantly complaining and incapable of having fun.[11]

Major depression is a more severe form. It may occur only once in a person's life, but more commonly people have multiple episodes. During these periods, a person experiences a significantly impaired ability to function at home and at work. Stress-related symptoms are more pronounced. People sometimes have thoughts of suicide and may even act on those thoughts.

In an article on the silent suffering of pastors, Fred Smoot, executive director of Emory Clergy Care in Duluth, Georgia, reported that when pastors can't live up to the excessive demands placed on them by their own perfectionism and the expectations of others, they often "turn their frustration back on themselves," which produces a downward spiral of self-condemnation and hopelessness. Furthermore, Matthew Stanford, professor of psychology at Baylor University, observed that depression in the Christian culture carries a "double stigmatization"—the culture's stigma about mental illness coupled with Christian "over-spiritualizing" depression by dismissing it as a lack of faith or a sign of weakness. This makes it very difficult for pastors to talk about the stress they suffer on the way down the long slide into hopelessness, and it makes it equally difficult to admit to themselves or anyone else when they hit the bottom.[12]

Honesty and objectivity—the first important components of dealing with depression—are as near as the pages of the Bible. The psalms are full of outpourings of grief, anger, disappointment, horror, and calls for revenge as well as love, praise, joy, and hope. In fact, theologian Martin Marty observed that half of the psalms are, in his words, "wintry." Laments aren't sub-Christian; they are part of a vibrant, authentic walk with God. Indeed, the prophet Isaiah asserted, "Those who hope in the LORD will renew their strength. They will soar on wings like eagles." But the verse doesn't stop there. In a life of faith, sometimes we soar but more often "they will run and not grow weary." And occasionally, the power of the Spirit enables faithful followers to face heartache so that "they will walk and not be faint" (Isaiah 40:31).

God's gracious assurance is that when we're at our worst, he hasn't abandoned us. The psalmist recounts his fury and God's tender touch:

When my heart was grieved
and my spirit embittered,
I was senseless and ignorant;
I was a brute beast before you.

Yet I am always with you;
you hold me by my right hand.
You guide me with your counsel,
and afterward you will take me into glory.
Whom have I in heaven but you?
And earth has nothing I desire besides you.
My flesh and my heart may fail,
but God is the strength of my heart
and my portion forever. (Psalm 73:21–26)

If we're open to the touch of God, he'll use even our deepest pain to draw us closer to him. Perfectionism wrecks us and poisons our hearts, but grace restores us. J. I. Packer explains how God's grace operates in our pain:

This is what all the work of grace aims at—an even deeper knowledge of God, and an ever-closer fellowship with Him. Grace is God drawing us sinners closer and closer to Him. How does God in grace prosecute this purpose? Not by shielding us from assault by the world, the flesh, and the devil, nor by protecting us from burdensome and frustrating circumstances, nor yet by shielding us from troubles created by our own temperament and psychology; but rather by exposing us to all these things, so as to overwhelm us with a sense of our own inadequacy, and to drive us to cling to Him more closely. This is the ultimate reason, from our standpoint, why God fills our lives with troubles and perplexities of one sort or another—it is to ensure that we shall learn to hold Him fast.[13]

In the book *Overcoming the Dark Side of Leadership*, Gary McIntosh and Samuel Rima contend that the pain that causes perfectionism, the thirst for approval, and the insatiable drive to succeed actually propel a leader to excel. Thus, pain can catapult a leader toward success.[14]

The Allure of Nothingness

People have different breaking points, but most people under unrelenting pressure eventually conclude that it's better to feel nothing than endure the pain any longer. I'm not talking about suicide; I'm talking about emotional numbness. It's easier to stay busy, watch television, and read every word of the sports section even though we don't give a hoot about Arena League Football, cricket, or curling. Distractions consume our time and our hearts. They rob us of joy, meaning, drive, and love. Temporary avoidance may be better than the pain we're suffering, but we pay a steep price for diversions.

When leaders go numb, they withdraw from their spouses, their children, and their teams. They may still relate to people who don't ask much from them. That's easy. Those people aren't threatening. It's harder to hide from those who are close, who notice and ask hard questions. These are the ones we must avoid!

When numbed leaders flatline their feelings, they try to go through all the motions, but their hearts are far, far away. They may not feel the crushing pain of the stress as much as before, but neither do they feel love, joy, and celebrations of God's blessings. It's easy to slip from taking responsibility to assigning blame when things don't go well. Numbed leaders become sour, crabby, impatient, and selfish.

Sam Ranier, writer and senior pastor of Stevens Street Baptist Church in Cookeville, Tennessee, compares emotional numbness to legs falling asleep after sitting too long in a cramped position. Usually, the numbness goes away as the tingles subside. The effect doesn't last long. But emotional numbness can last for years. "And the longer you are detached," he explained, "the more painful waking up will be. The longer you are asleep, then the more intense the wake-up process. You'll have to fight through that pins and needles feeling, shake yourself and start circulating again. Because to remain detached is to die. Slowly. Painlessly numb."[15]

God never wastes our pain. At the Aspen Ideas Festival, host Bob Schieffer of CBS's *Face the Nation* opened the floor for questions after interviewing T. D. Jakes. A woman said, "You're a preacher. Why don't you preach to us?"

Jakes had a simple sermon that day. He said, "When you're born, you're like a key with no cuts in it. As you go through life, each wound, failure, hurt . . . cuts into that strip of metal. And one day there is a clear *click*—your pain has formed the key that slips into the lock and opens your future."[16]

A church leader who trains hundreds of pastors each year told an audience that the pain we experience in the first forty years of our lives gives us the wisdom and experience for a far more profound ministry for the rest of our lives. Somehow that statement provides a wealth of hope as we go through heartaches, disappointments, and failure.

Know This

Stress isn't the problem. *Too much unrelieved stress* is the culprit.

Do This

Make a time line of your life. Identify the most significant events, pleasant and painful, even if the only person who knows about them is you. Then list the five most painful events of your life. How much do each of these haunt your thoughts, color your emotions, and compel you to please others, prove yourself, or hide from risks?

Think About This

1. What are some signs of unrelieved stress in your life?
2. Think about Dr. Swenson's tree branch. What shape has your branch been in over the past few years? How about right now? How can you tell?
3. What are some common causes of your stress? How do you normally handle the tension (pleasing, proving, hiding, getting busy, being distracted, becoming numb, etc.)?
4. Describe the double stigma of depression for leaders.
5. Do you agree or disagree with the statement, "God never wastes our pain"? Explain.

And remember: *you'll grow only to the threshold of your pain.*

4

GROWING PAINS

*Change is hard because people overestimate the value
of what they have—and underestimate the value
of what they may gain by giving that up.*
—JAMES BELASCO AND RALPH STAYER

Philip Wagner, Pastor of Oasis Church, Los Angeles, California

For many years, I didn't equate "leadership" with "pain." I equated leadership with vision, strength and success. I see it differently now.

I realize now that with responsibility come difficult decisions, painful seasons, as well as some tremendously rewarding victories. Leaders are problem-solvers. The better we are at solving problems, the better we are as leaders. People are the source of the great joys in our life. People are also the greatest source of our pain. Either way, Jesus asks us to love them.

A few years ago, Holly and I went to Cancun on vacation. We had three weeks to play and get refreshed. It was great... blue water, white sand, chips and salsa and no pressure. When I returned, one of the pastors on staff came into my office and sat down. He said hesitantly, "I think I may have made a mistake while you were gone."

The memories of white sand and blue water began to flow out of my soul like water going down a drain. I looked at him waiting, with a little fear, to hear what this "mistake" was. He continued, "I've started having meetings in my home, and we want to start a church."

A sick feeling slowly invaded my stomach. I blurted out, "Wait. What? You've started meetings in your home?"

He swallowed hard and told me, "I've wanted to start a church for sometime now, and I just felt God was saying to me that this is the time."

"This is the time?" I thought, *"While I was out of town?"* I said out loud: "So, while I'm paying you to help me pastor *this* church, you invited some members of this congregation to your home and are planning to start *your own* church? Does that sound ethical to you?" I was reaching for some logic.

He answered, "Well, several people had come to me and were thinking of leaving Oasis anyway, and I want to lead this new church."

I took a deep breath and looked him right in the eyes: "Did you wonder what it is about you that caused people to feel safe to tell you what they didn't like about the church and know that you would probably agree with them rather than help them see it differently?"

At this point I began to wonder if he would say anything in this conversation that didn't sound worse than the last statement he made. Then he said, "We've taken up an offerings to help get started."

I guess not. He paused for a second and then said apologetically, "I probably should've waited and talked to you about it."

I wanted to scream, *"You think!??"* But instead, I told him, "Bob," (let's call him,) "why didn't you talk to me first? You said you've always wanted to start a church—but you never mentioned that to me. Ever. Not even once."

Silence.

Then I asked, "Have I ever said or done anything that would make you think I would react negatively or wouldn't support you?"

He shrugged, "No. Never."

I pleaded, "Please don't do it this way. Please! If you do, relationships will be broken that will never be repaired. Some people will be so hurt they will never attend another church. Think about the people. There's a better way."

But in his mind, God had spoken.

That night I talked to a friend who is a pastor of a large church. He reassured me and gave me some welcomed advice. He said, "We've all been through this before and will probably go through it again. It'll be ok. It doesn't feel like it now, but it will."

I remembered hearing Pastor Bill Hybels say that it seemed like every four to five years a healthy, growing church has a major staff problem. *"Really?"* I thought. *"Great."*

Later, sitting with my wife staring at the wall in the darkened living room, I finally conceded, "I don't think I can take this anymore. This is too hard."

I thought to myself, *"Maybe I can get my old job back as a software salesperson or that limo driver position. Maybe, but probably not."*

In the situation with our staff member, every emotional issue that I've ever had (or thought I may have), surged to the surface, racing out of my insecurities like dogs when you open the back door to let them run. Some despair, a little shame, anger, confusion, not wanting to trust people, depression, feelings of betrayal and (throw in a little germ-o-phobia) you've got the picture. I was far exceeding Gideon's list of reasons why he was not the right guy for this job.

Over the next few weeks, people left Oasis—family after family and friend after friend. Friendships broke apart that may never mend. Some people left the church never to return to any church–ever.

The questions were unrelenting. "Is the bleeding ever going to stop?" "Can I ever trust people again?" "Could I get Michael Franzese, former Mafia boss, who's now a Christian, to be on our Board of Directors?"

As I met with people who were leaving, conversation after conversation began with, "I really love Oasis and all that the church has done for my family and me. I don't know where my life would be without this ministry." And ended with, "But I'm leaving the church."

Those weeks were about as enjoyable as walking through a minefield. In spite of the pain, I kept showing up each Sunday. We prayed and worshipped. We loved people. We taught the Word and led people to Jesus. I didn't end up quitting or raising someone from the dead. (I'm still working on it though.)

A miracle happened. People kept coming. I found that Jesus builds His church. I still try to help Him out a bit. Through every transition, especially the painful ones, He proves faithful to make us stronger and better than we were before. For thirty years, we have pastored a great church. And every four or five years a few people give us the chance to love them like we had not intended.

In these circumstances I have learned a few important lessons:

- First, we must keep loving people. We can't allow ourselves to lead from bitterness. Sometimes the greatest pain produces our greatest lessons.
- Second, people are going to do what they want to do. There's nothing you can do but keep doing the right thing and trusting God.

In transition and often in pain, some leaders lose faith or their sense of identity. Their story crumbles to the ground; their dreams fade. Others choose to face the pain and get stronger.

I'm glad that God has called me to leadership as a Pastor. But I've had to decide to keep going, to keep trusting, to face the pain and somehow get stronger. I wouldn't trade the opportunity I've been given for anything.

God reminds me, "Stand firm. Let nothing move you. Always give yourselves fully to the work of the Lord, because you know that your labor in the Lord is not in vain" (1 Corinthians 15:58 NIV).

**Bishop Walter Thomas, New Psalmist
Baptist Church, Baltimore, Maryland**

By 1991, our church had outgrown the building where we'd worshipped for the previous 13 years. It was an historic landmark built in 1844. As our congregation grew, we added services and expanded as much as possible. We were bursting at the seams. It was abundantly clear that it was time to move to another site.

At the time, we had purchased land about 15 minutes up the road. Our school was already built and meeting there. I told our church leaders and the congregation that it was time for us to build on the new land. I scheduled meetings with a project manager. We went over architectural plans for the new buildings, including a worship center, classrooms, office space, a gym, and everything else we wanted. I gladly told people about the progress we were making. I was excited!

Then, our key leaders and I had a meeting for the project manager to give us the cost of the new building. When the words came out of his mouth, I was stunned. He said, "Bishop, the cost of the new facilities will be $16 million."

In the previous history of our church, the most we had spent for any new addition to our campus was $215 thousand. I immediately told everyone in the room, "This meeting is over." As they walked out, a flood of emotions swept over me. I was devastated . . . disheartened. I felt ashamed that I had made a promise I couldn't keep. I was a failure . . . a foolish failure. I had encouraged the people to get their hopes up, and now those hopes were going to be shattered. How was I going to tell our people that we couldn't do what I'd promised?

I've only had three headaches in my life. This was one of those times. My head throbbed and my heart ached. We couldn't stay where we were, but we couldn't afford the new building. I saw myself as Moses leading the people of Israel at their moment of crisis: They were stuck with the Red Sea in front of them and the army of Pharaoh behind them. They needed God's deliverance. We did, too.

I pleaded with the Lord for wisdom. Suddenly, I had a breakthrough: We didn't need all the money at the beginning. We only needed the income stream to support the debt. The level of the income stream would dictate the amount we could borrow, which determined the scope of the new facility.

I met with our financial experts at the church. Together, we went through all the reasonable projections of income from our congregation, and we determined that the limit of the budget for the new facility would be $7.5 million. That's the size of the facilities we could afford and we would build—all of that and not a square foot more.

To build a facility of that size, we needed about a third of it at the beginning for a down payment—that's $2.5 million. We needed that amount in two years when the loan would be granted and construction begins. I had another meeting with our accountant. We already had some money saved, but we needed an additional $750 thousand each year for the next two years—which is roughly $15 thousand a week. I told our bookkeeper, "Every week for the next two years, we're going to transfer $15 thousand from our general fund checking account to our savings account."

It actually took us three years to reach our goal, but we made it. When we got the loan and construction began, we kept saving money every week and put it into savings. This gave us $60 thousand each month in savings. The mortgage on the new facility was $39 thousand, and the utilities averaged $10 thousand a month. This let us add about $11 thousand to our savings account each month, or about $130 thousand each year.

A few years ago, we realized we had outgrown that facility, and we needed to build again. This time, we used the same principles and processes we had implemented over 20 years before. The new mortgage was about six times higher, but the process remained the same. We put money into savings each week, paid the mortgage and utilities, and continued to build our savings.

Back in 1991, I was crushed by the news that our reach was so much farther than our grasp, but God gave us a solution. We stopped worrying about the total amount, and we focused on the level of our income stream. It's not about the total cost, but only about the cash flow.

My advice for a pastor who faces any kind of crisis is to give yourself one day to moan, whine, and feel sorry for yourself. Just one day . . . then get up, ask God for direction, and take your people where He leads you. Leaders can't afford to collapse for more than a day. They then have to seek solutions. We don't have the luxury to be paralyzed by anxiety and discouragement. We have an obligation to trust God for a workable solution and a plan of action. Begin with the positive assumption that God *always* has a plan. You may not have discovered it yet, but He has one for you.

Another piece of advice is to avoid promising your people more than you can deliver. In churches with congregational polity, members want to know as much information as possible at every stage in the planning process, but be sure to give only the facts as they develop. You may be excited and have a wonderful vision, but don't let your excitement run past the hard realities of numbers and dates. Know the budget before you make any pronouncements about the future of a building project. When the financial boundaries are set, don't color outside the lines. You'll save yourself from embarrassment, and you'll save your people from confusion and stress.

When Patrick became the senior pastor of a church in Chicago, he had plenty of ideas, visions, and dreams for the church. In fact, one of the reasons the search committee was so impressed with him was that his plans for the church were both visionary and practical. He knew where he wanted to lead them, and he had specific plans for leadership development, community outreach, and all kinds of other programs.

For the first six months, everything clicked. His small staff team and the lay members of the church leadership team were more than receptive to Patrick—they were thrilled! The church grew from 250 to about 350. Things were looking good. Patrick began to plan for a church of 500. As he thought and prayed, he realized some of the staff and key volunteers who could handle a church of 250 were straining under the load of leading a church of 350. He realized they didn't have the capacity for 500.

Over the next three months, Patrick began implementing a gradual plan to either replace or retrain and reassign many of the people who had been so excited about his arrival. He anticipated some pushback from a few people, but he hadn't expected the firestorm of resentment and accusations that seemed to come from all sides. In a few short weeks, he had gone from respected leader and friend to arrogant, unappreciative tyrant.

Actually, Patrick soon learned that the resistance was led by only a few people: one staff member and two people who led departments as volunteers. They were angry and vocal, and they talked to everyone with an ear. Patrick felt blindsided. He had tried to find a place for everyone, but he had to make some hard decisions about leadership if the church was going to grow. At first, Patrick tried to meet with each of the angry people. But instead of resolution, his attempted to explain his vision and their new roles were like throwing gas on a fire.

Patrick concluded that the heartache—theirs and his—simply wasn't worth it. He backed down. He apologized for pushing too hard too soon and asked them to stay in their current positions. For the next five years, the church fluctuated between 250 and 350 people. There was, during all this time, an undercurrent of distrust between Patrick and the ones who had defied him.

Their attitudes weren't evident all the time or to many people, but Patrick knew. He left the church because he realized he had lost his authority to lead. When he looked in the rearview mirror, he concluded that he knew what had to be done, but he was too afraid. He wasn't willing to handle the pain of change.

> Leaders have to be the midwife of the pain in the birth of new things. They have to hold the hand and help the body deal with pain productively.
>
> —Bill Easum

Paying the Price

Virtually all leaders in every field of business or ministry assume that growth will relieve stress, but growth actually increases stress. This misunderstanding adds a large measure of confusion to the considerable pains of leadership.

In conversations at conferences, some church leaders make a colossal—and colossally wrong—assumption about megachurch pastors. They shake their heads and say, "Those guys have it easy! They have all the resources in the world. Maybe someday I'll get there too." I shake my head too, but for a different reason. I know a lot of pastors of huge churches, and they tell me about the incredible chaos of leading a large organization.

Again and again, I talk with pastors who haven't yet grasped this fundamental principle of organizational leadership: if you want to grow, you have to learn the lessons of pain and suffering. Many disheartened pastors tell me, "I want my church to grow. I pray for God's blessing of increase, but the problems only multiply." These pastors are surprised by the obstacles, opposition, and strains they encounter. I can almost hear their prayers, "God, what happened? Won't you answer my prayers and fix this mess?"

I try to assure them that God is, indeed, answering their prayers. He's giving them the experience of pain—opposition, conflict, and resistance—to expand their capacity for more compassion and wisdom than they've ever had before. Difficulties are God's curriculum for those who want to excel.

In an article for *Church Leaders*, James MacDonald admits that, as a young man, he was often dismayed that the leaders of his Bible college, seminary, and church seemed to be clueless about some obvious problems. He wondered if their problem was blindness or timidity. Either way, their passivity was hurting the cause of Christ. Finally, he concluded that they couldn't see the problems at all.

Now, however, he has changed his opinion. With considerable organizational experience, he realizes there was (and is) a very different problem that causes leaders to remain immobile in the face of genuine needs. It's not blindness. They see the problems: poor performance by key people in leadership positions, toxic attitudes that spread dissension, outdated systems and structures, paralyzed leadership that effectively blocks innovation and creativity. MacDonald concludes, "THEY SEE IT ALL, but they are unwilling to pay the price to address it."

The price is the figurative blood of leadership: having your sanity or integrity questioned, the uncertainty of taking bold risks, the pain of hard conversations and replacing people (many of whom are friends) who no longer fit the larger scope of responsibilities, and the strain of being publicly positive while dealing with the myriad of private pains of change.

Leading a growing, changing, dynamic organization requires tremendous courage, wisdom, and tenacity. The leaders MacDonald saw when he was young weren't willing to pay the price to acquire those traits. For them and countless others, the price was simply too high. MacDonald concluded, "I understand their choice; I just don't respect it."[1]

Planning for Pain

For the past few decades, many consultants have observed particular (if somewhat arbitrary) points in a church's growth that require new insights and skills to break through to the next growth barrier. In *How to Break Growth Barriers*, Carl George identifies these levels at 200, 400, 600, and 800.[2] Pastor and consultant Nelson Searcy pegs the specific levels on a broader scale: 65, 125, 250, 500, and 1,000.[3]

Some pastors have a vision for growth but few specifics about how to get there. They assume better sermons, better children's ministry, or better donuts—coupled with fervent prayer—will cause people to flock to their churches. I'm all for prayer, better sermons, good programs, and great donuts, but pastors really need *anticipatory vision*. In other words, they need to anticipate what they'll need in order to get where God wants them to go. As they dream, pray, and plan to get all their resources in order, they'll be creating a ripple effect of change throughout the organization. If they're not ready for it—and if they're not willing to pay the price—they'll stay stuck at their current personal and organizational status. Growth always involves pain. In organizational growth, leaders actually cause pain, but for a very good reason. It's the only way to grow.

At every growth barrier, pastors need to deepen their insights and sharpen their skills. When they stop growing, their church will stop growing. The areas that often (if not always) need attention are people, structures, leadership development, space, being outward focused, and personal growth.

> Unless you are prepared to give up something valuable, you will never be able to truly change at all, because you'll be forever in the control of things you can't give up.
>
> —Andy Law, *Creative Company*

People

We'll start with the hardest area first. You may have hired your best friend to be the assistant pastor, your wife to be in charge of the women's ministry, your aunt to play the keyboard, and your son's best friend to be your youth pastor. Or you may have become friends with whoever has been in one of these roles, but now you realize that their capacity is limited. You patiently try to expand the staffer's skills and vision, and maybe you see a little progress—or maybe you think you see more progress than is really there. Slowly, grudgingly, you conclude there are key people on your team who can't take you and the church to the next level. The wrong people are holding your ladder.

First, you need to make people decisions slowly. Be kind and gracious, but always hire for at least the next level of growth. If your church is at 400, hire a youth pastor who can be effective for a church of 600 or 800. Yes, those people are harder to find, but you'll save yourself a lot of headaches by hiring for the future instead of later having to replace someone who has been in a role for a few years but doesn't have the wheels to take the church to the next level of growth.

No one has all the gifts, so you're not looking for superheroes. You may choose someone who is a visionary leader. Make sure that person has a team filled with team builders and administrators. You may choose someone who is terrific at building a great team. Make sure you keep the vision fresh so they realize their great relationships are making a difference on a wider scale. You get the idea. If everybody on your senior leadership team has the same gifts, you'll stagnate. Value diversity and welcome different perspectives, but be sure to recruit, hire, and train people for at least one level higher than your church is today.

With a few exceptions, almost every change in personnel is a traumatic experience for the leader, the team member, and the rest of the staff. Even if you hire well, you'll experience turnover because other churches will see the quality of your rising leaders and hire them. That's a compliment, not a threat.

Structures

In small churches you can have staff meetings in the front seat of a Fiat. As the church grows and team members are added, you have to be more intentional about every form of communication, delegation, authority, and reporting. Developing structures that fit a larger organization requires a blend of art and science. Clear lines of responsibility need to be established, and team members need to coordinate their efforts with others to avoid a silo effect, which occurs in an organization when departments don't share information, often resulting in suspicion and inefficiency. As the church grows, communication with the leadership team and key volunteers needs to continually improve.

I've talked to many leaders who were perplexed that their key people just didn't get it: they shared their vision and strategy, but their team members failed to act. But the problem may not be one-sided. Sometimes their key staff members and volunteers were frustrated because they didn't get enough information from the ministry leader. At every rising level of growth, new, more efficient structures of communication are required. The organizational chart may look similar to the last one, but more care needs to given to be sure everyone understands their role. Every new addition to a team adds an ever-expanding web of interconnections, which makes communication and coordination increasingly complicated.

Leadership Development

One pastor got the picture. He asked, "*How many* leaders and *what kind* of leaders will our church need to grow from three hundred to five hundred in the next two years?"

The size of your leadership team is like a layer of sand on a tabletop. The quality of leaders determines how much sand stays on top and how much falls off. It doesn't matter if you have a lot of leaders if they don't know how to lead.

I've consulted with a number of pastors who were frustrated with the ineffectiveness of their leadership development strategies. In many cases, these were entrepreneurial pastors who mistakenly assumed that other people were just like them—all they need is a little direction to figure something out on their own. That's seldom the case in reality. Yes, we love it when an enthusiastic, creative go-getter takes an idea and develops an effective ministry with little input from us, but most people need more help. A lot more.

> Settling is no fun. It's a malignant habit, a slippery slope that takes you to mediocrity. The art of leadership is understanding what you can't compromise on.
>
> —Seth Goddin, *Tribes*

Leadership conferences and delegation are important, but many people need the personal touch of encouragement and affirmation if they're going to thrive in a role, especially a volunteer role. In our culture, though, this gets tricky because a lot of connections between people happens on social media. I believe something crucial is lost if that's the primary means of communication for a team, but many people are so busy they don't have time—and they may think it's weird—when we ask them to actually meet us for coffee.

Your organization will grow only as fast as you can develop capable, godly leaders to broaden your base to connect meaningfully with more people. It's relationships that make these connections sticky. This puts more pressure on you to hire people who can be leaders of leaders as well as trainers of leaders. Another aspect of the complexity of leadership development is that the vast majority of people in your pipeline are volunteers, which means their motivation is primarily altruistic. You don't have the leverage of a paycheck to get them to do what you want them to do. This means you have to be more *passionate* as a visionary and more *compassionate* as a shepherd as you develop leaders for a growing church. And as your base expands, you can be sure some people won't be happy with you.

The pain associated with leadership development is the strain of pushing yourself to learn new strategies and change what's comfortable now into what's effective tomorrow. It's a lot easier to live with the familiar status quo than to stretch to acquire new skills—especially if the new strategies make others feel uncomfortable too.

Meeting Space

The most obvious growth barrier is the facility where your church meets. People may feel comfortable packing a concert hall shoulder to shoulder, but they don't like to be that close for worship. The rule of thumb is that a room is full if it's 70 to 80 percent of capacity.

Many churches solve the problem of limited space by adding services, but each worship gathering multiplies the complexities of administration and taxes personnel, to say nothing of the strain additional meetings have on the one who is speaking at each one.

A number of firms give sound advice about the seating capacity a church should consider when expanding or building a new facility. The point here isn't to give detailed instructions on architecture but to point out that a vision to grow inevitably produces the stress of enormously important decisions, such as the burden of raising funds, the coordination of transition plans, and the conflict of dissenting views. A vision of growth multiplies and intensifies the leader's pain significantly.

Outward Focus

Growing churches keep pushing themselves beyond the comfort of the members and regular attenders to reach out to the community in evangelism and mercy ministries. These efforts require more from the leader to be culturally relevant and inspiring as well as be an astute administrator. It is, of course, much less challenging to focus on the myriad of problems already existing in the church—and there are plenty to absorb a leader's time and energy. But a pastor who spends his time pleasing his congregants and solving existing problems will soon have a church that will plateau and soon decline.

Jesus, the Gospels tell us, saw that people were "harassed and helpless, like sheep without a shepherd" (Matthew 9:36), so he sent his followers out to care for them. We live in the most affluent country the world has ever known, but we don't have to look far in our own community to see harassed and helpless people. Some live in poverty, but even more suffer a bankrupt heart from the ravages of addiction, divorce, abuse, or abandonment. Single mothers and lonely elders need a smile and a helping hand. People notice when God's people care. More people come to Christ because they feel our love than because they're impressed with our building or our programs or our sermons.

Nelson Searcy identifies a benchmark for an outward focus: "In my experience, healthy, growing churches will have a 5:100 ratio of first-time guests to regular attendees. If you are averaging 200 people per week, you should average 10 first-time guests per week. Watch this ratio carefully, and take its waning as a warning sign."[4]

> Not everything that is faced can be changed. But nothing can be changed until it is faced.
>
> —James Baldwin

Personal Growth

The hours are long, the leaders need constant attention and encouragement, and the problems are complicated. That statement is true at every level of growth for a church. Some exhausted pastors tell me, "When our church gets to (fill in the number), then I'll have more resources and it won't be as much of a drain on me personally." They're dreaming.

When the well is running dry, we need to drill deeper. As a leader, your most valuable resource is your own heart. The greatest risk is becoming so tired, so discouraged, or so angry that your soul begins to shrivel. Then you're running on empty and running blind. When we're not replenishing our hearts with inspiration, encouragement, and insight, we have to strain just to make it through the next sermon or meeting. And if *we're* straining to make it through, we can be sure the people in our meetings are struggling, too, as they try to listen to us. When we remain dry for a long season, the desert often expands to our staff, key volunteers, and eventually the whole church.

In the other growing pains described in this chapter, leaders initiate change and subsequent discomfort. But in personal development, pain comes from inaction. The organization can only be spiritually, emotionally, and relationally healthy if the leader's heart is being nourished and strengthened. In the past couple of decades, Eugene Peterson has encouraged pastors to return to the time-honored practices of spiritual disciplines, the art of spiritual counsel, and the power of building intimacy through community. In *The Jesus Way*, he reminds us that spiritual vitality begins with a renewed focus on Christ himself:

> To follow Jesus implies that we enter into a way of life that is given character and shape and direction by the one who calls us. To follow Jesus means picking up rhythms and ways of doing things that are often unsaid but always derivative from Jesus, formed by the influence of Jesus. To follow Jesus means that we can't separate what Jesus is saying from what Jesus is doing and the way that he is doing it. To follow Jesus is as much, or maybe even more, about feet as it is about ears and eyes.[5]

When I've recommended personal development plans to pastors, some have shaken their heads and complained, "Yeah, yeah. You don't understand. I just don't have time." Yes, they'll pay a price if they carve out time to regularly replenish their souls, but they'll pay a higher price if they don't.

Insanity

My friend Scott Wilson is the lead pastor of The Oaks Fellowship near Dallas. A few years ago he realized his church had been bumping up against a numerical ceiling over and over again. No matter what new programs they tried, what new innovations they introduced, or what new staff they hired, they couldn't break through that barrier. Each effort brought a surge of growth, but it was never sustained. The brief blip was followed by a return to previous levels. Scott finally had an epiphany. He realized he had been trying to fix the wrong problem. Insanity, as the canard goes, is doing the same thing over and over again and expecting different results. Scott was committed to becoming sane and doing something different. He launched a comprehensive program to equip his staff and key lay leaders to be more passionate, knowledgeable, and effective.[6]

In an article for *Christianity Today*, Branimir Schubert noted, "There are two fundamental errors organizations make as they confront issues: ignoring the pain, and misdiagnosing it. . . . If organizations are unable to acknowledge their [organizational pain], the result will be a steady exodus of key people (if they have an option to leave), or will be manifested in a workforce that is detached, disillusioned, and does not perform to the best of their abilities. Ignoring the pain will not make the pain go away. Instead, it will spread."[7]

Many Christian organizations are reluctant to admit problems because they want to put on a face that says, "We're Christians. We walk with God. We don't have any problems . . . with anything!" Underneath the happy public face is the fear that their donors might not write a check or people might drive down the street to another church that seems to have it all together.

The other problem—misdiagnosis—focuses time, energy, and other resources on minor problems (or nonexistent ones) instead of the real issues facing the church. It's like having cancer, but the doctor looks at the x-rays and says, "You have a hangnail." You may, in fact, have a hangnail. It won't kill you, but untreated cancer will.

> Without change there is no innovation, creativity, or incentive for improvement. Those who initiate change will have a better opportunity to manage the change that is inevitable.
>
> —William Pollard

Some leaders see every problem through a lens they think they can handle. If they're excellent administrators, they see every difficulty as an organizational puzzle to be solved. If they're gifted counselors, they look for ways someone's family of origin shaped a poor performance for a simple delegated task. If the leader is theologically astute, he may assume the problem is caused by a doctrine that isn't properly understood by the conflicted parties. Of course, some problems are primarily administrative, have their roots in deep-seated psychological issues or unapplied doctrines, but it's a mistake to assume all problems have a single root cause.

Another problem of misdiagnosis is catastrophizing, that is, making every minor dispute, misunderstanding, or failure into an emphatic end-of-the-world disaster. When leaders make mountains out of molehills, people want to run for the hills no matter how big or small the problem may really be.

Pain Before Promotion

When you chart the course of your church toward growth, start with one basic assumption: your efforts to grow are going to create many, many problems. Expect them, anticipate them, and welcome them as God's instructors.

All the heroes in Hebrews 11 faced daunting challenges before they were rewarded. It's a principle of life that *pain comes before promotion*. David's experiences illustrate this point in several ways:

- He had to fight and kill a lion and a bear to prepare himself to face Goliath.
- He had to kill Goliath before Saul could invite him to the palace.
- He had to dodge Saul's spear and run for his life before he became king himself.
- He had to fight several wars to unite the kingdom.

People and organizations grow with the fertilizer of pain. We may not like it. We may resist it. But it's a principle of the kingdom. To live, something has to die. In order to give birth, a mother has to endure the suffering of the birth process. Before the resurrection was the pain of the cross. And Jesus said, "Whoever wants to be my disciple must deny themselves and take up their cross and follow me. For whoever wants to save their life will lose it, but whoever loses their life for me will find it" (Matthew 16:24–25). Before God promotes us, he takes us through pain to purify our hearts, deepen our dependence on him, and impart spiritual wisdom.

Joseph Mattera is a national and international church leader. He sees this pattern in his life and writes:

> I don't believe God has ever promoted me when I thought I was ready! Thank God He has waited until He knew I was ready for more responsibility! God loved David so much that He *didn't want him to be a king until he had every semblance of fleshly authority beaten out of him!* It has been my experience that, before God promotes me to the next level that I am already walking in that higher level anointing and authority, but without the position and the title. I have the anointing first, but then come a *series of challenging tests* meant to beat the flesh out of me so I don't explode with pride when I get to the next level! The transition has to take place internally before it ever manifests externally.[8]

As we've seen in these chapters, some of our pain is self-inflicted, the accumulation of unrelieved stress. Some is the result of external challenges, and we suffer heartaches and headaches because we're trying to grow and fulfill God's purpose for our churches. The goal, then, is sometimes to avoid pain, sometimes to relieve pain, sometimes to create the pain of growth, but always to learn the lessons God has for us in the midst of our pain.

Know This

We mistakenly assume growth will relieve stress, but it actually increases it.

Do This

Identify at least three ways your vision for growth has caused additional headaches and heartaches for you.

Think About This

1. What are some reasons many pastors (and other leaders) aren't willing to pay the price for growth and change?
2. What is your current size? How would you identify and describe your next growth barrier?
3. Describe how your vision for breaking the next growth barrier has created problems in these areas:
   - People
   - Structures
   - Leadership development
   - Space
   - Outward focus
   - Personal development
4. Think about leaders you know, or maybe your own experience, and describe the damage done by ignoring or misdiagnosing problems in their (or your) organizations.
5. Do you really believe that pain comes before promotion? Explain your answer.

And remember: *you'll grow only to the threshold of your pain.*

5

WHAT MAKES YOU TICK

A life isn't significant except for its impact on other lives.
—Jackie Robinson

Maury Davis, Senior Pastor of
Cornerstone Church, Nashville, Tennessee

On May 23, 1975, I found myself sitting in the Dallas County Jail waiting to be sent to a maximum security unit in the Texas Department of Corrections for the next twenty years.

Life had been painful for me. My father was an alcoholic who left my mother, brother and me at an early age. How many Friday nights did I sit on the front porch with my little suitcase packed waiting on Dad to come pick us up for the weekend, only to be told it is time to unpack and come back in the house. Dad wasn't able to get past the nearest bar to come see me. My Mom married a man who was extremely demanding. Until I ran away from home at 15, I was scared of what might happen to me when he got home each day. Living in fear, I explored and experienced the mind-numbing relief that drugs brought. By the time I was 18, I was hooked. One day in the middle of a crime, I committed a murder.

After the trial, I sat in jail, saved by God, and convicted by men—reality was stark and real. I had been sentenced to 20 years, but the God who sent His Son for me had given me the miracle of my lifetime. I wrote the following letter that night to my family.

"Hello! I hope you are all as contented with this [sentence] as I am. I feel like I was very lucky, and God was in the jury's heart. I am ready to go to prison and begin my sentence. The bailiff said I would be eligible for parole in 3 to 30 years, but I feel like the nature of my crime will make that very hard to achieve.

I'll probably be here [in the county jail] about three more weeks before they take me down [to the state prison]. I won't be in touch for about three weeks, but ya'll don't worry about that because I'll be fine.

For the first time in my whole life I know what I am going to do. I'm going to go back to school in prison and study psychology. Then I'm going to take correspondence courses and get a degree in ministry. When I get out, I will find a use for myself, and hopefully I'll be able to help others. One thing I would like ya'll to be at peace about is when I get out. I've worried that prison would just make me a colder person, and now I know it won't. I'm going to try and work in the Chaplain's office, but I don't know if that's possible. That's something we'll just have to wait and see. I'm going to get all the good time I can and make Class A trustee. That could take a year or two.

Ya'll were all so strong in court. That it made it easier on me. Thank you!

The thing that makes me happy is that I will be able to come home before my siblings are grown up completely. That is really something I am thankful for . . . my family.

I'm praising God for His decision for it was merciful, but I ask you to change your prayers a little. Let us all pray that God uses us as examples to others and lets us show our love and help them..."

I wrote that letter 39 years ago after receiving the jury's miraculously merciful sentence that stunned the D.A.'s office and the judge. My journey with Christ began with a miracle of amazing grace. As I wrote that letter, my newfound faith was full, my expectations were spectacular, and my naiveté was far greater than I realized.

During almost nine years in prison, I grew in the things of God, but I also experienced the most devastating of human emotions—loneliness. There were days it seemed like no one really cared. I knew in my head that people loved me, but they were outside and I was inside. They were free and I was imprisoned. During those dark hours of heartfelt pain, God began to teach me some truths. He allowed me to understand the "wilderness" where Christ was led was a place of power, and the wilderness is nothing worse than a "lonely place." The persecution of other inmates never stopped, and yet something inside said, "Don't give up on God." Sometimes I felt like I just couldn't endure another day, but His grace was always sufficient when my emotions were weak.

I was released from prison in 1983, and the journey took on a new sweetness: FREEDOM and FAMILY! I went to work as a custodian in a large church in Irving, Texas. The Pastor, J. Don George, took me under his wing to mentor and develop me.

Once again I discovered that just because God is good doesn't mean the world, or even church work, is all fun and games. There were those who didn't believe my conversion was real. I had to endure the naysayers who gossiped and waited for their preconceived doubts about me to come true. God gave me Gail to be my wife, and then began restoring the years sin had destroyed by allowing her to conceive and give birth to the TRIPLETS! Yet the joy of birth was mitigated by our son's underdeveloped lung and the life-and-death medical attention he received the first week of his life. Sitting beside an incubator, praying for a miracle, once again reminded me that life isn't easy. In this world you will have tribulations! Once again, God showed His mighty hand, and all the babies came home totally healthy for Christmas.

Over the years, Gail and I traveled with the kids as evangelists. In 1991 we came to Nashville, Tennessee, to pioneer a church, only to be asked to help save a small, struggling church in Madison. For 20 years, the church grew in every measurable category: numbers, mission outreach, salvations, water baptisms, community influence—in every way He added increase. Yet along the way, people I loved left for one reason or another, and the pain of pastoring was always there. I realized that when you pray for people, love them, and in many ways live your life for them, rejection will make you feel like you are back in the wilderness again.

God added a child to our family during that time. It was a blessing, but not without trauma. When he was 11 months old, I sat beside him after surgery. Again, I felt numb.

I've discovered God is good and life is tough. You can count your blessings or your problems. What you focus on will determine the condition of your heart.

After 20 years of growth, I made a tragic hire and brought

on a staff member who was a sower of discord, rebellion and division. For whatever reason, I was blinded to his character flaws and his personal agenda to draw people to himself at the expense of the church. The staff became divided, and the once flourishing church began to struggle. For the first time in my ministry, I questioned my assignment. Depression, anxiety and a spirit of confusion welled up in me, yet once again God came to my rescue. When I went to jail, He sent a Pastor to bring me out of darkness and into His light. In the latest spiral of destruction, God sent another man named Dr. Sam Chand to help me get my eyes focused, my heart healthy, and this incredible church back on track. It took him almost three years, but today we have moved forward, and the church is healthy and growing. I'm full of joy once again with a clear vision, and the future continues to be bright.

This morning I left what my children affectionately refer to as "The Compound" and counted my blessings. That little farm is the dream home Gail and I always wanted. My oldest son and his family just moved back to live on the farm beside us—we have adjoining driveways. They returned from Phoenix two days ago. Watching my 18-month old granddaughter dance in the rain for the first time with her Daddy will be a precious memory.

Life is made up of hard knocks and incredible blessings. Pain is unavoidable, but I've learned it isn't eternal!

Andre Olivier, Pastor of Rivers Church, Johannesburg, South Africa

It can be said with certainty that pain is inevitable. However, it can also be said with certainty that misery is optional. All people experience pain and disappointment—no matter how committed they are to God and no matter how flawless their character.

I have faced some very painful situations, but I have determined that misery and pain will not shape my life or darken my heart. Our family has lost a grandchild to a drowning at three years old; and we have seen one of our staff members murdered in an armed robbery on our church property. We have also experienced rejection and misunderstanding as we pastored churches split by hurt and bitterness. We have loved people only to have them lie about us, talk behind our backs, and try to engineer our departure from the ministry.

Life is full of pain. The sooner we learn to bounce back in God's grace, the better our daily happiness, joy and equilibrium will be. God's grace is sufficient, and we must not become victims of our pain, otherwise misery will set in. We cannot stop what happens *to* us, but we can certainly stop what happens *in* us.

One event was particularly difficult. One cold winter's night, Wilma and I were at a leaders' meeting; our daughter, Simónne, who was about 14, was at someone's home. At about 10:30 that evening, Wilma went home alone. I stayed to talk to some people and then picked up Simónne and headed home. I arrived home to find the door unlocked and open, and the alarm deactivated, which was unusual. As I walked into our home with Simónne, it was dimly lit. I couldn't understand why Wilma had left the lights off and the door open. I was about to call out and ask her why she hadn't closed the door when I walked into the bedroom and saw her tied up on the bed with five armed gunmen standing around her. It was a nightmare!

In a flash I grabbed Simónne and darted down the hallway.

I ran for the door, but one of the men grabbed my daughter and held a gun to her. Another ran up to me with a gun and put it to my neck. I froze. They took us to the bedroom, tied us up tightly and began to threaten us with death if we didn't show them our safe and give them money. We had no safe or money. I tried to explain that we don't keep money at home, but they didn't relent. They ransacked the house and repeatedly came into the room, waving the gun in my face, demanding money and threatening us all.

After an hour of shock, terror, and much prayer, they came into the room again, lifted Simónne from the bed and took her toward another room. I realized they were about to rape her, so we continued to pray and trusted God for her safety. In South Africa a woman is raped every 3 minutes. The thought of having to watch or hear this event sent me into a state of shock I had never experienced before. Suddenly, they miraculously changed their minds, turned around and brought her back into the bedroom.

This threat occurred several times during the course of the evening. We stayed calm, prayed and trusted God for his deliverance while they packed up my vehicle and filled it with our jewelry, clothing, household items and electrical appliances. They then took me into a bathroom and locked the door. I thought they would surely kill or rape the girls, and I was powerless to stop them. Fear began to rage within me, so I continued to pray earnestly. They then put my daughter in a second bathroom and covered Wilma with a pile of clothing. Then they left and tried to drive away. They had difficulty driving my car because they couldn't locate the brake release. They spent a long time trying to get it going. During this time I escaped and alerted the neighbor. He fired a few shots in the air, and they ran off. By this time it was well past midnight. We called the police. The officers came to investigate, and some friends came to comfort us. They all left at around 2:00 in the morning, and we lay awake unable to sleep.

We recovered most of our things, but we lost some very valuable and sentimental jewelry Wilma had inherited. We were finally safe, but quite traumatized and fearful. In our country many people are scorched with hot irons, shot or raped during home robberies. For the next few months, we had 24-hour security guards before moving to a safer, more secure, gated complex.

The experience deeply affected each of us for several months. You look over your shoulder, and you don't trust anyone anymore. Everyone is treated with suspicion, and your life takes on a different tone, which can color all your relationships. The threats in our country are very real. Many Christian leaders have abandoned their calling out of fear for their safety, but we determined we would press on and trust God for fresh grace!

We have now moved past this experience and are wiser and stronger. We no longer live in fear, but with wisdom and caution so that we don't become victims of another home invasion. We have relied on God, forgiven the thieves for their actions, and have chosen to live a large life confidently, not allowing this experience to shrink our lives and our world. We are walking in the confidence and grace of God and relate well to all types of people without undue suspicion.

This hurtful and traumatic experience has enabled us to empathize with others who have been traumatized by crime, and it has served the purposes of God in our lives. People have seen how God carried us and renewed us by his Word and his Spirit, and they have been emboldened to trust God in their crises. It was a shocking and painful event, but it has not destroyed our faith in God or our hope in the future of our country. We are building a great church, investing in property and opening more campuses despite the crime and violence in our nation.

Pain is inevitable, but misery is optional! Don't allow your pain to define you or limit you. Let it make you wiser. Become a person who has learned to bounce back in life.

Despite the experience, Wilma, Simónne and I are involved in building people up despite the hurt that people may inflict on us. We have moved past the pain into our future and will not allow any painful experience to limit us or keep us under a ceiling.

At a national conference, a denominational leader who had been a pastor for more than twenty-five years met with two dozen young pastors and church planters and their spouses. At the beginning, he asked a simple question: "What are the expectations you shoulder in your role?"

It didn't take long for the answers to begin flowing:

"Great team leader . . . so everyone on the team is fulfilled."
"Skilled CEO, handling every opportunity and problem perfectly."
"Therapist, marriage counselor . . . and, oh, yeah, hospice nurse."
"An outstanding teacher."
"Yeah, Tim Keller, Joel Osteen, and T. D. Jakes rolled into one!"

A few people laughed, but not because it was funny. They laughed because it hit home. Then more responses came:

"Outstanding fund-raiser."

"And CPA. All the money has to be accounted for down to the last cent."

"Gifted evangelist, with dozens coming to Christ every week."

"With fresh, meaningful, unique things to say at every funeral and wedding."

"Leading every meeting, hiring the right staff, resolving every conflict, on top of cultural trends, finding incredible quotes and stories for sermons, always available to help those in need, weeping for those who are hurting."

Then the wives began to inject the expectations they felt:

"My husband is on call twenty-four hours a day, seven days a week. But people expect him to be the consummate family man, the best husband in the world, and for our kids to be the most godly, best-behaved children in the city! Let me tell you, they're not!"

"And people expect our marriage to be perfect. Believe me, it's not!"

"And don't forget, they expect us to see the face and hear the voice of Jesus every morning at 5:00 . . . if we have time for devotions."

At this point, nervous laughter mingled with a few sobs. Then one of the young pastors offered this insight: "We come to conferences like this, and we hear from pastors who are given a platform because they are the very best at one thing they do exceptionally well: evangelism, discipleship, church planting, multi-sites, fund-raising, assimilation, community outreach, and all kinds of other things. The implication, at least—this is the way I feel after a conference like this—is that if I'm going to be a good pastor, I need to do everything all these experts are doing. But I can't. Believe me, I've tried. It's almost killed me."

The discussion among the group lasted about an hour. The leader rarely said a word. He just let them talk, cry, and share their hearts. When it was over, people felt heard, they felt understood, and they realized they weren't alone. Their expectations had been very unrealistic. Now they had permission to be more honest with themselves and their spouses, and they could finally adjust their hopes and fears to a more normal level. It was, by the account of many of them, a remarkable moment of clarity in the lives of the couples in the room.

> A man should carry two stones in his pocket. On one should be inscribed, "I am but dust and ashes." On the other, "For my sake was the world created." And he should use each stone as he needs it.
>
> —A Rabbi

Readjusting

Idealism is a wonderful thing—until it becomes a crushing burden. Most pastors sign up to lead because they want their lives to count for the glory of God. Leaders in business imagine creating new, revolutionary products or changing the way people communicate. Leaders in every field have great dreams of having an impact on countless lives, but if they aren't careful, unrealistic expectations—coupled with genuine disappointments and conflicts—can make them feel *less than*. All of us, and I mean *all* of us, from the most successful to those who are just starting out, need to realize the blessings and limitations of the gifts God has given us to lead our churches. Only Jesus had all the gifts. Here's a news flash: you and I aren't Jesus!

Your happiness is inversely proportionate to the shoulds in your life.

Exaggerated expectations inevitably lead to disillusionment: a common form of leadership pain. We can significantly raise our pain threshold, then, by having a more realistic view of ourselves, our God-given talents, and our need for others to fill in the gaps. We may want to see a super Christian in a cape when we look in the mirror each day, but this illusion will eventually ruin everything beautiful in our lives.

Church leaders and consultants have many different ways of identifying categories of leaders. A popular one describes the offices of prophet, priest, and king. Some pastors are primarily prophets: God uses them to proclaim his Word and transform people through the power of the spoken word. Others are priestly: they represent the people to God and they represent God to the people. They are compassionate, great listeners, and patient counselors. Still others have kingly gifts: they rule over their churches with wisdom and organizational skill. When pastors can identify their primary God-given talent, they can bring plenty of resources to excel in that area and can find others to function effectively in the other roles. An accurate analysis of their gifts and limitations doesn't threaten them; it humbles them and makes them deeply appreciate those who are strong where they are weak.

But I prefer to use somewhat different terms to describe the strengths and limitations of four kinds of pastoral leadership: entrepreneur, shepherd, teacher/preacher, and administrator.

Entrepreneurs

I have the privilege of working with many extraordinary visionaries. These people look into the future and see things the rest of us could never imagine. They set a course to achieve the seemingly impossible, and their ability to inspire others brings people along and invites their commitment. A favorite verse for them is Paul's quote of Isaiah's glowing picture of the future—"What no eye has seen, what no ear has heard, and what no human mind has conceived"—to which Paul adds, "the things God has prepared for those who love him—these are the things God has revealed to us by his Spirit" (1 Corinthians 2:9–10). More to the point, God often reveals a glorious future to entrepreneurs who refuse to settle for anything less than its fulfillment.

Entrepreneurs accomplish greater things than anyone else but often at considerable cost. A number of people think they're crazy. Amazon founder and CEO Jeff Bezos noted, "Entrepreneurs must be willing to be misunderstood for long periods of time."[1]

Shepherds

Many pastors don't have much of a vision for growing their churches into megachurches, but they have a clear sense that God has called them to care for the hurting, reach the lost, comfort the grieving, and provide direction to those who are wandering. When they walk into a room, they sense the level of love or tension. They are often insightful about the complexities of a strained relationship. Shepherds are peacemakers. They see themselves in Paul's explanation of his relationship with the Thessalonian Christians:

> We were not looking for praise from people, not from you or anyone else, even though as apostles of Christ we could have asserted our authority. Instead, we were like young children among you.
>
> Just as a nursing mother cares for her children, so we cared for you. Because we loved you so much, we were delighted to share with you not only the gospel of God but our lives as well. . . . For you know that we dealt with each of you as a father deals with his own children, encouraging, comforting and urging you to live lives worthy of God, who calls you into his kingdom and glory. (1 Thessalonians 2:6–8, 11–12)

Shepherds are treasured at the bedside of a sick church member, but they may not give their congregation a clear direction for the future. Entrepreneurs get frustrated with them because they don't seem to care about growth, and administrators get frustrated with them because shepherds are so busy with the people they let a lot of details—and important details at that—slide.

Teachers/Preachers

People love to hear God's Word opened up to them so that it challenges them, inspires them, and transforms them. Some pastors have a special gift to study and uncover rich insights into the Scriptures, find wonderful illustrations and metaphors that connect the points with the hearers, and provide clear applications so the truth can make a difference in their lives. This kind of speaking is certainly a gift, but it's one that is coupled with a love of truth and a commitment to study for long hours. These pastors aren't entertainers; they disclose God's message to the hearts and lives of those who are listening.

In Paul's last communication with Timothy, his protégé, he gave this instruction:

> In the presence of God and of Christ Jesus, who will judge the living and the dead, and in view of his appearing and his kingdom, I give you this charge: Preach the word; be prepared in season and out of season; correct, rebuke and encourage—with great patience and careful instruction. (2 Timothy 4:1–2)

Pastors who are gifted in teaching and preaching take Paul's charge to heart.

Sometimes a church's existence can become based solely on the talents of a phenomenal speaker. When this happens, the pews may be full each week, but the leadership team may not have clear direction, programs are poorly led, and a world of conflict bubbles beneath the surface. As long as the plates are full of donations, the disaster can be averted—at least from week to week. Sooner or later, however, the neglected aspects of the church's life will cause problems that can no longer be avoided.

Administrators

Pastors who are administrators aren't just gifted at counting pencils and keeping their desks straight. They are talented in crafting strategic plans for the church. They may not have the biggest vision in the world, but they make sure every person involved in the church has a crystal-clear understanding of the responsibilities, resources, time line, and reporting structure. They create detailed, workable systems so that no one has to ask, "What's my role?" or "What are we trying to accomplish?" Pastors with this gift often have one main emphasis, and they pour their considerable energies into making it successful. For instance, they may craft a detailed plan for a leadership pipeline. The plan covers every contingency from A to Z, and quite often is very successful.

Administratively gifted pastors want "everything . . . done in a fittingly and orderly way" (1 Corinthians 14:40), but even more, they try to enlist the effective service of every leader so that everyone contributes to the success of the church's mission. For them, Paul's directions to the Ephesians is their mantra:

> So Christ himself gave the apostles, the prophets, the evangelists, the pastors and teachers, to equip his people for works of service, so that the body of Christ may be built up until we all reach unity in the faith and in the knowledge of the Son of God and become mature, attaining to the whole measure of the fullness of Christ. (Ephesians 4:11–13)

Sometimes administratively gifted pastors drive entrepreneurs crazy because they insist on clearly defined steps before they begin *and* plenty of time to reach every goal. Shepherds may assume that the focus on structures and systems misses the hearts of the people, especially the leadership team. Occasionally, administrators are so driven to create the perfect system, they can't pull the trigger to start the always messy process of growth. Administrators love paper trails, but others see this as wasted time, or worse, a leadership flaw of micromanaging people and events.

> To love what you do and feel that it matters—how could anything be more fun?
>
> —Katherine Graham

Shadows and Secrets

When pastors try to be experts at everything, they lose their sense of reality and sense of identity. As pressure mounts and frustration (from all sides) multiplies, they feel even less secure. They try to stay idealistic and upbeat, but the foundation underneath is cracking. Some leaders lose sight of pleasing God and, instead, live to please the next person who walks into their office.

Their compulsion to please reminds me of a man who took a seat on an airplane next to a beautiful woman. After some small talk, he asked her, "What do you look for in a man?"

She instantly replied, "I like someone who can think on his feet and be swift like an American Indian." She thought for a second and then said, "I also appreciate men who have made a lot of money. Many Jewish men I've met are great businessmen." After a moment, she added, "But I also like cowboys who drive pickup trucks with a gun rack in the back." She paused, turned to the man and asked, "By the way, what's your name?"

He looked her in the eye and answered, "My name is Geronimo Goldstein, but my friends call me Bubba."

We may think this story is absurd, and it is, but some of us aren't too far from the man in the story. In our insecurity, we become chameleons, changing our attitudes, perspectives, and values to suit the person in front of us. Our life's goal has gradually shifted from bringing glory to God to winning approval from others. In his book *Overcoming Your Shadow Mission*, John Ortberg contrasts the Persian king Xerxes and Esther. The king's driving goals were to demonstrate his greatness. Shaping and shining his reputation was his shadow mission. In contrast, Esther was willing to risk her life for a higher cause. No matter what the price, she was devoted to honor, courage, and truth. Ortberg wrote:

> [The story of Esther] tells us that our shadow missions have enormous destructive potential. The mission we devote ourselves to will shape us. Our unplanned, involuntary thoughts and wishes will spring out of it. Noble missions will give rise to noble thoughts, but shadow missions will produce an inner life of hidden darkness and destructive discontent. Shadow missions always destroy at least one person—the one who lives for them.[2]

It doesn't take much to create a shadow. We can be doing all the right things but gradually shift to motives that are more about applause, comfort, power, and control rather than the glory of God. Ortberg explained, "Our shadow mission leads us just five or ten degrees off our true path in the direction of selfishness or comfort or arrogance. But those few degrees, over time, become the difference between light and shadow."[3]

When we live in the shadows, we keep secrets. We don't want people to know our hidden fears and selfish dreams, so we hide them from everyone. We may become so adept at the deception that we soon can't even admit them to ourselves. Mark Love is a furniture maker and former minister in Wimberley, Texas. In an article for *Church Leaders*, he identifies eleven significant secrets in the lives of pastors—certainly not every pastor, but enough of them to be worthy of note. Here are the six that strike me as the most important:

1. "Our Greatest Fear Is Irrelevance."

Many ministry leaders are afraid that what they do every day, what they've devoted their lives to accomplish, is not really changing lives. People come in and out of worship services, in and out of small groups and meetings, but they have the same emotional problems, the same relational conflicts, and the same spiritual lethargy toward God. These leaders wonder if their lives really count.

2. "We Think About Quitting a Lot."

Many leaders feel discouraged because they don't see any visible, tangible results of their efforts, and they feel jealous because their friends make a lot more money and enjoy far better perks. Secretly they wonder if they've made the right career choice, and some of them spend a lot of time daydreaming about a different job.

3. "We Envy People Who Can Be Themselves."

Like it or not, people put ministry leaders on a pedestal, and a few delight in knocking them down. The high position sometimes feels good, but they realize it's dangerous. They just want to get off the pedestal and be, well, normal.

4. "We Are Often Spiritually Starving."

People in ministry give, love, and serve until they're running on fumes. They craft and lead worship services for others to sense the presence of God, but as they lead, they seldom sense the wonder, beauty, and power of these experiences. Mark Love remarks,

> Like a worker at the chocolate factory who no longer likes the taste of chocolate, . . . we deal with spiritual matters so much that they often no longer have meaning to us. . . . We can't read the Bible without thinking of sermon ideas. We can't pray without thinking of leading prayers. We can't meet with other church people without talking shop. So we'd rather play golf, or watch TV, or anything else.

5. "We Are Sinful, No Different than You."

A few leaders harbor the secrets of the "younger brother" sins, such as illicit sex, greed, pornography, and addictions. But far more often, leaders in ministry commit the "elder brother" sins of self-righteousness, resentment, and arrogance. The first kind gets more attention from the media when these sins are exposed, but Jesus had harsh words for the Pharisees, the quintessential elder brothers. Pastors don't want people to know they commit either kind. Oh, they may occasionally admit they have a weakness or a flaw, but they don't want anyone to know about their genuine God-grieving sins. (I'm not advocating a tell-all message every week, but appropriate authenticity is refreshing—and rare.)

6. "We Are Lonely Because It's Hard to Trust."

Ministry leaders are in the center of the lines of communication for the church and the community. They know the dirty laundry and have heard secrets shared as prayer requests. And worse, they've heard gossip about themselves and their families. Maybe they took the risk to trust someone in the past, but their private life was exposed in a shameful, embarrassing way. Whatever the cause, many leaders (and especially their spouses) are very reluctant to expose themselves again.[4]

> You and I live in an age when only a rare minority of individuals desire to spend their lives in pursuit of objectives which are bigger than they are. In our age, for most people, when they die it will be as though they never lived.
>
> —Rusty Rustenbach, *Giving Yourself Away*

Love, Honesty, and Security

In the twelve-step world, people know you're only as sick as your secrets. As long as we try to hide our insecurities, sins, and limitations, we'll suffer far more leadership pain than is necessary. Instead, we need to be completely honest with ourselves, with God, and with at least one other person. If you don't have a friend who is supremely trustworthy, find a therapist. They're paid to understand *and* stay quiet.

You don't have to be Superman. In fact, you *can't* be Superman. Know your leadership style: celebrate the fact that the sovereign God of the universe has given you particular strengths and embrace your limitations. Be honest with your leadership team about what you enjoy, and resist, and thank them for filling in the considerable holes you leave behind. Arrogance and resentment create many wounds; gratitude is a wonderful salve to heal them. Dive deep into the grace of God. Let his love, forgiveness, and acceptance flow into your soul, and find security in his matchless grace instead of your performance. It makes a difference, a huge difference.

First, we are recipients. We live in a transactional world, but we need to get the order right or our whole lives will become confused. We are recipients, not givers. We come to God with empty hands and open hearts, and we depend on him to fill them. Only then, when we are overflowing with his goodness and greatness, can we give to others with no strings attached. If we give, love, and serve to win approval or gain control over others, we're not really giving at all; we're only manipulating people for our benefit.

For this reason, some of us are compulsive givers but poor receivers. When we can give and receive with equal grace, we can have real relationships with God, with our spouses and children, with friends and neighbors, and with those in our churches. In *Bread for the Journey*, Henri Nouwen said that giving is important. When we give we express love, show support, and make connections on a personal and emotional level. When we give we offer our time, our possessions, and even more, ourselves. But leaders need to learn to be gracious receivers, too. When we take something someone has offered, we validate them as human beings, as valuable members of the community, and as equals. Nouwen explains that genuine gratitude is essential for the exchange to have real meaning. Looking people in the eye and saying, "Thank you" validates their gift, their hearts, and their lives. Giving isn't enough to form real community, and receiving isn't enough. It takes both to form the circle of genuine connections.[5]

Insecure, threatened, stressed-out leaders give, but they don't know how to receive. Secure leaders receive with humble, thankful hearts, and the grace multiplies in glad giving and sharing.

No Exceptions

Throughout the Bible and church history, we see a clear pattern in how God works with people. No matter how gifted they were, God humbled them before he used them. A. W. Tozer believed that the experience of pain is essential for any leader to become pliable in the hands of God. In one of his most famous books he wrote, "It is doubtful whether God can bless a man greatly until He has hurt him deeply."[6] God's methods may vary, but he always manages to get a person's undistracted attention to teach the most fundamental lessons of trust:

- God told Noah to build a huge boat on dry ground. The deluge didn't come for 120 years. Noah had to trust God while all the people around him thought he was crazy.
- Abraham was promised that he would be the father of a great nation, but his life was a study in infertility for 25 long years.
- Joseph had two dreams that his family would someday bow down to him. His brothers resented his arrogance and his father's favoritism. They sold him to a caravan, and he became a slave in Egypt. There, too, he was betrayed and forgotten in a dungeon. But when the time was right, Joseph was ready. God used him to rescue two nations: Egypt and his family.
- Moses grew up in luxury in Pharaoh's palace. When he realized he was a Hebrew, he tried to defend a slave by killing an Egyptian. He spent 40 years at the backside of nowhere to realize he wasn't in charge.
- Joshua had seen God do miracles in drying up the Jordan River and making the walls of Jericho fall down, but one man's sin caused a military calamity. That got Joshua's attention!
- Elijah saw God perform one of the great miracles of the Bible by sending down fire to consume the altar and the sacrifice on Mount Carmel, but he became so fearful of Jezebel that he fled for his life and became deeply depressed. In the depths of his despair, God met him.
- David was anointed king, but it took years of flight and fight to finally claim his throne. Later, his sins of adultery and murder required a prophet's rebuke and God's amazing grace of cleansing.
- Daniel was an exile in Babylon, but he was selected for the king's court. Jealousy prompted reprisals from the king's officials, but Daniel was delivered from the lions' mouths.
- Peter made a grand proclamation of loyalty to Jesus just hours before he denied even knowing him. After the resurrection, Peter

gave up on the mission and went fishing. But Jesus found him, restored him, and made him the leader of the young church.

- Paul despised Jesus and all Christians. With ferocity and tenacity he set out to destroy the people of faith, but Jesus met him and changed his heart. His passions were totally transformed to spread the news of the Lord Jesus!

Are we better than these people (and countless others we could mention)? Does God work in us in a different way than he did in their lives? Pain isn't an accident in God's world. Even when it's self-inflicted through doubt and sin, God graciously weaves the strands of these experiences into something beautiful—if we'll let him.

We claim to follow Jesus, to be committed to let him conform us into his image. But just what image of Jesus might that be?

- The circumstances of his birth were questionable. His parents were the topic of gossip.
- He became an African refugee for the first years of his life.
- His parents didn't understand him or his mission.
- After he began his ministry, his family thought he was insane.
- He was criticized and condemned by those who claimed to represent God.
- He was misunderstood and abandoned by his closest friends.
- He chose to endure the most excruciating torture.
- At his supreme moment of pain, the Father abandoned him.

Sooner or later, the God who has transported us out of the kingdom of darkness into his marvelous light takes us out of the light and into a dark night of the soul. It's part of the way of the cross—to some degree for every believer, but especially for those of us who have been called to lead God's people. We find true spiritual strength when we trust God when we're weak. Similarly, our leadership is far more attractive and authentic when we've been broken and then lead out of humility instead of pride.

> To live by grace means to acknowledge my whole life
> story, the light side and the dark. In admitting my shadow
> side, I learn who I am and what God's grace means.
>
> —Brennan Manning, *Ragamuffin Gospel*

When we experience a sudden crisis or prolonged season of agony, we find out what really makes us tick. If we open our hearts to experience more grace than ever before—even though God may seem a million miles away—we'll sooner or later find him sweeter than ever. When pain has its way *in* us, the lesson can have its way *through* us as we become channels of the compassion, love, and courage we've found in our pain.

Have you been there? Are you there now? Get ready; it's coming—and always to draw you close and shape you a little more into his likeness.

What makes you tick? We may be leaders in the world of business, nonprofit organizations, or churches. Wherever we serve, each of us is an incredibly complex blend of God-given strengths and deficiencies, noble goals and selfish desires, drivenness and apathy, giving and grasping, love and fear. If we aren't aware of the powerful forces at work under the surface of our lives, we'll be caught off guard when we encounter pain; we'll be reactive and defensive instead of wise and strong.

Know This

Exaggerated expectations inevitably lead to disillusionment:
a common form of leadership pain.

Do This

What is the leadership style of the pastors you most admire
(entrepreneur, shepherd, teacher/preacher, or administrator)?

Identify how their excellence has inspired you and perhaps discouraged you because you didn't measure up.

Identify your limitations, your shadow mission, your secrets, and your resistance to brokenness.

Think About This

1. If you had been in the room with the leader and the young pastors and their spouses, how would you have felt when you heard them list all their expectations?
2. How would you define and describe a shadow mission?
3. Which of the descriptions of leadership styles best fits you (entrepreneur, shepherd, teacher/preacher, or administrator)? What are your strengths? What are your limitations and frustrations? And how do you frustrate others?
4. Which of the secrets listed is the biggest problem in your life? Who is one safe person you can talk to about this issue? How will it help to talk about it?
5. Do you agree or disagree with Tozer's statement, "It is doubtful whether God can bless a man greatly until He has hurt him deeply"? Explain.
6. In light of Jesus' suffering, what does it mean to be "transformed into his image with ever-increasing glory" (2 Corinthians 3:18)?

And remember: *you'll grow only to the threshold of your pain.*

6

ROOT CAUSE ANALYSIS

Adversity is the diamond dust Heaven polishes its jewels with.
—Thomas Carlyle

Michael Pitts, Bishop,
Cornerstone Church, Toledo, Ohio

Early in my ministry, I had a wonderful mentor, Dr. Lester Sumrall. I learned a lot from him, and he poured his wisdom and knowledge into an eager young pastor. When he passed away, I looked for another mentor. I found a man who was the leader of Azusa Fellowship. He had a big vision, and he believed in my wife Kathi and me. Under his leadership, I grew and our church grew. He invited me to speak to larger audiences than I'd ever spoken to before. I was thankful for our relationship and his leadership in my life.

A few years into our relationship, he began to talk to me about a theological position, a form of universalism, that was, of course, quite controversial. At first, the discussions were lively . . . and private. Soon, though, he began teaching his position from the pulpit. That was alarming, but it got worse. He began to sound to me like a martyr. He announced, "I'm prepared for the body of Christ not to receive this message during my life-time." He seemed to feel people were abandoning him, when it seemed to me that although they loved him, they felt he was abandoning fundamental truths. His message didn't line up with Scripture! He claimed that he was leading a new reformation movement, and he was going to change the face of Christianity.

I had the greatest respect for this man's intellectual brilliance, his educational background, and his ministry expe-rience. But I realized someone could be much smarter than me and still be wrong. I initiated a number of conversations to try to reason with him and point him to passages that refuted his position, but he only hardened his stand.

I wasn't alone in my alarm. A number of national and inter-national leaders contacted him and pleaded with him to back away from his position. His former denomination issued a doc-ument declaring him to be a heretic, but he again refused to back down.

We continued to talk, and he remained very gracious to me even though he knew I disagreed with him. I decided to change my tactics. Instead of arguing points of theology, I rattled off a list of leaders who had pleaded with him to return to theo-logical orthodoxy. There were probably many more than the ones I knew about, but those on my list were formidable. I said, "Every respected leader I know has asked you to reconsider your views, but you haven't listened to any of them. I have a question: Is there one person on the planet alive today who, if he or she challenged you, you'd reconsider your position?"

He didn't wait long before he said, "No, I don't know of anyone whose opinion would change mine."

During this controversy I'd seen many yellow flags. Now I saw a big red one. I replied, "How can I be under the authority of a man who refuses to be under the authority of anyone else? "

This wasn't just a theological or academic debate to me. This man had been a dear friend, he had poured himself into my life, and I had trusted him. Yet, when I realized he was fixed in his position and was not open to the counsel of other leaders, I knew a separation had to be made. The pain of separation was intense. Kathi knew how much this man had meant to me. When she realized how far he had gone off the rails, she wept because she understood the loss for me, for him, and for the body of Christ.

By this time, a number of people in our church were also following the controversy, so I decided to release a brief written statement to our church. I explained he had made several large fundamental shifts in his theology, and he had taken himself out from under anyone's authority. Therefore, being responsible for the wellbeing of others, he and I could no longer walk together. One of the values that I have always believed in and sought to live by is one of honor, so it was important to me for my words to convey that without the hint of superiority or spite. I reiterated that he had always been very kind and gracious to my family, and me. I always appreciated his generosity of spirit and his willingness to promote others. I asked people to think of him as a brother and to pray for him; although I saw him as being in error, my love for him remained.

I placed this brief statement on our church website. This was in the early years of the Internet, and I wasn't exactly media savvy. I had no idea the local newspaper and a major magazine would look at our web site and run stories about the controversy.

The debate, of course, wasn't over. It was necessary for me to take a clear stand, but my objection put me at odds with my friend and all those who continued to follow him. Many old and valued friendships became strained.

Actually, I got hammered from both sides. The ones who called him a heretic were upset with me for not blasting him, and the ones who agreed with him blasted me for opposing him. I understood their hurt. I was hurt, too. One of the values I hold most dear is loyalty. Breaking away from a good friend and mentor was excruciating to me. It was a hard choice that had to be made, but it was still very painful.

Now I found myself in a position I did not agree with theologically, which was, I had no oversight. I knew that needed to change, but the pain and disappointment, as it often does, caused me to withdraw and want to crawl into a hole to hide. I didn't feel as if I had the energy to sow the time and trust I knew would be required to engage and be vulnerable again; but I also knew that I needed to have covering, and that would require me to take the risk of being disappointed again.

Many people were aware of my devastation at the loss of my mentor, but Bishop T.D. Jakes called to check on me. I remember him saying, "If you need anything, please let me know."

I am sure many others would have heard his words as the huge open door and invitation to a new and wonderful relationship that they were. But I was hearing through my hurt and though I thanked him, our conversation ended without my reciprocating.

About a year later, I was flying back from Africa with another pastor. As we were boarding the plane he asked, "Do you know Bishop Jakes? I think the two of you would hit it off."

I answered, "Yes, I've had some contact with him, but it's been a while."

About a minute passed, and then he handed me his phone. He said, "I just text Bishop Jakes. He said to give you this number."

I didn't miss the second open door for this relationship. He has been my mentor and friend since that day.

Though the previous season had been painful, I did learn a few valuable lessons. First, I learned that there is always a right way to do something. Even during stressful situations a person should not abandon the values and ethics that they hold dear. It seems that too many times people use the faults of others to disregard their own Christian values, the old saints used to say it this way, "God don't like ugly." Second, I solidified my belief in having Godly authority. It was not imposed on me, but something I sought because of a fundamental belief that everyone needs someone they are accountable to, someone who has the right to ask the hard questions, challenge our thinking, and someone whose very presence modifies your behavior. Many people only seek covering when they are in trouble and find themselves trying to deal with long-term problems with short-term friends. Being uncovered isn't just inconvenient; it's dangerous.

It's important for leaders to conduct rigorous self-examinations to see what makes them tick, but they also need to evaluate their organizations. This broader analysis—looking through a wide-angle lens—often gives new perceptions about the pain they experience.

Warren had been the senior pastor of the biggest church in town for more than thirty years. He was a fixture in the community, respected and beloved. His assistant pastor and youth pastor had been with him for years. They were a solid team. As his retirement approached, Warren met with the chairman of the executive team to talk about succession. One person was the obvious choice. Dan was a close friend of the youth pastor and several others in the church. He was serving as an assistant in a church in a neighboring state. If anybody seemed ready to lead the church, it was Dan. The youth pastor was thrilled that Dan might come.

It seemed like a slamdunk. The hiring process was accelerated because many of Dan's references were on Warren's team or leaders in his church. Dan accepted the call, and everyone looked forward to a bright future.

Warren officially retired three weeks after Dan arrived. Only a few days later, Dan's shining reputation began to show signs of tarnish. He failed to communicate with the team, his sermons fell flat, and he seemed more interested in golf than the church. For a few weeks the murmurs in the office were coupled with reassurances. "He's just getting established. Give him time. I'm sure it'll work out great."

But things only got worse. Over the next few months hairline cracks of suspicion widened into canyons of distrust. Factions began to form. The youth pastor, formerly Dan's best friend, tried several times to have honest conversations with him—the kind they had shared so often in happier times—but these weren't happy times at all now. The assistant pastor defended Dan at all costs, and he was furious that the youth pastor was confronting their new God-anointed leader.

Every staff meeting, every worship service, and every event at the church now carried a heavy load of doubt and resentment. People took sides, and each side blamed the other. After Dan had been in his new role only six months, the acrimony led to a nasty church split. The ones who left, including the youth pastor, the board chairman, and at least thirty other families—about a third of the church—were branded as malcontents and even demon possessed. Virtually every person on both sides wondered, "What in the world happened? Couldn't this have been resolved before it got to this point?"

> The worse thing that can happen to any of us is to have a path that's made too smooth. One of the greatest blessings the Lord ever gave us was a cross.
>
> —Charles H. Spurgeon

The Inherent Questions

When people suffer in any way, it is human nature to ask, "Why did this happen?" "Why did this happen to me?" These questions are part of our DNA. The goal, then, is to make a searching and fearless assessment to assign appropriate responsibility. The problem is that most people lack at least one and perhaps both of two essential elements: insight and courage. Instead, they tend to become either blame sponges or blame throwers to affix blame quickly and get the conflict over as soon as possible.

In times of conflict, some people readily accept the responsibility for a problem even if they didn't do anything (or much) to cause it or prolong it. In their insecurity, they can't stand living with tension. Their answer is to claim that they're the ones at fault. They're sponges, absorbing the blame.

On the other side—the blame throwers—are more than happy to come to the same conclusion. They impulsively defend themselves at all costs and point to any target, especially those who willingly and foolishly accept all blame.

This pathological dance happens in business offices, church teams, and marriages. In fact, the more it happens, the harder it is to change the pattern of accusation and acquiescence. The pattern may become relatively comfortable because it's entirely predictable, but it never leads to love, understanding, courage, and growth.

Root cause analysis is a method of identifying and resolving the underlying causes of problems, failures, and conflicts. It doesn't simply try to manage the symptoms of a problem, even though the symptoms may be severe.

Instead, those who use this method invest time and energy to unmask the hidden but powerful root cause, which, when it is addressed, substantially resolves the problem and its consequences.

In business, the failure to ask and answer the hard questions—to address the root cause—can mean the difference between life and death. In 2014, General Motors CEO Mary Barra admitted to a congressional subcommittee and the public that the company had failed to recall cars made with a defective ignition switch, a problem that led to at least thirteen deaths and many more injuries. An investigation discovered that GM executives had known about the problem for years and could have fixed each switch at a cost of less than a dollar per car. One of the investigators summarized the findings for the subcommittee:

> There was a lack of accountability, a lack of urgency, and a failure of company personnel charged with ensuring the safety of the company's vehicles to understand how GM's own cars were designed. We found failures throughout the company including individual errors, poor management, Byzantine committee structures, lack of training, and inadequate policies.[1]

At the time of the investigation, Barra had only recently been tapped for the top role in the company, but she did not back away from a brutal (and accurate) analysis of the problems with the auto giant. She explained, "I know some of you are wondering about my commitment to solve the deep underlying cultural problems. The answer is, I will not rest until these problems are resolved. I am not afraid of the truth."[2] For over a decade, GM designers, engineers, and executives knew the problems existed, but in their analysis and solutions they valued their reputations (and pensions) over integrity. They hoped the problem would go away. When it didn't, they hoped no one would point a finger at them. In the end, their wrong analysis cost lives and ended the career for one designer.

For pastors of churches and leaders in any type of organization, the results of failing to identify root causes don't lead to crashes and deaths, but they often produce a myriad of soul-killing consequences:

- **They feel confused.** They're trying as hard as they can, but they get resistance and lethargy instead of an enthusiastic buy-in from those they lead.
- **They feel disillusioned.** They look around at other churches that are growing and other pastors who are being asked to speak at conferences, and they feel like failures.
- **The lack of resources frustrates them.** They worry about finances—their own and the church's—and they don't seem to have enough time, space, or leaders to get things done.
- **Their families are imploding.** The pastors are deeply devoted to the cause of Christ, and they're willing to suffer for it, but their families often feel neglected and resentful.
- **They're chronically tired.** They love to cut the grass, work on a furniture project, or do something else that lets them see what a completed project looks like. No matter how many hours they put in, there are always far more hospital visits, phone calls, sermon illustrations, and prayers that scream for their attention.
- **They're lonely.** It seems that no one really understands—even the spouse. Everyone wants more from the pastor than he can give. He feels alone and empty.
- **Their minds and hearts drift.** They begin to think the unthinkable, then imagine the unimaginable, and then act on those things—ranging from bailing out of the ministry and getting a nonchurch job to failing morally.

In response to these very real threats, most ministry leaders desperately try to manage the pain, minimize the damage, and live to fight another day. But they seldom accurately identify the underlying causes of their heartaches.

Stages of Growth and Pain

Not all pain is personal. Sometimes the pain is the direct result of the organization's stage of development. I've consulted with leaders in churches and businesses for many years, and I've noticed predictable stages as they take steps to implement their vision for growth. In each of these stages the leaders and the organization suffer particular pains.[3] Let me outline the five stages I've noticed and describe the pain in each one:

1. **The entrepreneurial stage:** At the beginning, a new vision captures the leader's heart and mind. All things seem possible, and a bright future looks very promising. However, all the ideas are conceptual; nothing concrete has been established. The leader tries to articulate the beauty and power of the new vision, but his team may look at him like he's speaking a foreign language, because, in a way, he is. People point out the lack of resources, and they throw up dozens of what-ifs and what-abouts. The leader feels the pain of being misunderstood and perhaps even opposed by those he's counting on to move the plans forward. Some leaders have told me that during this stage they sometimes wake up in the middle of the night in a cold sweat of fear even though they were really excited about the possibilities of fulfilling a new dream. Entrepreneurs always take bold risks, but many of their people are reluctant to commit entirely to that course of action. These leaders often face significant costs. They may have to invest more time, money, people, and their reputations than ever before. In light of the risks, they have to calculate if it's really worth it.

2. **The emerging stage:** As the new plans are implemented, the leader and the organization are squarely in no-man's-land—in between the certainty of the past and the hopes of the future. Instead of resolving all the questions from the previous stage, the first steps of implementation surface far more struggles than anyone anticipated. Everyone expected growth to happen immediately, but unforeseen obstacles

and resistance stand in the way. This causes confusion, and people react by questioning the leader's credibility. Why, they wonder, would he have started something if he didn't have all the answers? A *Forbes* magazine article reports that eight out of ten businesses fail within the first eighteen months.[4] A major reason for such failures is the inability of leaders to answer the questions in the emerging stage so that staff and customers trust them and the product. For established churches with a new vision, at this stage the devils view the vulnerable leader as ready to admit failure. At the same time, leaders in the emerging stage may feel great about the direction in which the organization is headed, but they have little to show for it.

3. **The established stage**: In businesses, churches, and other organizations that have functioning systems, leaders who press for change often feel like they're pushing a huge mass of jelly. Organizational inertia is very difficult to overcome, even for the most passionate leader. Board members are often firmly committed to existing systems. Leadership teams have gotten promotions and bonuses by excelling in accomplishing the old goals. Behind the scenes, technicians have invested countless hours to establish and fine-tune current operating systems. Industry standards, government regulations or denominational rules, and other standardized policies have to be considered. At every point and at every level the leader faces an intransigent reluctance to change. In addition, when the organization was young and growing, staff could be hired and fired by the leader, but now every staff change requires the input and expertise of a human resources department. Small companies and churches can make relatively quick turns, but large organizations, like aircraft carriers, need much more time and space to turn in a different direction.

4. **The erosion stage**: I've talked to many leaders who woke up to realize their organizations had stopped growing and were actually declining. When they took a closer look, however, they realized the acid of erosion had been introduced years before. The momentum

from previous years of growth had carried them forward for a while, but no longer. The vision no longer captures anyone. Passion has turned to lethargy. Encouragement has given way to blame and resentment. Their business or church had been established and running well, but the leader began making too many assumptions. Then something happened that caused them to ask, "What's really going on here?" Sometimes leaders know instinctively that something is terribly wrong with their organization, but until they dig deeper and ask some hard questions, they can't figure it out. At this moment of awakening, leaders often discover their assumptions about some of their key people. They had trusted team members who were responsible for important tasks, but these things have been neglected, and the staff members may have undermined the leader. Sometimes it takes a cataclysmic event—like the realization of embezzlement or a staff member going rogue and taking a portion of the congregation to start a new church down the street—for the leader to realize the depth of the decline.

5. **The enterprising stage:** Leaders can't afford to stand still and watch their organization continue to grow. It won't happen. To stay in touch with the people they must stay sharp and continually reinvent the product and their services. Companies like Apple and Amazon come out with new, innovative, awe-inspiring products on a regular basis. Not long ago Samsung came out with a new phone. Their marketing didn't talk about the features of the telephonic connections but the fact that their new device took superior pictures. They studied their audience and gave them something they wanted. Blackberry famously failed to innovate, and it's faded from the marketplace. For leaders in the enterprising stage, the challenge is to stay ahead of the curve so the organization doesn't begin to erode. Leaders fear being left behind.

Does the pain you're feeling correspond to any of these stages? Certainly our painful experiences may be the result of unrelieved internal stress or external challenges, but the pain we endure in the stages of growth often compound these hurts. Don't overlook them! Be objective, identify the pains inflicted in the stage of your business, church, or nonprofit organization, and take the steps you need to take.

> Suffering so unbolts the door of the heart, that the Word hath easier entrance.
>
> —Richard Baxter

Human and Divine

When we face difficulties, we often make two categorical mistakes: we look for quick, obvious answers, and we blame God for not protecting us or providing in the way we expected. We need to take a closer look and uncover a more accurate and more soul-satisfying analysis.

We may be able to identify the surface problems fairly easily: resistance from a staff member, a workload that's too heavy, a spouse's anger, lack of funds, and so on. But one layer down is a very significant *perception of these problems*: we feel out of control, and we believe we have to be in control to be happy and successful. The perception that we're out of control multiplies our anxiety. Then, instead of dealing with the surface problem, we're wrestling with a far bigger, deeper, more threatening danger of believing we're weak, worthless, and, worse, people may find out that we're weak and worthless!

For leaders, recognizing the limitations of their ability to control people and events lowers anxiety and provides welcome relief. For many leaders, however, controlling others isn't a haphazard choice—it's an obsession. The *illusion of control* is an observed tendency for people to overestimate their ability to control individuals, groups, and events. They believe they have the power to determine others' responses, attitudes, and outcomes. Psychologist Sandra Sanger observed her clients and herself:

The issue of control is ubiquitous in my practice as a therapist. Clients wish they could control others, detest feeling out of control, fear being controlled by others. And let's face it, there are times when my own illusion of control directs fantasies of wielding more influence in my clients' lives than is surely possible. If only I could wave the magic wand that, spoken or not, many clients seem to long for.[5]

In healthy forms, the desire to control drives us to be meticulous and try our best, but many of us go beyond this level. Our concern for excellence morphs into demands for compliance. When this happens, every decision is a competition of wills, with a loser and a winner. Relationships are soon strained because no one feels valued when compliance is demanded.

Of course, pastors who are a bit too controlling don't operate in a vacuum. Many churches suffer from an epidemic of control freaks! On the human level, one of the most helpful and positive things leaders can do is to recognize the limitations of their ability to control others. The answer isn't to give up and quit, but to realize that trying to force change, compliance, and a pleasant attitude almost always backfires. Concern shouldn't slip over into worry, encouragement need not morph into demands, and invitations to join the effort can be given without manipulative, guilt-driven strings attached. Don't misunderstand. Leaders can and should hold people accountable for the tasks they've agreed to do, but this perspective changes everything about the interactions—at the beginning when the offer is made, during the task when the person is doing well or poorly, and at the end at the evaluation. The illusion of control causes leaders to become anxious and demanding, and the people they serve often feel used. An understanding of the limits of control changes the atmosphere, the expectations, and the language on both sides.

The Point of Pain

As we know, there's another dimension to life, including our pain. Throughout the Bible we see godly men and women endure heartaches and adversities of all kinds. In many cases they realized much later God's divine purposes for their pain, but in some, like Job, they never got an answer to the *why* question. And Joseph was the victim of his brothers' betrayal. They were jealous of his status as the favorite son, and they resented his assumption, from his dreams, that he was superior to them. They sold him to a passing caravan and told their father wild animals had eaten him. His bloody coat served as evidence for their lie. As a slave in Egypt, Joseph's master's wife tried to seduce him. When the young man refused, she accused him of attempted rape. Joseph languished in prison for many years.

Through a series of God-ordained events, the betrayed, accused, abandoned, and seemingly forgotten man was brought before Pharaoh, the most powerful king on earth. Again God used dreams in Joseph's life. This time, he explained Pharaoh's disturbing dreams of harvest and famine, and the ruler was impressed. He made Joseph second in command over all of Egypt. When famine hit the area a few years later, Joseph's brothers traveled to Egypt to find grain to stave off starvation. Joseph tested them to see if they had changed, and they passed the test. After their father died, the brothers then feared for their lives. Joseph explained his divine perception of all that had happened and the brother's sinful role in God's plan: "Don't be afraid. Am I in the place of God? You intended to harm me, but God intended it for good to accomplish what is now being done, the saving of many lives. So then, don't be afraid. I will provide for you and your children" (Genesis 50:19–21).

When we suffer, we seldom see the reason *during* the pain (unless the suffering is a direct result of sin, and even then we may not connect the dots easily, quickly, or well). When we're in pain, our instinctive conclusion is like the disciples in the boat in the middle of a terrific storm while Jesus slept. Above the noise of the wind and waves, they shouted to him, "Teacher, don't you care if we drown?" (Mark 4:38).

When we're tempted to conclude that God doesn't care, we need to look at the cross. In that moment, God poured all the evil, sin, and horror of the human condition on his sinless son. There has never been and will never be any greater act of love. In Christ's willing, sacrificial death for sinners, he has made the ultimate statement of his affection for us. We may not know the reasons for our pain, but we can be absolutely sure that one reason is ruled out: it can't be that God doesn't care, because he has proven his love beyond any doubt.

In *Walking with God through Pain and Suffering*, pastor Tim Keller wrote:

> According to Christian theology, suffering is not meaningless—neither in general nor in particular instances. For God has purposed to defeat evil so exhaustively on the cross that all the ravages of evil will someday be undone and we, despite participating in it so deeply, will be saved. God is accomplishing this not in spite of suffering, agony, and loss but *through* it—it is through the suffering of God that the suffering of mankind will eventually be overcome and undone. While it is impossible not to wonder whether God could have done all this some other way—without allowing all the misery and grief—the cross assures us that, whatever the unfathomable counsels and purposes behind the course of history, they are motivated by love for us and absolute commitment to our joy and glory.[6]

From the divine perspective we can draw a number of important conclusions that help us endure:

- God never abandons us, even when we can't sense his presence.
- Our faith and character are developed most powerfully in times of adversity.
- God sometimes delivers us *from* pain, but more often he delivers us *through* it.
- When we trust God in difficult times, our stumbling blocks become stepping-stones of growth.
- When we face our deepest fears, our faith grows because we find God to be faithful.
- When doubts cloud our minds, it's time to refocus on God's grace, greatness, and wisdom.

- We may not like the path God has chosen for us, but we need to humbly accept pain as part of his plan.

Paul's Perspective

At least one spiritual leader was under no illusions about the fact that God would use pain to shape his character and provide a platform for his ministry. After Saul (later called Paul) met Christ on the Damascus road, he was led into the city where he met a man named Ananias. For good reason Ananias was afraid of the man who had been terrorizing Christians. When he expressed his doubts about God's leading to go to Saul and lay hands on him, the Lord told his reluctant servant, "Go! This man is my chosen instrument to proclaim my name to the Gentiles and their kings and to the people of Israel. I will show him how much he must suffer for my name" (Acts 9:15–16).

For years Paul traveled from city to city to take the gospel of Christ to anyone who would listen. When the Corinthian Christians wondered about Paul's credentials as an apostle, he reminded them that his authority didn't rest in a polished résumé but in God's divine calling and his willingness to endure any pain God's call might include. Paul gave them a short list of his experiences as he traveled to tell people about Jesus:

> I have worked much harder, been in prison more frequently, been flogged more severely, and been exposed to death again and again. Five times I received from the Jews the forty lashes minus one. Three times I was beaten with rods, once I was pelted with stones, three times I was shipwrecked, I spent a night and a day in the open sea, I have been constantly on the move. I have been in danger from rivers, in danger from bandits, in danger from my fellow Jews, in danger from Gentiles; in danger in the city, in danger in the country, in danger at sea; and in danger from false believers. I have labored and toiled and have often gone without sleep; I have known hunger and thirst and have often gone without food; I have

been cold and naked. Besides everything else, I face daily the pressure of my concern for all the churches. (2 Corinthians 11:23–28)

In the same letter, Paul related another experience of pain. This time, however, the source was different. God had given Paul a stunning vision of heaven. He had seen something only the angels had ever seen before, and he was tempted to think he was privileged. To humble him, God allowed Satan to give him a "thorn in the flesh." We don't know exactly what it was, but it was so painful that Paul asked God three times to remove it. Relief wasn't God's purpose. He answered Paul with a "no" and an explanation: "My grace is sufficient for you, for my power is made perfect in weakness." God's reasoning was enough for Paul. In fact, it gave him a renewed sense of gratitude for the pain he was suffering. He wrote, "Therefore I will boast all the more gladly about my weaknesses, so that Christ's power may rest on me. That is why, for Christ's sake, I delight in weaknesses, in insults, in hardships, in persecutions, in difficulties. For when I am weak, then I am strong" (2 Corinthians 12:9–10).

Let me paraphrase Paul's perspective:

- Life's most defining moments are usually painful experiences.
- When we encounter pain, we often default to previous coping styles. It takes perception, courage, and help to create new habits.
- We grow by design, not default.
- We need to realize that painful incidents are rocket boosters that can propel us to a higher orbit.

Responding in Faith

When we experience heartaches and difficulties, no matter what the source, we need to look beneath the surface to identify the root causes from a human and a divine perspective. An accurate analysis requires courage, perhaps to admit we were intellectually wrong, morally flawed, and relationally controlling. Yes, we may be victims of other people's demands, lies, abuse, or abandonment, but we have a responsibility to respond with integrity, wisdom, forgiveness, and love. We can't control what other people say or do, but we can control what we say and do.

> Our expectations of becoming paragons of piety, great contemplatives, attaining higher stages of consciousness—all subtly aimed at carrying us beyond the daily troubles of ordinary life—are not the way into the kingdom. Rather the kingdom consists in finding God in our disappointments, failures, problems, and even in our inability to rid ourselves of our vices.
>
> —Thomas Keating

Quite often an accurate appraisal shows us that a dream has died or people we trusted let us down and don't care. When we suffer loss of any kind, we need to grieve. Americans aren't very good at grief because we believe God has promised us a happy life. He hasn't. But he's promised us a meaningful life, one that involves pain and the necessary response: grief. As we grieve we choose to forgive those who have hurt us. Our capacity and willingness to forgive is a direct result of the depth of our experience of Christ's forgiveness for our sins (see Ephesians 4:31–32 and Colossians 3:13). If we have a hard time forgiving, we need to go deeper into God's grace that has forgiven our sins.

When we let go of the tight grip of control and hold on to only what we are responsible for handling, we realize we aren't as powerful as we thought. This brings a new level of humility, and it demands new levels of trust in God, who is sovereign over all. He's God; we're not. In all of this, we realize that God is using the most painful events and most difficult relationships in our lives, not to destroy us, but to create something beautiful. But this lesson may take a while to learn, so we need to wait on the Lord for his answers and for our strength to endure.

As we become more honest and secure in the grace of God, we stop controlling those around us. They may be amazed at the change, and they may feel uncomfortable for a while because they have become accustomed to our telling them how to think, feel, and act. But now we can have rich, authentic relationships based on honesty, trust, and love. Objectivity opens the door to real change in us and in those around us. And there's no real change without it.

One of the most powerful and lasting ways to raise your pain threshold is to accurately analyze the deeper source of our pain. Then, instead of avoiding it or managing it, you can invite God to use the pain to teach you life's most important lessons. And you'll be a far better leader.

Know This

Life's most defining moments are usually painful experiences.

Do This

Identify the short-term benefits of ignoring pain, blaming others for it, and trying to control people so you feel more powerful.

Describe the long-term consequences of these behaviors.

Think About This

1. How would you define and describe root cause analysis?
2. Where have you seen blame sponges and blame throwers do their dance? How does it usually work out? Why do families and teams stay stuck in this pattern?

3. What stage are you and your organization in right now? What are the inherent pains in this stage? How does it help to identify them?

4. What are some ways the illusion of control inflames anxiety for leaders and their teams? Do you see any of those traits in yourself and your people? Explain.

5. Even if we don't know the reason why we're experiencing pain, why is it crucial to know the reason can't be that God doesn't care?

6. How would it change your life if you, for Christ's sake, "delight[ed] in weaknesses, in insults, in hardships, in persecutions, in difficulties"?

7. What is the most significant point you will take from this chapter? How will it change your perspective, your attitude, your response to pain, and your relationships?

And remember: *you'll grow only to the threshold of your pain.*

7

YOU GOTTA LOVE IT

You will never understand pleasure without pain.
—T. D. Jakes

Scott Wilson, Lead Pastor of
The Oaks Fellowship, Red Oak, Texas

"Little" sins aren't so little. They are a dose of spiritual poison, a gap in the defense that lets Satan shoot his arrows at us, a crack in a pot that lets our integrity and joy leak out. God, in His great mercy, has been shining His light on my "little" sins. It's been exceptionally painful . . . and exceptionally necessary.

There is nothing in the world as wonderful as knowing that everything is right with you and the Father, knowing you are forgiven and clean. I don't mean knowing that you're going to heaven when you die. I mean knowing that everything in your past and present is in the open. You've brought everything into the light. You aren't hiding anything from God or anyone else.

The Father invites us to come into the light. But we're reluctant. We resist the exposure because we're afraid the guilt will be too much for us. This is the truth: we won't ever fully come into the light until we are convinced that the pain of staying in the dark is worse than the fear of being exposed by the light.

God has made me acutely aware of the darkness in me. He loves me too much to let me fool around with half-truths and falsehoods. He has called me to attack my lies and my pride with a fierce humility and radical truth.

I didn't lie on my tax return, and I didn't misrepresent my degrees on my resume. It was much smaller, and more significant, than that. I was at a restaurant with a couple from out of town. One of them asked about our church's attendance. I replied, "Well, last week we had about 2500, but we had over 5,800 at Easter. And if you take all the people who say they attend, we have 6000, or maybe even as many as 6500."

Seconds later, the Spirit shined the light of truth on my words and my heart. I had exaggerated the truth to look better in the eyes of strangers. An exaggeration is a lie. It's not a mistake; it's a lie. My motive was a toxic blend of fear and pride. I wanted our church—and me, of course—to look a little better in another person's eyes. And I quickly realized, I told that kind too often . . . far too often.

The lie revealed more than just an untruth. It showed a lack of faith in the goodness and greatness of God, and deep sense of insecurity in me. It grieved the Father to know that a son he loves didn't trust Him enough to speak the unvarnished truth.

That night, the Father continued to deal with me. I asked the Lord what I needed to do to shine his light on the recesses of my dark heart. He said, "Go, confess your insecurity and your lies to the people at the table tonight. Don't just confess the number confusion. Confess the heart issue."

The next day I went to the couple and I told them everything. It was humiliating. I didn't want to do it, and I felt rotten while I told them the truth. I felt stupid, but the pain of staying in the dark is worse than the humiliation of confessing my darkness and coming into the light.

As a pastor, I'd always taught the importance of confession and repentance. Now I was learning to practice these essential disciplines of discipleship. Here's what I learned, I'm learning, and I'll continue to learn for the rest of my life:

I need to be quick to confess my sins. I need to quit hiding, rationalizing, minimizing, and justifying them. I need to find someone and speak the truth out loud, just like James 5:16 tells me to do. I don't have to tell everybody, but I need to tell somebody. Confession opens my heart to the flood of God's love, forgiveness, acceptance and healing power. Without it, I stay stuck in the quicksand of denial. If I want to live in the light, I have to be radically committed to the truth.

Living in the dark not only impacts my relationship with the Father; it also negatively impacts my relationships with all the people in my life. I often need to ask: "Do I have any unresolved issues with people? Have I forgiven everyone who has done me wrong?" If I haven't, I need to bring that issue into the light.

Then I need to ask the Lord if there is anyone that I need to forgive. When I've asked Him, He often has brought things to mind that I haven't thought about in a long time. Forgiveness seems pretty important to Him! "Little" hurts are like "little" sins. They can fester and produce the poison of bitterness and superiority.

And further, I need to take steps to restore broken or

strained relationships when it's possible and appropriate. Sometimes it isn't appropriate to try to bring restitution to a relationship if it was abusive, if the other person is unwilling, or if the person has passed away, but we can still forgive them. It is very important to offer restitution to pay back for the damage we've done to our spouse, children, parents, friends, or anyone else we've wronged.

I've had very important—and very scary—meetings for restoration. These conversations were difficult for me to initiate. In them, both sides were at fault to some extent, but I didn't accuse the other people. Instead, I owned up to my sins and flaws. I asked them to forgive me for what I did wrong, or for not doing what I should have done. I confessed hidden things that I hadn't told them before. These meetings went surprisingly well. After them, I felt clean, lighter, and more hopeful. These encounters terrified me, but they were necessary if I was going to walk in God's light.

It's easy for me to wear a mask and fake it with people around me. Until God showed me the depth of my deception, I had no idea how much I lived in lies. I've made a new decision to live in the truth—God's truth about Him, about me, about others, about our church, and about every aspect of life. No more faking. No more pretense. No more masks. I'm committed to walk in His light, whatever it takes.

Matt had been ready to quit. The strains of being a pastor had finally gotten to him. As he thought about his fifteen years as the pastor of a medium-sized church in Virginia, he couldn't point to any cataclysmic event—there had been no moral failures, no palace coup, no church splits, no furor over the direction of the church. But ten thousand moments of giving out a little more than he was taking in had finally emptied his tank. Actually, he had been running on fumes for the past several years, but like a good soldier, he had kept moving forward.

When Matt told his wife, Rachel, he was thinking of leaving the ministry, she tried to act surprised, but she was glad. She had watched his spirit dissolve very slowly over all these years like it had been bathed in a weak acid. Together they began to come up with ideas about what kind of job he could do. How many executive positions in respected companies are impressed with a seminary degree and years in the ministry? Still, anything would be better than another year in the acid bath.

For several months before the decision to leave the church, Matt and Rachel had planned to attend a pastor's retreat. When he told her that he was going to call to cancel their reservation, she stopped him. "Let's go. This will be one last thing we can do before you tell the team you're leaving. We need some refreshment . . . and you could use a break."

A week later, at the retreat, the speakers were warm and encouraging, and the other couples seemed very approachable. One morning after breakfast and before the first meeting, Stephen, a pastor Matt had met the day before, approached him and said, "Hey, Matt, I don't want to jump in your soup or be weird or anything like that, but if you're willing, I'd like to tell you something that's on my heart."

Matt wondered if the guy was going to share a secret sin and unburden his soul, but he nodded and said, "Sure." They walked out to a quiet spot as the early morning sun broke through the trees. They sat down, and Stephen said, "I know this sounds really odd, but I think the Lord gave me something to tell you."

Matt instantly thought, *Oh, God. Not that! I sure don't want some nut case to have "a word from God" for me. I've got enough craziness in my life as it is.* But he smiled and said, "Great. Go for it."

Stephen swallowed hard and said, "The Lord told me to tell you that self-pity isn't a good foundation for a life of faith and hope."

Matt felt his face turning red. He was furious that a stranger would be so cruel, but Stephen wasn't finished. "He also told me that you've been busting your butt to serve him and the people of your church. You're a good leader . . . a kind and compassionate pastor, but you've slipped off the ledge into a hole."

Stephen stopped for a second to see if Matt was going to walk away or slug him. When neither of those happened, he continued. "Matt, God's not finished with you. He still has a lot more for you to do at your church, so don't quit. Whatever you're thinking, don't do it. But to make it, you're going to have to give up the self-pity. Stop thinking of yourself as the victim, and build a whole new way to think about your life."

After a long pause when neither said a word, Stephen got up, put his hand on Matt's shoulder, and said, "That's all I've got, brother. Now it's up to you."

The insight of an accurate analysis of our pain may come as gradually as a sunrise or as suddenly as a lightning bolt. The moment of clarity, though, isn't the end. It's only the beginning. We've spent years thinking, talking, and acting according to the old perceptions of pain. Now we are finding a new path, and we're just beginning to take a few steps down it. We need to learn to walk in wisdom. The wisdom we need to acquire redefines how we've thought about pain: instead of despising it, we begin to see the inherent value in it. In fact, we will learn to love it!

> For the believer all pain has meaning; all adversity is profitable. There is no question that adversity is difficult. It usually takes us by surprise and seems to strike where we are most vulnerable. To us it often appears completely senseless and irrational, but to God none of it is either senseless or irrational. He has a purpose in every pain He brings or allows in our lives. We can be sure that in some way He intends it for our profit and His glory.
>
> —Jerry Bridges, *Trusting God*

Reframing

At some point, we need to radically reframe our concept of happiness, realistic expectations, and the purposes of God. The problem, of course, is that these things are as solid as concrete in our minds, hearts, and habits, so God often uses the jackhammer of pain to get through to us. In those vulnerable moments, we can become hardened and resentful . . . or we may become softened and receptive.

As our perspective begins to change and pain becomes less of a threat, we gradually embrace it as the best teacher. At some point, we actually welcome pain because the effects are so positive. Those who have embraced pain as a way of life are seldom surprised by suffering, seldom devastated by difficulties, and seldom reactionary when things aren't what they hoped.

Dean Karnazes is an ultramarathon man. He ran fifty marathons on fifty consecutive days. He ran 350 miles in three days, without stopping and without sleep. He has run the Badwater Marathon seven times, which begins in Death Valley and finishes 135 miles later halfway up Mount Whitney. In an interview for *Outside* magazine, he shared his view of American culture:

> Western culture has things a little backwards right now. We think that if we had every comfort available to us, we'd be happy. We equate comfort with happiness. And now we're so comfortable we're miserable. There's no struggle in our lives. No sense of adventure. We get in a car, we get in an elevator, it all comes easy. What I've found is that I'm never more alive than when I'm pushing and I'm in pain, and I'm struggling for high achievement, and in that struggle I think there's a magic.[1]

Leadership expert Michael Hyatt reflected on Karnazes's life and drew three conclusions about why we should embrace discomfort:

1. **Comfort is overrated.** It doesn't lead to happiness. It makes us lazy—and forgetful. It often leads to self-absorption, boredom, and discontent.

157

2. **Discomfort can be a catalyst for growth.** It makes us yearn for something more. It forces us to change, stretch, and adapt.

3. **Discomfort is often a sign we're making progress.** You've heard the expression, "no pain, no gain." It's true! When you push yourself to grow, you will experience discomfort.[2]

The Substitute Teacher

Children get comfortable with their teachers. When these teachers are absent, especially for a prolonged period of time, the kids (especially those in junior high and high school) often think the substitute will be an easy target for all kinds of craziness. They are sometimes shocked when the substitute is a better teacher than their regular teacher—like Albert Einstein walking in to teach a physics class or David McCullough sitting down for a history lesson. Pain is a surprising substitute teacher in our lives. We've gotten used to the way things are in our leadership strategy, thoughts, perceptions, and practice. Pain is the new teacher we want to avoid or get rid of as soon as possible, but in reality it's the best instructor we could ever have.

Pain teaches us five crucial lessons (among many others):

1. We Are Weaker, More Self-Absorbed, and More Fragile Than We Ever Imagined

As long as things are rocking along pretty well, we feel confident and in control. Heartaches and conflicts, however, have a way of bringing the dark side to the surface. We instinctively blame others, speak harshly to innocent people, argue about the smallest things, demand our way, wallow in self-pity when we don't get our way, and harbor bitterness instead of forgiving those who have hurt us. We may feel completely justified in all these attitudes and behaviors, but if we'll let it, our new realization of these harmful perceptions and attitudes becomes the beginning point of repentance, wisdom, and growth.

2. Actually, We Don't Have a Clue What God Is Up To

We thought we were pretty sharp. We assumed we were in control. We exercised authority over our domain, and we were pretty darn successful at it—until we weren't. Our theology may have been accurate that God is the only omniscient being in the universe, but some of us assumed we had an inside track on knowing what God knows. Now we realize we aren't even close! God, clothed in infinite glory and full of infinite wisdom, is the king and ruler of all. We have no idea how he can weave the flaws, sins, and evil of the world into something redemptive and beautiful, but he promises he will if we'll trust him. The experience of pain brings our intellectual pride down a notch or two. Suddenly, we realize we understand maybe a millionth of a billionth of a zillionth of the magnificent and mysterious plan of God for the ages. At that point, we have the choice to trust him or not.

3. We Become More Grateful

When our sense of entitlement fades, we see all the gifts and blessings of God through new eyes. Instead of taking love, health, salvation, time, and friendships for granted—and focusing our hearts on the things God hasn't done for us—we reassess what's really important. We may realize we've made the success of our ministry, or the applause or power that comes from it, into an idol that we've treasured more than God. With appropriately grieving hearts, we confess our sin, accept the wonder of his forgiveness, and thank him for so many things he has graciously provided. Even if the barn is empty, the cupboards are bare, and the natives are hostile, we can give "joyful thanks to the Father, who has qualified you to share in the inheritance of his holy people in the kingdom of light. For he has rescued us from the dominion of darkness and brought us into the kingdom of the Son he loves, in whom we have redemption, the forgiveness of sins" (Colossians 1:12–14). We have him and he has us, and maybe for the first time, that's enough.

4. We Find God to Be Beautiful Instead of Just Useful

When we were focused on success, we may have made God the means to the end of our growing, dynamic ministries instead of the only One who rightly deserves worship, love, and loyalty. We led with excellence, and we were devoted to build the kingdom, but maybe, just maybe, it was more about our kingdoms than his. When God didn't come through for us to make a program thrive, we were more than disappointed. Somehow we felt betrayed. Hadn't we done enough? Didn't God owe us . . . just a little?

Sooner or later God puts the brakes on to let us see what's really in our hearts. If we're too devastated by failure, there's a good chance we were using the ministry as a means to burnish our reputations instead of pointing to his glory. God has a way of putting his finger on our most treasured possession—just ask Abraham about the day on the mountain with Isaac—to test us to see what's most important to us. In pain and times of testing we have wonderful opportunities for God to purify our hearts, change our motives, and delight more than ever before in the beauty of his grace and greatness.

5. We Become More Tender, More Understanding, and More Compassionate

Compassion doesn't come out of a vacuum. It's a character quality that has to be instilled in us through our experience of God's kindness when we're hurting. As we experience God's comfort, we can then comfort others. We may have visited people in the hospital before, but now we hurt with them and for them. We may have preached funerals before, but now we share the family's grief. We may have given solid counsel to a couple who was considering divorce, but now we weep with them.

The apostle Paul was the ultimate tough guy—a man's man, a leader of leaders who never quit. But he was open to have his heart tenderized by the experience of God's tenderness during a time of heartache. He explained this transformation in the opening verses of a letter to the Corinthians: "Praise be to the God and Father of our Lord Jesus Christ, the Father of compassion and the God of all comfort, who comforts us in all our troubles, so that we can comfort those in any trouble with the comfort we ourselves receive from God. For just as we share abundantly in the sufferings of Christ, so also our comfort abounds through Christ" (2 Corinthians 1:3–5). If God can soften Paul's heart and make him more compassionate, he can soften yours and mine.

As we've already said, pain either hardens us or softens us. Jesus became supremely soft when he willingly suffered humiliation, torture, abandonment, and death so that he could shower us with love, forgiveness, and acceptance. Let pain soften you. Experience God's comfort and then shower others with tenderness, understanding, and compassion.

Choosing a Different Response

Change is hard, but sometimes it's absolutely essential. No more excuses, no more delays. It's time to make the necessary adjustments in our intentional planning and our responses to people and situations. Superficial change may not take much effort, but changing how we think and how we instinctively respond requires discipline, determination, and accountability. The variables are unending, so I can't give a formula for success in every area. But I'd like to make some general suggestions that can be adapted for many circumstances. All of them require complete honesty and tenacious discipline to internalize principles and practice new skills.

When we hit overload on internal stress, we may need more than just a good night's sleep and a ball game to snap back. As shown by Dr. Swenson's tree branch illustration in chapter 3, we may need time and space to relieve the pressure so that we gradually come back to a relatively normal state of mind and body. Rest is essential, but we also need to set up systems to limit pressures, and we need skills to manage stress more effectively. Here are some important principles:

- **Define the limits of your control:** You can control only your thoughts, choices, and priorities. You can't control the behaviors and attitudes of other people, the national economy, or the responsiveness of the people in your church and community.
- **Put rest, family time, and fun into your schedule—and stick**

to it: Part of what you can control is your schedule. (Yes, you can! If you think you can't, go back and reread this book again.)

- **Make sure you do a few things you really enjoy:** All jobs include some drudgery, but don't let the pressures of the job keep you from doing things that give you pleasure inside or outside your normal job description.
- **Watch for hidden stressors: guilt, perfectionism, and worry:** It's not wrong to be honest about faults, to want to excel, and to care about people, but stress is often the result of these good things going too far. When over responsibility feels completely good, right, and normal, it's time for a change.
- **Aggressively address the biggest pain producers in your life:** Don't be passive and don't just accept things as the way they have to be. Your family and career and maybe your life are at stake. Identify the things that make you stay up at night, give you cold sweats, or cause you to dread. It shouldn't be very hard to identify them. The hard part is crafting a reasonable, workable plan to deal with them.
- **Triage the stress.** You probably can't resolve the most significant causes of stress in a short time, so pinpoint the most important ones first. Work though them while you're also crafting new skills and new perceptions about what it means to live a healthy life.

To walk in wisdom in handling external challenges, you may need to put up your guard to be less vulnerable to the attacks of the few ornery people who are tormenting you.

In a *New York Times* article, Stanford professor Robert Sutton commented, "One nasty person can bring down a whole group. That can happen because the group members devote more energy to dealing with the bad apple and less energy to the task at hand. Moreover, anger and hostility are contagious, so the whole group can become infected."

Sutton talked to a woman named Ruth who worked in a particularly toxic office environment. She learned a lesson about survival when she was whitewater rafting in California. When she fell out of the raft, fighting against the current only created more anxiety and made her feel less in control. She decided to apply that principle to her office relationships. Whenever a meeting turned hostile, she chose to avoid fighting. Suddenly Ruth no longer saw herself as a victim. Instead, she felt strong and in control. Sutton commented, "In a healthy workplace, being emotionally engaged is great, but when you can't escape a disrespectful environment, practicing the fine art of indifference and detachment can help you endure the onslaught. Detachment can also help you to quell the temptation to respond in kind—and thus avoid fueling a vicious circle of hostility."[3]

> In order to arrive at what you are not
> You must go through the way in which you are not.
>
> —T. S. Elliot

If we think detachment is appropriate only for the business world and not for the church, we need to think of how often Jesus engaged his enemies and then withdrew from them. John tells us, "Jesus would not entrust himself to them, for he knew all people. He did not need any testimony about mankind, for he knew what was in each person" (John 2:24–25). We will be smart to follow the Lord's example and be as shrewd as snakes and as innocent as doves (see Matt. 10:16). Strategic withdrawal isn't apathy; it's wisdom.

Psychological distance gives us room to respond instead of reacting in fear, hurt, or anger. In our communication with staff, the leadership team, volunteers, our families, and the person at the grocery store checkout, we need to adjust the hair trigger on our reactions so we become quick to hear, slow to speak, and slow to anger (see James 1:19).

Try to understand what people are saying, and look for the message beneath the words. Quite often a person's inflammatory words are an indication of a deeper hope or hurt. Take time to look for the content of a person's heart. Ask a second or third question—at least a first question!

When others feel understood, they are much more likely to hear your side of things.

Today, a lot of communication is done through email and texting, but the intent of the heart often doesn't come through to us digitally. A good principle is to move up at least one medium. If you'd normally send a short text, send a longer email. If you'd regularly email, make a phone call. If you'd usually call, ask for a face-to-face meeting. Relationships are forged on trust, and trust can't be built when hearts fail to connect.

Whenever possible, own up to your part in any misunderstanding or dispute. The three little words that are vital to cement relationships aren't "I love you" but "I was wrong." Blame is instinctive; confession and restoration are beautiful, powerful, and cleansing—and, sadly, rare.

When you and your church experience growing pains, learn to ask the right questions. Too often we focus on the immediate hindrance to growth, but we may miss the bigger picture. It's fine to ask, "What do we need to fix here?" But also ask, "How can we create a vibrant, healthy, creative, faith-filled, celebratory culture that brings out the very best in every person involved?" This question is important whether your church has twenty members or twenty thousand.

To identify the health of an organization's culture (or lack of it), I recommend having an open-ended conversation to discuss the following questions:

- Who are the heroes? What makes them heroes? Who determines who the heroes are?
- When someone inquires, "Tell me about your organization," what stories are told?
- How much does the average staff member feel he or she has input into the direction and strategy of the organization?
- Who has the ear of the top leaders? How did these people win a hearing with the leaders?
- What are the meaningful rituals? What message do they convey to those in the organization and those outside it?

- Who is rewarded and for what accomplishments? What do these awards say about the values of the culture?
- What is the level of loyalty up and down the organizational chart? What factors build loyalty?
- What is the level of creativity and enthusiasm throughout the organization?
- When an objective observer spends an hour watching people interact in the offices, what mood does he or she pick up?
- How are decisions made, deferred, or delayed?
- Who are the nonpositional power brokers? How do they exercise their authority?
- Where are control problems and power struggles most evident?[4]

Work hard to build or rebuild trust. With it, you can fulfill the greatest dreams. Without it, you'll crush people's spirits. It's much easier to change staff members and programs than to change the culture of an organization. Ask the right questions and keep on asking them. At every level of growth, work hard, communicate well, and pray like crazy that God will produce a healthy culture. And remember, it begins with you. If you aren't healthy, your organization's culture doesn't stand a chance.

Always on Display

Leaders, especially pastors, are always in the public eye. When they suffer, their families are watching, their staff teams are watching, their church members are watching, and often the community is watching to see how they handle adversity. Recently, my friend Michael Pitts was diagnosed with prostate cancer and had surgery. He was aware that he was giving a public demonstration of how he was handling his private pain. He is on television every week, and he asked me to help him figure out how to be appropriately vulnerable but continue to be a voice of hope.

Leaders are teaching others how to handle pain at the exact moment they are learning these lessons themselves. The pain is felt and the lessons are taught in real time. The psalms of lament give us direction about how to communicate. In about half of the psalms, the writers pour out their frustrations, disappointments, doubts, fears, and anger—often toward God! But in all but two, they eventually come around to a fresh perspective of the goodness and greatness of God, and their faith is renewed. And all these complaints are in God's songbook. Obviously, God isn't shocked or offended by raw honesty.

The pain may come from any cause: children arrested, illness, staff rebellion, financial strains, personal sin, betrayal, or opposition from trusted friends. In each one, you have to figure out what's appropriate to share and what needs to remain private, how much information is too much and how much is too little, how to be honest without being foolishly vulnerable, and how to point people to hope without being superficial.

Jack Hayford was succeeded at The Church on the Way by his gifted son-in-law. Jack looked forward to a wonderful retirement, but his son-in-law had an aneurism and suddenly died. Jack's agreement with the church was that he would come back if anything happened to the new pastor within a specific time. In a single tragic moment everything changed for Jack and his family. He had to grieve the loss of his daughter's husband, comfort the family and the church, and then step back into the role of senior pastor, a role that was suddenly much harder because of the terrible loss. Jack had to recalibrate his life and figure out how to communicate both grief and stability to his congregation.

Phony faith teaches nothing helpful. My advice to pastors and other leaders in pain is to realize God has put you in a position to teach people some of the most valuable lessons they will ever learn by watching you as you are appropriately vulnerable and honest, trusting in the darkness, and continually reaching for God's hand and heart as you struggle. You may not be able to identify the lesson for a long time—maybe never—but you can trust that a sovereign, wise, and loving God is using the pain to shape you and use you in some way. Honesty and steadfast faith—especially in the darkness—forms a powerful and enriching message for everyone in pain.

I've seen leaders stand up in front of people during times of intense stress, loss, and heartache. I've seen them confess moral failures and explain complicated organizational difficulties. Sometimes they communicated very clearly, and at other times they should have taken more time to craft their message. Sincerity and humility are essential. The heart comes across loud and clear even if the words aren't articulate. But I've never seen anyone recover after publicly losing his cool. Expressions of outrage at a staff member in a meeting shatter trust. Publicly denouncing others from the platform casts more doubt on the communicator than the one being blamed. Moses faithfully led God's people in the wilderness for decades, but when he angrily struck the rock twice, everybody saw his outrage, and his leadership role was effectively over (Numbers 20:10–12).

Leaders in business and the church need to be very careful to avoid expressing outrage in public arenas. Instead, talk about the hurt that is beneath the anger. People can identify with that, and they'll respect you more for framing it as a gnawing or intense pain. Own your responsibility for the problem and have the guts and humility to say, "I'm sorry," without shifting the blame for your part to anyone else. Humble leaders are attractive leaders. Angry, arrogant leaders may effectively dominate, but they don't build lasting trust. Eventually, their kingdoms crash around them.

For leaders, perfect privacy is a pipedream. They suffer privately, but they also inevitably suffer publicly. They need wisdom to know how.

Always in Progress

One of the most enduring and endearing truths in the Bible is that God is more than willing to use flawed men and women to accomplish his purposes. That's a good thing because none of the other kind is available! At best, we grasp only a fraction of God's greatness and his purposes, but he's thrilled when we sign on for the adventure of a lifetime. Pastor Craig

Groeschel encourages pastors to embrace their flaws and trust God to use them. He said, "God uses insecure, risk-taking, pain-enduring idiots!" When pastors realize their insecurities, they trust God instead of their knowledge, skills, and ability to control events. The kingdom of God is all about taking risks. The heroes in Hebrews 11 laid it all on the line. And the point Groeschel makes that is most pertinent to our study of leadership, which I also call *bleedership*, is that the way of the cross always involves pain. The amount of pain we're willing to endure sets the limit of our effectiveness. If we avoid it or numb it, we'll risk nothing, sacrifice nothing, feel nothing, and accomplish nothing.[5]

To put this in context, I have to say something outlandish: Jesus' disciples were idiots. They were insecure and clueless most of the time, but after Pentecost, they risked everything and endured persecution because their lives were flooded with the love and power of God. Luke recorded, "When [the Jewish leaders] saw the courage of Peter and John and realized they were unschooled, ordinary men, they were astonished and they took note that these men had been with Jesus" (Acts 4:13).

Knowledge can be acquired in an instant, but wisdom comes only with time, experience, reflection, honesty, and affirmation. In every aspect of heartache, difficulty, crises, and pain, learn to walk in wisdom.

John Newton, a former slave trader who became a pastor, wrote a song describing his transition from false expectations to rugged realism:

> *I asked the Lord that I might grow*
> *In faith, and love, and every grace;*
> *Might more of His salvation know,*
> *And seek, more earnestly, His face.*
>
> *'Twas He who taught me thus to pray,*
> *And He, I trust, has answered prayer!*
> *But it has been in such a way,*
> *As almost drove me to despair.*

I hoped that in some favored hour,
At once He'd answer my request;
And by His love's constraining pow'r,
Subdue my sins, and give me rest.

Instead of this, He made me feel
The hidden evils of my heart;
And let the angry pow'rs of hell
Assault my soul in every part.

Yea more, with His own hand He seemed
Intent to aggravate my woe;
Crossed all the fair designs I schemed,
Blasted my gourds, and laid me low.

Lord, why is this, I trembling cried,
Wilt thou pursue thy worm to death?
"'Tis in this way," the Lord replied,
"I answer prayer for grace and faith.

"These inward trials I employ,
From self, and pride, to set thee free;
And break thy schemes of earthly joy,
That thou may'st find thy all in Me."[6]

Know This

At some point we need to radically reframe our concept of happiness, realistic expectations, and the purposes of God. You've got to learn to appreciate the lessons you learn from pain.

Do This

Name one person who has learned important lessons from experiencing pain (internal stress, external challenges, or growing pains). Pick up the phone and call that person. Ask at least three or four questions and then listen.

Think About This

1. How would you explain to a staff member or friend how discomfort is actually good for you?
2. Which of the (at least) five lessons we learn from pain is most meaningful to you? Explain.
3. Which point under "Choosing a Different Response" can you apply right now? What difference will it make?
4. What are the right questions you need to ask your team about your organization's culture?
5. To become one of God's "insecure, risk-taking, pain-enduring idiots" you have to learn to be honest about your flaws and comfortable always being *in process* instead of *having already arrived.* To what extent are you there? How can you tell?

And remember: *you'll grow only to the threshold of your pain.*

8

THE PRIVILEGE OF LEADERSHIP

*Leadership is the lifting of a man's vision to higher sights,
the raising of a man's performance to a higher standard, the
building of a man's personality beyond its limitations.*
—PETER DRUCKER

Lisa Bevere, Messenger International, Colorado Springs, Colorado

Recently I found myself traveling on a plane alongside a brilliant gentleman in his eighties. For many decades he consulted organizations as diverse as Johns Hopkins Hospital and the US Department of Defense. Even at his advanced age he was still in high demand, speaking at leadership summits and retaining seats on prestigious boards. It wasn't long before I found myself caught up in stories from a long, successful career.

I asked the man what were some of the most essential elements to growth and success. He answered, without any hesitation, *the involvement of women.*

He explained that if a company he was consulting did not have women on their board, or had not enrolled any women in his seminar, he gave them two options. He invited them to choose a few of their brightest females, and he would consult them for free. If they declined, he refused to consult the company altogether.

When I asked why he was so adamant on this point, he assured me that women have innate talent for things many organizations lack, yet need to move confidently into the future—three of them being intuition, communication, and compassion. Far too many women are not involved in areas of leadership that desperately need them.

My experiences in church leadership have been quite the opposite of this man's experiences in the corporate world. I remember an incident when my husband, John, invited me to be part of a meeting with a number of church leaders. When I arrived, I discovered I was the only female present.

Even though the group knew I would be joining them, my presence was met with almost open hostility by the host. From the onset he did his best to invalidate my input with condescending comments, heavy sighs, and the rolling of his eyes.

Any communication that involved our organization was singularly directed to John. John kept encouraging my involvement, saying, "I would like Lisa to weigh in on this." But if I spoke, I was completely ignored.

A very clear signal was sent to those present: *Lisa may be in this room, but she will not be acknowledged.* John tried to include me, but I was not going to jump into the mix again.

After the meeting, another leader attempted to comfort me: "Hey, he just doesn't like processing things with women."

What do you say to that? "I'm sorry for being female"?

John was uncomfortable with what had transpired as well,

but I wanted to avoid further conflict. When John raised his concerns, I echoed the input of the associate. "It's okay. He just doesn't process things with women...but I am glad you do."

I decided then and there that John would go to all future meetings alone. I was just a hindrance to the process. But though I was not willing to pursue the issue further, the meeting had set off an alarm within my spirit.

Time passed and I heard other women who knew nothing of my encounter share about similar experiences with this leader. I began to wonder why he viewed what God called a "good" addition to the world of men (women) as a hindrance. Why did he feel their contribution was unnecessary? God was the one who said it was not good for men to do life without the voice of women!

Time marched on and sadly the leader's organization fell apart. It was discovered that he was very conflicted in his personal life, causing him to limit the input of women in his world. Because I had not known this, I drew back and discounted my involvement in a project that would have been enriched by my input. From this incident, I learned some valuable lessons.

It's Not Personal: Albert Einstein stated, "No problem can be solved on the same level at which you meet it." I cannot think of anyone who could have stated this with more clarity or authority. Einstein was a brilliant physicist and a logics genius, but he was most powerful in his approach to theories. He understood that natural appearances could be very limited.

In my conflict with this leader, an attempt to resolve the problem on the level where I'd met it could have meant outrage at the disrespect. I could have forced my involvement and demanded equal treatment. But the truth is...I was never really the issue.

My mistake was making the conflict personal and

withdrawing. When we personalize what needs to change, we make it about us rather than about the need for a lasting solution. Taking things only personally robs us of perspective we need to move forward.

Women are needed in the mix of leadership. It would be easier for us to opt out, but what would we be building for the women coming after us? I decided to embrace temporary pain to open paths for others.

Often men who are strong or opinionated are celebrated while women with the same characteristics are not. Rather than being viewed as confident, they are seen as aggressive and controlling. This is rarely accurate. But such is the world right now. We can rage against it, or we can build a better world by rising above prejudice and exceeding expectations.

I have wasted far too much time and energy trying to make sense of the senseless...and so have you. We must decide those days are over. Daughters, you will face problems and conflicts. You may be tempted to take them personally. I implore you, fight this temptation. I learned that every step I took backward created a bottleneck for others.

Calling for Change: For years our organization was called John Bevere Ministries, and our board consisted of four men and me. It came into my heart that our name was tied to an individual, not to our function. It limited our ability to expand and created no pathways for spiritual legacy. I proposed the name be changed to Messenger International, and each and every year the board shot down the suggestion.

"Why aren't you content to serve under your husband's name?"

"Are you ashamed to carry John's name?"

When I wasn't around, board members would suggest that John wasn't in control of his wife.

There were two dynamics at play. In a board meeting, I was not relating to John as his wife but as a board member answerable to the organization. The problem came with the second dynamic: the other members decided I was only on the board by default because I was John's wife.

This went on for years. Each year I brought it up; each year they shot it down. The name change only came when a non-profit accountant suggested it would be better.

At first I thought, *Really? Isn't the board going to attack this man's character?* But then I realized...change had come! I didn't want to sabotage what I had waited so long to see by getting angry over how it came about!

That was nearly ten years ago. Our board now includes other women, and such issues no longer arise.

Moving Forward: The demographic of leadership is changing on every front. We can be part of that change or be angry that it didn't happen sooner. Don't dwell on the past; we need you to be part of moving things forward.

Here are some things I've learned the hard way:

Don't be so concerned about being heard that you don't listen. People listen better when they know they've been heard.

Don't make it hard for others to hear you. Give your input respectfully.

Don't become negative and fearful.

Be objective, but don't dumb down your intuition.

If you endure the pain of being misunderstood, misrepresented, and misjudged, the next decade will be better for everyone!

Adapted in part from *Nurture: Give and Get What You Need to Flourish* (FaithWords, 2008).

A good deal of this book points out the complexities and difficulties in the role of leading an organization. I'm not now diminishing those pressures, challenges, and pains, but I'm going to suggest that *managing* the causes of leadership pain (what I call bleedership) is only part of the solution. We can only raise the threshold of our pain if we *deepen the gratitude* in our hearts. Sometimes we have to overcome some faulty thinking about our connection with God and the faulty expectations that come from that thinking.

A heart of thankfulness is the appropriate response to our perception of generosity and kindness shown to us. In his book *Finding God*, author and psychologist Larry Crabb observes that many of us think of God as "a specially attentive waiter."[1] When we get good service from him, we give him a nice tip of praise. When we don't get what we want, we complain. Or do we trust that the sovereign Lord of the universe just might know more than we do about how the world should work? Have we experienced enough of his grace and greatness to convince us to have ambidextrous faith, trusting that he will use both blessings and heartaches to produce wisdom, faith, character, and hope in us? Thanking God for his love, power, and wisdom—no matter how or where he leads us—renews our hope, lightens our load, and puts steel in our soul.

> The authority by which the Christian leader leads is not power but love, not force but example, not coercion but reasoned persuasion. Leaders have power, but power is safe only in the hands of those who humble themselves to serve.
>
> —John Stott

Modern Pharisees

We usually give the Pharisees a hard time. They opposed Jesus at every turn and plotted to kill him. But if we correctly understand first-century Jewish culture, we see they were the good guys. When the Romans occupied Palestine, the Pharisees defended the traditions and the Scriptures. When Jesus offered grace to all sinners—including the outcasts and misfits the Pharisees would never invite to a dinner party—the religious leaders were outraged. The more Jesus talked about love, a supernaturally changed heart, and caring for the poor, the more the Pharisees detested him. They concluded that Jesus threatened their sense of control, which is ironic, because the Romans were really in control. The Pharisees were living under an illusion.

You might recognize my insinuation and you may vehemently protest, "I'm certainly not a Pharisee! I teach grace all the time!" But Jesus might ask us some uncomfortable questions:

- "Do you measure your worth by your numbers from last week?"
- "Are you a workaholic but resentful of how much is asked of you?"
- "Are you more committed to your ministry or to me?"
- "Is your heart truly broken for the poor, the lost, and the hurting?"
- "Do you pray more in public than in private?"
- "Do you try to earn respect from people but harbor secrets from your spouse, your friends, and even yourself?"
- "Are you missing too much of your children's lives?"
- "Are you no longer amazed that I came to earth, suffered, and died to rescue you?"

In a talk to pastors about creating a culture of self-awareness, Craig Groeschel warned and admitted, "Some of you will do what I did years back. I became a full-time pastor and a part-time follower of Christ. I'd pray when I prayed publicly. I'd study when I was preparing for a sermon.

My self-worth was based on last week's numbers." Another red flag for him was his assumption that he had all the answers. Then he realized, "The more I tend to believe that I'm right, the more likely I might be wrong." For Groeschel, the solution is the fundamental and profound answer found on every page of the Bible: "The more I humble myself and listen to God, the more broken I am, the better my relationship with my spouse is, the better my family is, and the better my church is."[2]

Pride shows itself in two very different forms. *Superiority* is the assumption that we know better than God how life should work and we're making it happen. *Inferiority* is based on the same initial assumption, but with the opposite conclusion: we can't make it work, so we're colossal failures. We instantly know that superiority isn't humility, but sometimes we mistake inferiority for a humble heart. It's not. A truly humble person doesn't feel compelled to put himself down. He knows he's deeply flawed—in fact, he's brutally honest about his sins and limitations—but he's also convinced that the grace of God is more wonderful than anything he can imagine. He's free from the bondage of defending himself or proving himself. He's beyond the temptations of praise and the ravages of blame.

> Trust is not a passive state of mind. It is a vigorous act of the soul by which we choose to lay hold on the promises of God and cling to them despite the adversity that at times seeks to overwhelm us.
>
> —Jerry Bridges, *Is God Really in Control?*

Peter Should Know

Few leaders have fallen as hard—or as publicly—as Peter. When Jesus told the disciples he was going to be arrested, falsely accused, tried, and executed, Peter boldly announced for all to hear, "I will lay down my life for you" (John 13:37). Only a few hours later, a few people warming their hands over a charcoal fire asked Peter if he had been with Jesus, and three times he denied knowing him. When Jesus looked him in the eye shortly after that, Peter was crushed. He wept bitter tears of shame and grief.

One of the most poignant conversations in the Bible occurred a short time after the resurrection. Peter and some others had gone fishing. By early morning they hadn't caught a single fish. A man on the beach called to them to lower their nets again, and they hauled in a huge catch of big fish. Instantly, Peter knew it was Jesus on the shore. He jumped in and swam to him.

Jesus had prepared breakfast for them. In his account, John makes the point that he was cooking fish over a charcoal fire. As Peter approached, the smell of the fire reminded him of the night of the arrest, the moment of his greatest sin, his deepest shame, and his betrayal of the one to whom he had professed complete loyalty. Then Jesus asked him three times, "Do you love me?" The questions must have stabbed Peter's heart like a dull knife. The smell of the charcoal fire and now the words forced him to confront the deepest darkness in his life. But Jesus wasn't being cruel; he was being thorough, kind, and gracious. He knew that restoration could only happen with complete honesty. This painful and tender moment was the turning point in Peter's life. After that, he was no longer just talk. When he spoke about the wonder of God's forgiveness, he was speaking from experience. When he talked about the privilege of serving Jesus, it came from the depths of a forgiven, restored, thankful heart.

> What do some leaders do when they get a challenging vision from God? They abort secretly. I believe that God has sent millions of visions to leaders all over the world. No one knows that all of these visions are being aborted though.
>
> —Bill Hybels

Peter's letters were written to people who were strangers who had been scattered by persecution. What did they need to hear? What did their leaders need in order to lead during a time of pain and confusion? Peter gave the people a fresh sense of identity founded on grace, not their performance or pleasant circumstances. He wrote, "You are a chosen people, a royal priesthood, a holy nation, God's special possession, that you may declare the praises of him who called you out of darkness into his wonderful light. Once you were not a people, but now you are the people of God; once you had not received mercy, but now you have received mercy" (1 Peter 2:9–10). They may have been outcasts running for their lives and barely able to provide for their families, but God had a different perspective of them: they were kings and queens, priests who represented God to man and man to God, and prophets who proclaimed the grace of God to the world.

Can you imagine how Peter's words made the exiles feel and think about their role in God's kingdom? It reminded them that it's all about grace and that pain can't diminish their identity and responsibility. No matter what their circumstances, they had the incredible privilege of being God's dearly loved children, children who delighted in advancing the family's name.

Near the end of the same letter, Peter addressed the leaders of the exiled church. First, he reminded them of his own experience of God's grace, and then he instructed them to carefully examine their hidden motives in ministry. Control, power, and greed are temptations for every leader, but honesty, repentance, and loving service will receive a reward: "When the Chief Shepherd appears, you will receive the crown of glory that will never fade away" (1 Peter 5:4).

For leaders, there will always be a fight against our culture's values and our sinful nature. We can't afford to go with the flow. We have to be intentional. Peter reminds us:

All of you, clothe yourselves with humility toward one another, because,

"God opposes the proud
but shows favor to the humble."

Humble yourselves, therefore, under God's mighty hand, that he may lift you up in due time. Cast all your anxiety on him because he cares for you.

Be alert and of sober mind. Your enemy the devil prowls around like a roaring lion looking for someone to devour. Resist him, standing firm in the faith, because you know that the family of believers throughout the world is undergoing the same kind of sufferings. (1 Peter 5:5–9)

Peter ends his instruction to these leaders with another reminder that what we see in this world isn't all there is. A strong hope for the future gives us strength to face pain today: "The God of all grace, who called you to his eternal glory in Christ, after you have suffered a little while, will himself restore you and make you strong, firm and steadfast. To him be the power for ever and ever. Amen" (1 Peter 5:10–11).

If Peter can raise the threshold of his pain, so can we.

When we sense the overwhelming privilege of being God's children, and the wonderful privilege of being called by him to care for those Jesus died for, we have a very different view of pain, whatever its cause. Exhaustion, entitlement, and self-pity erode our threshold of pain, but a fresh sense of the privilege of grace raises it to the skies. And with that, we're secure. And with that, we can endure.

> Twenty years from now you will be more disappointed by the things that you didn't do than by the ones you did do. So throw off the bowlines. Sail away from the safe harbor. Catch the trade winds in your sails. Explore. Dream. Discover.
>
> —Mark Twain

It is a paradox of a grace-filled spiritual leader that he can be a bold visionary yet humble and willing to listen to anyone at anytime; he can be driven but his heart is at rest; he can be tenderly compassionate yet brutally honest when the occasion warrants. He has nothing to prove and nothing to lose.

Be certain of this: when you suffer the pains of leadership, God is trusting you to weather the storm and represent him to a watching world. Your church's executive team looks to you to lead them; they trust you. The people in your business or nonprofit organization are looking to you; they trust you. Your family sees you when you aren't your best; they trust you. No matter what the source of difficulties you endure, God has put you in a position to display his kindness, wisdom, and power in the midst of your heartache.

> We found that for leaders to make something great, their ambition has to be for the greatness of the work and the company, rather than for themselves.
>
> —Jim Collins, *Good to Great*

Esther became the queen of a foreign land. When her older cousin Mordecai learned of a plot to wipe out the Jews, he realized God had strategically placed Esther in that *exact* place at that *exact* moment. Understandably, she hesitated to speak to the king to try to convince him to change his mind. She was risking her life. But Mordecai gave her a warning not to miss that opportunity: "Do not think that because you are in the king's house you alone of all the Jews will escape. For if you remain silent at this time, relief and deliverance for the Jews will arise from another place, but you and your father's family will perish. And who knows but that you have come to your royal position for such a time as this?" (Esther 4:13–14).

When we're in pain, it may not seem like much of a privilege to represent God at that moment and at that place, but God himself has appointed us, empowered us, and placed us "for such a time as this." He trusts us to endure with grace. The moment of pain, then, is a point of high honor earned by faithfulness, effectiveness, reputation, and proven character. It's an honor and a challenge to be God's representative in a time of heartache. People are watching us. It's an incredible opportunity. We dare not miss it.

Know This

It is a paradox of a grace-filled spiritual leader that he can be a bold visionary yet humble and willing to listen to anyone at anytime. He can be driven, but his heart is at rest. He can be tenderly compassionate yet brutally honest when the occasion warrants. He has nothing to prove and nothing to lose.

Do This

Look at the questions listed in this chapter. Put a check mark next to the ones you have sensed or said in the past month.

Think About This

1. How would you define and describe "the privilege of leadership"?
2. On a scale of 0 (not in the least) to 10 (all day every day), rate your level of genuine gratitude toward God and others. What does this say about your perspective? What can help you dive deeper into God's love, kindness, and generosity?
3. Do you agree or disagree that it's easy for ministry leaders to become Pharisees? Explain. If you agree, how does this happen? (It might help to review the uncomfortable questions in this chapter.)
4. What are some signs that a pastor has become "a full-time pastor, and a part-time follower of Christ"? Are any of these true of you? If so, what will you do about them?

5. How do you think Peter's failure and restoration shaped his sense of gratitude and humility? What kind of leader would he have been without the painful but cleansing encounter with Jesus on the beach?

And remember: *you'll grow only to the threshold of your pain.*

9

THE POWER OF TENACITY

*At the timberline where the storms strike with the
most fury, the sturdiest trees are found.*
—Hudson Taylor

**Wayne Alcorn, National President of Australian
Christian Churches, Senior Pastor of Hope
Centre International, Brisbane, Australia**

I still remember the phone call in September 2011. I had just finished speaking at a conference of our groups of churches here in Australia. It was my son, Brendan, on the phone. He sounded distraught as he broke the news that he'd incurred a hamstring injury to his left leg.

This couldn't have come at a worse time for him. He was playing his first game of a new cricket season—one that he hoped would see a major escalation of his accomplishments playing at an elite level. People reading this story may have their own opinion about cricket. Mine is that it's baseball . . . played properly!

Twelve months earlier, Brendan started playing with a new team in a major metropolitan area. He enjoyed immediate success, drawing the attention of influential and experienced people in the sport. They believed that with the right assistance, Brendan had the potential to achieve great things.

From his earliest years, Brendan always had a ball of some shape or form. One day, a casual observer noticed Brendan bowling a ball (that's like pitching, for those who aren't familiar with cricket) in a different way than all the other kids. He would later be described as a "left arm orthodox spinner." This unique skill gave him special opportunities in junior grades, and he progressed through the minor leagues. Honors flowed, and with them, the hope that one day his childhood dreams, ones that many Aussie boys share, could be realized.

Then came the injury. Assessments by sports medicine specialists discovered the cause of his hamstring tear was seriously bulging discs in his lower back. This was devastating news to a young bowler who relies on a strong and flexible back to deliver the ball. All of a sudden, the dreams he had carried from early childhood seemed to come crashing down. The idea of playing as a professional, of trying his hand in the English County Cricket System, seemed, in an instant, to be dealt a death blow. It became apparent that there would be no cricket for him that season. The extent of the injury restricted movement, and in the short term, made it impossible for him to run.

Despite every therapeutic avenue Brendan pursued, he experienced very little relief from the pain and discomfort. Good people tried a range of things to help, but with little success. Then came the dreaded word from sports medicine specialists that his playing career was over. He was advised to give up the sport he loved for the sake of his own wellbeing.

Where do Christians go in times like this? They turn to the Lord, believing that He is a God who heals today, as He did in Bible times. Regularly, Brendan stood in prayer lines at the end of Sunday services, asking God for a healing of his body and a restoring of his dream. The fact is, however, not everybody gets healed. To date, neither has he.

We all have a choice when we encounter personal pain. Brendan's choice was to do all he could to manage the injury in order to regain a quality, active lifestyle with the hope of playing some level of competitive sport.

Then came a phone call that would have a profound effect upon him. A friend of a friend had heard about Brendan's injury and offered to examine the scans and x-rays of Brendan's back to determine whether he could assist in his recovery. This man is a wonderful Christian physiotherapist. He had a highly successful practice and was the personal therapist for some very high profile sports stars. Brendan's medical records were sent to Sydney. The specialist called the following day to say that he believed that the injury was treatable. He concluded the conversation by confidently stating, "I know I can help him because I'm good at my job, and I'm a man of faith." A new journey began.

For the next year, Brendan traveled from Brisbane to Sydney (a 1-½ hour flight), then caught a train to the specialist's office to undergo a unique treatment regime. Initially, he went weekly, eventually tapering off to fortnightly. Fortunately the school where he worked was very accommodating, changing his class timetable to facilitate this arrangement.

Brendan also participated in specialized gym sessions a

few times a week, as well as the daily stretching and exercising required to strengthen and mobilize damaged areas of his body. This was all done with low expectations of ever returning to the standard of play that he had once known. Nor was there any hope of fulfilling his dream of playing in the United Kingdom.

It was quite a surprise for Brendan to get the call that he was to resume playing in the senior side on the first game of the new season. This meant he would be playing at a much higher grade—and much earlier than anyone expected.

That first game back from injury was a bittersweet experience. There was the sense of elation that he had made it back on the field. However, he was well aware that he was now playing with a damaged body, one that would not allow him to fully perform at a level he once enjoyed. He often played in pain. It was the love of the game that kept him on the field.

There have been a number of setbacks in the seasons that have followed. On occasions, the injury has flared to the point where he has been unable to continue playing. He has needed regular professional help to assist him with the pain management. There's never been a season, however, where he has not been able to fulfill his responsibilities to his team.

At the time of writing this, I have just returned from Scotland where Brendan is competing in the Scottish League as a professional cricketer. We had the privilege of going to a game and watch him perform brilliantly as both a batsman and a bowler. It was a joy to hear local officials applaud his efforts on the field and his character as a man.

Admittedly, this is not the lofty heights of playing at one of the world famous cricket grounds. It was, however, the fulfillment of a desire to play his beloved sport in an international context. It was Brendan's reward for the tenacity and persistence shown in managing an injury that so far has not gone away. He's played through pain, and ultimately, he has reaped the rewards.

The statistics on the longevity of pastors isn't encouraging. As we saw earlier from a major survey of pastors, 80 percent leave the ministry within five years.[1] Jimmy Draper, former president of the Southern Baptist Convention and former president of Lifeway Research Group, observed that for every twenty people who enter the ministry, only one retires from it.[2] That's only a 5 percent retention rate.

I don't know any leaders—of churches, businesses, or nonprofit organizations—who haven't thought about quitting at some point. Leadership is a magnet for pain, and sometimes our capacity to endure is severely challenged. We can receive some encouragement by looking at the world of sports.

The way to Heaven is ascending; we must be content to travel uphill, though it be hard and tiresome, and contrary to the natural bias of our flesh.

—Jonathan Edwards

Contact

Hockey is for tough guys. High sticks to the face, body checks against the boards, hard falls, fights, missing teeth, and multiple cuts and bruises. And that's a normal game. Plenty of fans smile when they hear the common snide remark, "I went to a fight and a hockey game broke out." Sportswriters Jeff Klein and Stu Hackel cataloged the pain suffered by players on the San Jose Sharks during the 2011 play-offs:

> Joe Thornton, the Sharks' captain and best player, skated in the last [play-off] game with a badly separated shoulder that will require surgery. He played throughout the playoffs with a broken pinkie, which was surgically repaired Thursday. The tip of the finger was just floating, and that forced Thornton to adjust the grip on his stick, exacerbating a wrist problem.
>
> Dan Boyle, the team's top defenseman, played since mid-March with a sprained medial collateral ligament in a knee, an injury that normally requires six weeks to heal. . . .
>
> Forward Ryane Clowe, a key playoff performer, had his shoulder separated in the second round against Detroit. He missed one game but returned. . . . He needed help pulling on his jersey, and needed a trainer to tie his skates. . . .
>
> Wing Dany Heatley . . : played with a hand that had been broken during the season. . . . He also sustained a high ankle sprain.

To these players and their coach, the hope of winning the Stanley Cup gave them a steel will to endure pain. Their coach was pleased with their effort, and general manager Doug Wilson expected nothing less. He was philosophical about playing through the injuries: "Did we drain our tank and leave us susceptible to injuries because we didn't leave ourselves any margin of error?" The lesson, he concluded, was to play even harder from the beginning of the next season. "We have to be ready from Day 1 next year."[3]

Pushing Through It

Athletes who participate in endurance sports—such as long-distance running, cycling, and swimming—realize that gut-level tenacity is as important as raw talent. Mary Wittenberg, president and CEO of the New York Road Runners, the organization that sponsors the New York City Marathon, identified the secret of successful marathoners: "Mental tenacity—and the ability to manage and even thrive on and push through pain—is a key segregator between the mortals and immortals in running." She described runners who come to the finish line with saliva streaming from their faces. "We have towels at marathon finish to wipe away the spit on the winners' faces. Our creative team sometimes has to airbrush it off race photos that we want to use for ad campaigns."[4]

Tom Fleming, a two-time winner of the race and now a coach, described his mind-set in races: "I was given a body that could train every single day, and a mind, a mentality, that believed that if I trained every day—and I could train every day—I'll beat you. The mentality was I will do whatever it takes to win. I was totally willing to have the worst pain. I was totally willing to do whatever it takes to win the race."[5]

Sports doctors have analyzed the tenacity of the best marathon runners. Dr. Jeroen Swart, who works for the Sports Science Institute of South Africa, concluded, "Some think elite athletes have an easy time of it," but that's a wrong assumption. "It never gets easier" as your time improves. "You hurt just as much." Accepting the reality of pervasive pain, he explained, leads to more realistic expectations and faster times: "Knowing how to accept [the reality of the pain] allows people to improve their performance."[6]

During points in races when the pain is most intense, some runners tend to dissociate, to try to distract themselves from the pain by thinking of something else. This strategy seems to work for a while, but sooner or later they hit a mental wall that hinders their efficiency. In contrast, Dr. Swart discovered, the best long-distance athletes concentrate even more intensely on their running, cycling, or swimming when they experience grueling pain. He concluded, "Our hypothesis is that elite athletes are able to motivate themselves continuously and are able to run the gauntlet between pushing too hard—and failing to finish—and underperforming."[7]

The best of these athletes don't avoid the pain; they push into it and past it.

Close to Home

The pain we experience may be caused primarily by the bumps and bruises inflicted by others, by our desire to reach higher and do more for the kingdom of God, or it may come from a closer source: our families.

Rev. Jesse Jackson has been a lion of the civil rights movement. He worked closely with Martin Luther King Jr., spoke eloquently for racial equality in America, and campaigned for the Democratic presidential nomination in 1984 and 1988. In recent years Jackson's struggle has come closer to home. His son, Jesse Jr., was ousted from his seat in the U.S. Congress as a result of an investigation of former Illinois Governor Rod Blagojevich. Investigators uncovered evidence that the younger Jackson may have been involved in paying Blagojevich to name him to the Senate seat vacated by Barak Obama after the 2008 election. But Jackson wasn't charged with anything in the Blagojevich case; he later stepped down for mental health issues as well as two other federal investigations. Eventually he was found guilty of misusing campaign funds and sentenced to thirty months in prison, and ordered to repay $750,000 he had spent on personal items.[8]

During this long and difficult saga, the elder Jackson felt deeply troubled. "My heart burns," he related. "As I always say to my children, champions have to play with pain. You can't just walk off the field because you're hurt."[9]

> By perseverance the snail reached the ark.
>
> —Charles H. Spurgeon

For Seth Barnes and his wife, Karen, the personal heartache in his family wasn't about politics. When their daughter Leah was a child, she suffered a chronic and severely painful ear infection. The sickness affected her ability to hear, so she had a hard time connecting to family and friends. A few years later other problems surfaced: her palate hadn't fully formed, and she also had speech difficulties as well as learning disabilities. Then, when she was a teenager, Leah began having seizures. Seth wrote, "We as parents have carried the burdens of crushed hopes while trying to meet all the special needs. I don't have any answers for her when I see her heart broken because other people have friends and she doesn't. When she looks at me with eyes that say, 'Daddy, it's not fair,' I don't have answers for her."

At many points in this journey, Seth and Karen realized they had a choice: to shake their fists at God and incubate a vindictive spirit or choose to trust him, "knowing that somehow he will redeem it." Instead of dissociating—ignoring the pain, engaging in endless distractions, or blaming anyone and everyone—Seth and Karen concluded they had no choice but to trust God:

> Our Creator God is the author of all life. Somehow in the midst of the pain, even through the tears, we have to trust him. He is the "Father of lights" who, the Bible tells us, gives us good and perfect gifts. As we trust him, we do so believing that he does answer. We believe that if that answer doesn't stop our pain, at least it redeems it. Yes, we don't understand what we've had to go through. Still, we will stand with Job and say, "Though he slay me, yet will I hope in him." We'll follow Leah as she follows God, knowing that her faith is often stronger than ours. When sometimes we half-step our way to God, she is usually able to trust him with her whole heart.

The Lord gave Seth, Karen, and Leah a picture of love, joy, and hope. Leah went to a dance for young people with special needs. As they danced with all their might, Seth saw something beautiful: "If you looked closely, for a second, I swear you could see Jesus dancing, right in the middle of them."[10]

Refusing to Quit

When we're in pain we quickly notice the default setting on the human heart: run, blame, smother the hurt in busyness, or act like nothing's wrong. To persevere, we need a vision for the future that's bigger than our pain. We may not see it clearly, and we may not like the process of getting there, but we have to be convinced in the depths of our hearts that enduring the pain will someday be worth it. This confidence enables us to raise the threshold of pain so we can respond with courage and hope.

> Go forth today, by the help of God's Spirit, vowing and declaring that in life—come poverty, come wealth, in death—come pain or come what may, you are and ever must be the Lord's. For this is written on your heart, "We love Him because He first loved us."
>
> —Charles H. Spurgeon

Pastor, broadcaster, and author Bob Gass identifies four primary traits of resilient people:

1. **They take control of their lives** instead of spending energy trying to blame others or waiting for them to bail them out. They may want to quit, but they don't. Instead, they look at the past and think about how they've handled adversity before, and they look at the present with clear eyes as problem solvers.
2. **They surround themselves with the right people.** We may have grown up in an addicted, abusive, or abandoning family, but we can make choices today to spend time with people who live in truth and have hope for tomorrow.
3. **They allow their pain to spur growth instead of collapsing in self-pity.** Even when a life goal is completely blocked by disease or any other cause, resilient people find an open door when others only saw the one that's closed. They creatively invest themselves

in a new venture, often one that focuses on helping others who are experiencing pain from similar physical, emotional, or relational heartaches—and they make a difference.

4. **They insist on changing what they can and not worry about the rest.** For resilient people, encounters with pain enable them to sift through their responsibilities and priorities. Suddenly, many things that seemed important are no longer on the top of the to-do list. But other things, such as people they love and a cause they can champion, are now on top.[11]

The Necessary Process

Wayne Cordiero wrote an eye-opening and challenging book, *Sifted: Pursuing Growth Through Trials, Challenges, and Disappointments*. He insisted that all Christians, especially leaders, go through a necessary process of sifting. He identified it this way: "The process of sifting, coming to that moment when our strength is spent, is how God builds our faith. It's a process that forms new character, tearing away old perspectives and putting fresh truth in its place. Former habits are discarded and wrong tendencies abandoned."[12]

Failure isn't the end of the world for those who are open to God's tender, strong hand. It's the beginning of a new wave of insight, creativity, and effectiveness—but only if we pay attention and learn the lessons God has for us. When we receive a vision from God, we're excited, and we dream about the steps it will take to fulfill it. We generally assume God will supply everything to accomplish the goal he's given to us, but we often fail to realize that he needs to do a deeper work in us so we can do what he has called us to do. And the way he works deeply in us is through all kinds of opposition, stress, heartache, loss, and obstacles. In other words, God works most powerfully in and through our failures. Cordiero explained:

> The truth is that you *will* fail. You simply won't have what it takes when you begin. You may have the calling, the zeal, the energy, and the support.

You might even have the location, the invitation, and even the money. But when you begin you won't have what it takes to finish. "What is that?" you might ask. What's missing is that inner core, the tensile strength of faith that is revealed only under strain. It is a quality of character that is tested not in port but in the open seas. And it is this testing that ratifies your calling. . . . It is something that can be acquired only through failure, learning your limits and learning to trust not in yourself but in the God who has called you.[13]

As long as we see failure, stress, and difficulties as intruders, we'll fail to let them teach us, shape us, and strengthen us. When we expect God to use pain in our lives to sift us, prune us, and build us, we'll have the tenacity it takes to endure hard times.

> How you think when you lose determines how long it will be until you win.
>
> —G. K. Chesterton

No Regrets

Great athletes know they have to invest everything in their sport. Every decision they make about eating, sleeping, training, and relationships goes through the grind and grid of decision making. As Christian leaders, the grind of ministry sometimes causes us to look more deeply at what we really value. We may realize some (perhaps a lot) of what seemed so important is extraneous and maybe detrimental to what God really wants to do in our lives. God often uses difficulties to clarify our purpose, purify our motives, and give us a clearer sense of direction.

J. R. Briggs was asked to be the heir-apparent pastor of a large church near Philadelphia. During his first year he preached several times to the congregation of three thousand people. One Sunday as he was walking back to his office between services, a couple approached him and said, "We just know you are going to be the next Andy Stanley."

Suddenly, the bar of expectations was raised through the roof!

A few months later the pastor was forced to resign under a cloud. Since J. R. was the pastor's hire, the lay leaders of the church were suspicious of him. During his time at the church he realized that being the pastor of a megachurch wasn't God's best for him. He asked the church leaders to bless him as he charted a course to plant a new church, but instead of a blessing, they ordered him not to plant one anywhere near the city. J. R. reflected on the moment he resigned and walked away: "I left the church staff two years to the day of my hiring. That season of our lives could be summed up with one word: loss. I was wrestled to the ground by loneliness and despair. I felt like my soul was bludgeoned, dumped in the back alley, and left to die."

J. R. raised enough funds and found enough interested people to start a new church of about forty adults. Some people accused him of wasting his talents, and others said it was bad stewardship to leave a church of three thousand to minister to only forty. And the old church didn't leave him alone. He received hate mail for over a year.

Starting the new church didn't relieve the gnawing sense of loss. J. R. remembered, "My perceived ministry failure had created a virtual prison that left me living in a cramped cell. I was suffering from spiritual claustrophobia."

J. R. realized his path led only further into spiritual, emotional, and relational darkness, so he found a counselor who provided insight and hope. He knew the normal response to threat is fight or flight, but he wondered if the Scriptures speak to those reactions. Was there a third, more productive way to respond to failure? Gradually, new perspectives began to dawn—or more likely old truths that had seemed irrelevant now seemed vibrant and new. Instead of running from God and fighting with people (or the other way around), J. R. began to see himself as a loved, forgiven, accepted child of the King:

When I choose this third way—yielding—the Father moves me from a posture of rejection to acceptance, and from a place of shame to honor.

Despite my failure to live up to some standard (which invariably leads to being rejected by others), God did not reject me. I belong to him. And regardless of how I perform, he still loves me.

> Be of good cheer. Do not think of today's failures, but of the success that may come tomorrow. You have set yourselves a difficult task, but you will succeed if you persevere; and you will find a joy in overcoming obstacles. Remember, no effort that we make to attain something beautiful is ever lost.
>
> —Helen Keller, *The Story of My Life*

The moment of failure, Briggs noted, is a watershed experience: it has the power to transform or destroy. God invites us into a process of transformation, a classroom where he is the wise, loving instructor. As he continues to learn this lesson, Briggs has increasingly experienced the paradox of faith: he is becoming stronger and more humble, bold but at peace, honest yet compassionate. Though he is now comfortable in his role as the pastor of a small church, questions about his value as a small-church pastor occasionally return to the dark corners of his mind. But now he has an answer: "When my heart whispers these questions, I remind myself of the truth of the gospel: my identity and worth—as a pastor and as a person—is not wrapped around what I do or how large my congregation is. It's not tied to how much clout or influence others think I possess. It is only based on one thing. I am a cherished child of the King." [14]

I can relate to J. R.'s experience. Before I began to learn the lessons of tenacity, I grossly *overestimated* what God wanted to do in the short term, and I grossly *underestimated* what God wanted to do in the long term. Today, I have more of a long-term view, which gives me "peace like a river" when trials "attendeth my way, when sorrows like sea billows roll." In spite of the obvious headaches and heartaches near me, I'm convinced that God is still the gracious King.

Longer, Deeper

As believers we have something hockey players and distance athletes don't have: certainty about the future. They play through the broken bones and dislocated joints with the hope of a championship, and they rivet their minds on the finish line as they endure grueling pain. But they can't be sure they'll win the cup or finish first. We have the assurance that someday God will make all things right. The sweeping arc of Scripture is creation, fall, redemption, and restoration. God's solemn promise is to bring everything back into perfect alignment: no tears, no regrets, no sin—only unfettered love, joy, and purpose in the new heaven and new earth of God's fully consummated kingdom.

> There are two pains in life: the pain of discipline, or the pain of regret. You choose.
>
> —Wayne Cordeiro

Our perspective about tomorrow radically affects how we respond to today. Spiritual myopia enables us to see only what is right in front of us, and we're often alarmed. But hope gives us courage to face any calamity or nagging difficulty. God has given us a magnificent promise for our future in the new heaven and new earth. In fact, it's so wonderful that it overwhelms us. The process begins here and now.

Do we really believe what we say at funerals or is it empty comfort for grieving people? Do we grasp the full weight of God's promise that

Christ's resurrection is the firstfruits of the transformation we'll experience someday? To the extent we believe it, we'll be able to endure the pains we experience today. Teresa of Avila had it right. She explained how certainty about the future affects our ability to handle today's trials: "The first moment in the arms of Jesus, the first moment of heaven, is going to make a thousand years of misery on earth look like one night in a bad hotel."[15]

The longer perspective of eternity helps us endure, but so does a deeper view of the ultimate example of endurance. When we're tempted to quit, the writer to the Hebrews tells us to take our eyes off our misery and look to Christ: "Let us run with perseverance the race marked out for us, fixing our eyes on Jesus, the pioneer and perfecter of faith. For the joy set before him he endured the cross, scorning its shame, and sat down at the right hand of the throne of God. Consider him who endured such opposition from sinners, so that you will not grow weary and lose heart" (Hebrews 12:1–3).

> Shouldn't we suppose that many of our most painful ordeals will look quite different a million years from now, as we recall them on the New Earth? What if one day we discover that God has wasted nothing in our life on Earth? What if we see that every agony was part of giving birth to an eternal joy?
>
> —Randy Alcorn, *90 Days of God's Goodness*

Do we face opposition? The civil and religious authorities opposed Jesus at every turn. Do we encounter evil in all its forms? Satan himself tempted him. Do we feel betrayed and abandoned? The crowds that yelled "Hosanna!" soon cried, "Crucify him!" And almost all of his best friends ran for their lives at his greatest hour of need. Do we feel misunderstood? The Lord of glory stepped out of heaven to rescue sinful people, and they killed him. Do we feel vulnerable? He was stripped, beaten, and hung on a cross in public humiliation. Why did he do all this? Out of love for the very ones who had run away from him, who had driven spikes into his hands, and who jeered him as he hung on the cross. People like you and me.

When we feel like quitting, we can think about Jesus. In the greatest act of love ever known, when he was unjustly dying for those who despised him, he could have come down from the cross and killed them all—but he stayed.

Know This

To persevere, we need a vision for the future that's bigger than our pain.

Do This

Think of pain as a watershed to transform or destroy. Who are some people you know who have been transformed (character proven, faith deepened, hope secured) by their experiences with pain? Who are some who have been destroyed? What's the difference in their pains and their responses?

Think About This

1. Does it surprise you that only one in twenty people who enter the ministry retire from it? Explain.
2. What can you learn from the tenacity of athletes, either in contact sports or endurance sports?
3. Are there particular kinds of difficulties that cause you more anxiety than others and tempt you to quit? What have been the crises in your life and ministry that caused you to want to bail? Do you see a pattern?

4. Which of the four traits of resilient people is already present in your life? Which one(s) need some work? How will you develop this trait?

5. How would it change your response to difficulties if you were convinced that God would use them to sift you and transform you?

6. How do the longer view of the certainty of restoration in the new heaven and new earth and the deeper view of Christ's endurance give you at least a little more tenacity?

And remember: *you'll grow only to the threshold of your pain.*

10

PAIN PARTNERS

Friendship is a sovereign antidote against all calamities.
—SENECA

Joe and Gina Cameneti, Pastors
of Believers Church, Warren, Ohio

From Joe . . .

At the 20-year mark of our church's history, which was 11 years ago from today, I took some time to do an inventory of our growth. We had pioneered the church, and it grew to about 1600 people in attendance on a weekend. I realized, though, that 99 percent of the growth was from transfers. We were leading people to Christ with door-to-door witnessing, and even a few in our services, but none of them were being retained. My heart broke when I looked at the numbers. At that point it didn't matter that we grew a big church in a small demographic area. We weren't reaching the unchurched (non-Christians), and we weren't teaching the Christians to reach the unchurched. I asked the very tough question: "Why?" After several years of research, I realized the problem was the way we were doing services. Our services were actually pushing unchurched and new Christians away.

I figured out a way to grow strong Christ-following believers and relate to unchurched and new Christians without compromising my charismatic Christian beliefs. We began to implement some changes in our service to reach the unchurched in our community: shortening worship to four songs, eliminating some elements that newcomers considered awkward, and tailoring each week's sermon to connect people with God in every area of their lives, both believers and unbelievers.

The changes began to make a difference, and Gina and I were excited about it! But at the time I was making changes in our services, I was also making changes in other departments of the church. I was doing what every pastor has to do at the 20- to 25-year mark: streamlining the direction of the every department to be in sync with the main vision of the church. Because of those changes, a long-time staff member left in a negative way. His departure, coupled with the service changes, started a 700-person exodus that lasted about four years.

Two years after the exodus began, I thought we hit bottom. It seemed that everyone that was going to leave had left. Then, it got even worse. Another staff member told us he was getting out of ministry for personal reasons. I threw him a party, received a special offering for him. Very soon after that, he popped up in a new church plant in town. And another exodus began.

Those days, weeks, months, and years, were traumatic for me. I had never experienced such pains of rejection. I'm not blaming the people that left; I'm simply saying it hurt. During that time, I often ran into people that I knew from church at a restaurant or store, but I didn't know if they had left or were still with us. It was a very awkward and painful time for me. I felt hurt, ashamed, confused, and alone. It seemed that more than 20 years of building our church had crumbled to dust.

My confidence was shattered. I felt that my name, even though I did nothing bad, was ruined in the community, so I planned to leave the church. Gina and I decided to move to Chicago, her hometown, to start over and pioneer another church. But Gina felt so burned-out emotionally that she didn't want to be in ministry any longer. I was going to be on my own. I told our church's board of trustees that we planned to leave, but to my surprise, they didn't want us to go. Now I was really confused. I had assumed everyone thought we were the problem.

I called two mentors to ask for their help. Sam Chand and Tony Cooke each flew into Warren, on different days, to meet with us on their own nickel. Dr. Chand gave me a template of questions to help me figure out if leaving was God's will. That was incredibly helpful. Tony also gave me incredible advice and talked to our board to help them walk through this difficult season.

I followed one of the steps in Dr. Chand's advice and flew to Chicago to scout out the land. He also gave me several names of successful pastors in Chicago who were willing to help me. Then several weeks later, Gina and our daughters went to Chicago for a vacation. While we were on vacation, I continued scouting the area to see where we might plant a church. During that time, God made it very clear to my heart that he wanted us to stay where we were. The move was off.

The board was excited to have us back. They treated us with exquisite kindness and generosity, and they gave us time to heal. I regularly met with a Christian counselor who walked me through the dark valley of hurt, anger, and shame . . . and to the other side of forgiveness, hope, and renewed joy. This experience was a godsend for me. I built spiritual muscles that I'm so excited to have and use! Finally, the painful and confusing events of the past few years no longer haunted me. I was free to pursue God, Gina, and all God had for us. I was no longer willing to live in the past. I was going to walk with God, enjoy life, and move forward.

About a year after we decided to stay at the church, things began turning around. We saw some signs of a positive momentum. We were really excited! The changes we had begun years before were reaping results. I did another analysis of our church, and I found that 61 percent of our growth was new believers, and only 39 percent was people who had come from other churches. I was amazed and gratified. We developed a new vision statement: "We exist to see a city connected with God." Our goal is to turn unchurched people into *fans*, *friends*, and ultimately *followers* of God. Our people love it. They are so excited because they can bring their loved ones and friends to a service knowing it will be a positive experience. And many of them are coming to Christ!

What's happening now is really cool. We are averaging 15 adults accepting Christ per weekend! That works out to 81% of our first-time visitors making a commitment to Christ. Plus, we're retaining a large portion of them and pulling them into membership.

None of this would have happened if God hadn't brought two mentors into my life at a pivotal juncture. Sam Chand and Tony Cooke were instrumental in helping me regain my perspective and my confidence. I learned that God always comes through, even when it looks like he's a million miles away—if we trust him with all our heart. God was at work even in our darkest days. Change always brings pain—sometimes years of pain—but the fruit is well worth the struggle.

From Gina . . .

Joe and I were both shattered by the events that led to the exoduses from our church. Those who left weren't just numbers; many of them had been dear friends of ours. I felt terribly fragile and broken. A lot of people blamed us for the problems, which felt so unfair. We experienced the blows of betrayal and a crushing sense of shame—we had been misjudged and condemned, and our reputations were in tatters.

Soon, the person I had been was unrecognizable. I lost the enthusiasm, joy, and insights I'd had before. I became a shell of who I had been. Leaving seemed like the only good alternative, but I simply couldn't go back into ministry—in Chicago or anywhere else. I was too damaged to give out to anyone. Joe stayed strong; I fell apart.

I took a break to meet with mentors and a counselor. For two years, I focused on finding the love and power of God to restore my soul. Grieving losses isn't quick or pretty, but it's necessary. I had a few safe people who loved me when I was at the bottom and who gave me courage to take steps out of the quagmire of hopelessness. I was willing to pay any price to get the help I needed—money for counseling, time away, energy and effort, and being misunderstood for taking so long to heal. It was humbling to be on the receiving end instead of being the strong, resourceful minister who always had cared for others.

Eventually, I realized this whole experience was the very best thing that could have happened to me. After the overwhelming wave of grief subsided, I came back with more wisdom, strength, and joy than I'd ever had before. One of my mentors told me, "You wouldn't go through all that again if someone offered you a million dollars, but you wouldn't trade it for a million dollars." It was excruciatingly hard, but it was worth it.

Joe and Lori Champion, Celebration Church, Georgetown, Texas

From Lori . . .

When Joe and I had been married about two years, I was seven months pregnant. We were serving on the pastoral staff at the church where my father had been the pastor. We were so excited about the arrival of our first child! On a Saturday afternoon, we went to a craft fair to buy some things to decorate the nursery. As we walked around the booths, I reached up to scratch my neck and felt a lump—a large lump—at the edge of my collarbone. I didn't say anything, but I knew something was very, very wrong. By the time we pulled into our driveway at home, I broke down in tears and told Joe about the lump.

For several weeks before that day, I had a sense that something wasn't right. It as more than that: it was a spirit of death.

During those weeks when I felt so strange, Joe assured me it was only the normal hormonal change associated with pregnancy. His words sounded reasonable, but I knew it was more than that. My fear wasn't unfounded. Four years earlier, I had seen my father drop dead from a heart attack as he preached one Sunday morning. He was only 45 years old.

Everything with the pregnancy had gone amazingly well. I had felt really good, and our ministry was growing. But I had a strange sense of foreboding. I was afraid something would happen to Joe, and I'd be alone with a newborn. I told Joe, "We need to pray that God will protect us. I feel that we're going to be under attack." I suggested that we get life insurance. We signed the papers for the insurance the morning before we went shopping at the craft fair.

As soon as we got home that afternoon, I called my doctor and made an appointment for Monday morning. He, too, thought it might be normal hormonal fluctuations associated with pregnancy, or maybe something related to my allergies, or maybe an infection that caused my lymph nodes to be so swollen. He tried a number of treatments, but nothing worked. After three or four weeks, he decided to do a biopsy. When I woke up from the anesthesia, the doctor gave me the diagnosis: Hodgkin's lymphoma. He said they needed to deliver my baby immediately because he didn't know how far the cancer had spread.

I was now eight months along. Mason was born, a very healthy little boy, but the next four weeks were the hardest of my life. I was thrilled to have a baby, but I couldn't get over the fear that I might die and leave Joe and Mason alone. I felt so sick, and I had no appetite. One day, I told Joe that I was afraid to close my eyes at night because I didn't know if

I'd ever open them again. As soon as I said those words, he got on the phone to call friends to ask them to pray. They'd already been praying, of course, but now it was urgent.

From Joe . . .

When Lori told me she was afraid she'd die any moment, I knew we couldn't make it on our own. I called people who know and love us to ask them to pray—to care for us in a way that would hold us up before the throne of God. At a terribly difficult time in his life, David had his mighty men. David was alone when he killed Goliath, but in his fight against Saul's army, he had a group of men who were totally loyal to him. They knew him, they loved him, and they noticed when he was in need. He didn't have to ask them to come alongside; they saw when he was exhausted and hurting, and they gladly supported him. They were true friends. Our friends were like David's mighty men.

We can't wait until we're in trouble to create friendships like these. They have to be in place before the crisis hits. I've known pastors who prided themselves on being Lone Rangers. Many of them didn't survive the crises they inevitably faced. Thank God, Lori and I had true and trusted friends we could count on in our darkest season of life.

We need friends who aren't there only for professional purposes, but for personal purposes—friends who don't necessarily make our ministries more successful, but who know us intimately and care for us deeply.

During the worst four weeks of fear and doubt, God used some mighty men and women in our lives. I had spoken at a church in California years before, and there, I met Jane Manley. When Lori and I felt desperate, I sensed the Lord leading me to call Jane to ask her to pray. God had prepared her: when she answered, she said she already knew I was going to call, and she knew Lori was having difficulties. Ed and Nancy Werner walked with us, step by excruciating step, through the valley of the shadow of death. When Lori couldn't eat, Ed came to our home and sat patiently with her to help her get some food into her body.

There are times in all of our lives when our faith falters. In those times, our friends carry us along. When the four friends of the paralytic dug a hole in the roof and lowered him in front of Jesus, it wasn't the paralyzed man's faith Jesus saw, but the faith of his loving, compassionate, assertive friends. Without friends like that, we won't make it during our most difficult seasons in life.

There are some fights we can't fight alone, but we need to choose our friends wisely. Some friends are pleasant in the good times, but we discover our real friends during hard times. We need to find those life-giving friends who believe God with us for the future.

From Lori . . .

God never forgets us. He sends his messengers with a word when we need it most. When I was almost beyond hope, Robert Barriger came to our church as a guest speaker. After he spoke, he asked to see me. We found a quiet place, and he said, "Today, you said that you might die. I'm telling you that you're going to live. You're going to see your children and grandchildren, and in your old age, you're going to lead worship in the house of God." That conversation changed everything for me. I had never met that man before that day, but God used him to infuse me with a new hope for the future. I'm very thankful for friends, old ones and new ones.

Our secrets will kill us. They will haunt our dreams, cloud our plans, and distort our relationships. We may harbor secrets because the truth about a single evil past act or a continuing bad habit is too shameful to tell, or we may keep our secrets hidden because we don't have any real friends who will genuinely listen. Either way, we remain alone, isolated, and desperate to stay hidden.

Kill us? you might object. *Surely it's not that serious.* Sometimes it is. When leaders have no place to vent their frustrations and no one to understand their pain, they internalize all the hurt, fear, confusion, and anger. Some experience severe physiological problems that can result in prolonged disease and premature death. And others give up completely. Suicide can become an attractive alternative for leaders who can't see any light in their future. They feel utter isolation and abject hopelessness. When I need gas for my car, I go to a gas station. When I need food, I go to a grocery store or restaurant. Every leader needs to ask: "Who is filling my emotional tank? Who is giving me the sustenance of hope, joy, and understanding?"

Leaders in business, nonprofits, and churches desperately need to find someone who has no agenda except to listen without judging and love without any strings attached. The existential angst of hopelessness and despair can only be addressed in community—close relationships with at least one, preferably a few, who genuinely care for us. Nothing less will do.

Almost three out of four pastors say they regularly think of leaving the ministry,[1] many because they don't have a single close friend. Only a few have been loners all their lives. Most of them had wonderful, meaningful connections in the past, but something happened: people moved away, the stress of the job sucked the time and life out of one or the other or both, people got too busy and stopped calling and having coffee, a simple misunderstanding grew into an irreparable schism, or betrayal shattered a trusted bond. Whatever the cause, most pastors have no one to lean on, no safety valve, no understanding ear, and no shoulder to cry on.

Pain can only be effectively managed in a trusting, affirming, honest community—not necessarily a large community, but at least a few people who genuinely understand. Most leaders have to endure seasonal storms that last for a while and then subside. For pastors, however, the storms never stop. The torrents keep coming. Without a strong, supportive community, pastors wither away under the pressure. Consider the following questions:

- Who in your life "gets you" and doesn't think you're weak or strange when you wrestle with the complexities of your role?
- Who listens to you without feeling compelled to give you advice?
- Who asks second and third questions to draw you out instead of giving pat answers, simple prescriptions, and easy formulas?
- Who is your safe haven so you can be completely honest and open?
- Who fills your spiritual and emotional gas tank?

The answer to these questions identifies your *pain partner*—a most cherished friend. In my consulting, I strive to be a safe person with whom people can honestly share their pain.

A friend told me about his conversation this morning with a pastor, we'll call him James, who is showing signs of mild depression. He has been at his church for two years. When James was an assistant pastor, he had three close friends who somehow found time to get together every other week. They went to ball games and movies, fished, or just sat and talked for hours. The other three all moved to other positions at about the time James took on his new role.

When my friend mirrored his discouragement over coffee, James admitted, "Yeah, I'm on the edge. Frankly, some days I'm over the edge. I took a pay cut to become senior pastor at our church. Go figure. Who does that? And I had no idea our leadership team was such a mess. After two years, I'm finally getting a handle on resolving the tension that has existed since, oh, since the church was founded fifteen years ago."

"Who are your buddies? Who can you talk to?" my friend asked.

"Right now, you. I used to have three friends. We could say anything to each other—and we did. We were honest and supportive. That's a great combination, especially for people in ministry. But they're gone, and it shows. Every day I feel more isolated, even though things are finally going pretty well at the church. I'm glad you're here." He paused and then asked with a hint of desperation, "You *are* here for me, aren't you?"

> People with deep and lasting friendships may be introverts, extroverts, young, old, dull, intelligent, homely, good-looking; but the one characteristic they always have in common is openness.
>
> —Alan Loy McGinnis, *Friendship Factor*

No Options, No Excuses

I've known leaders who have *survived* without friends because they had the sheer willpower to keep showing up day after day, even though they were always on guard in every relationship. But I've never known any leaders who *thrived* in their roles, in their families, or in their personal lives without at least a few trusted friends. A spouse can be a wonderful encourager and a leader's number-one fan, but church leaders need a peer or two who are shouldering similar loads and who understand the complexities of the role.

In other words, if you don't have a friend or two, you probably won't make it very long. And if you gut it out on willpower, you won't have the emotional resources to genuinely connect with people. You'll be an empty shell going through the motions.

Some ministry leaders insist, "All I need is God. God and me . . . that's plenty." Nonsense. This is a statement of either arrogance or ignorance. God has made us relational beings—even pastors! To function as the people God has created and redeemed, we need both the vertical connection with God *and* meaningful horizontal connections with people.

Oh, we have plenty of horizontal connections as leaders in ministries and nonprofits, but the vast majority of those are draining our emotional tanks, not filling them. It doesn't take long before we're running on empty. We simply have to find people who will pour into us instead of always pull out of us.

Starting Points

People expect ministry leaders to be the epitome of warmth, perception, gentleness, kindness, and humor. Few of us can even approach this pedestal, but some begin with greater resources than others. I know some leaders who stand on the shoulders of loving, strong, supportive parents. A few of these leaders are the latest in a long legacy of spiritual leadership going back generations. They are powerful, wise, loving leaders in large measure because they saw that kind of leadership modeled in front of them every day as they grew up. But I also know plenty of great leaders whose parents weren't wise, loving, and strong at all. Still, the men and women I know broke the cycle—they imparted plenty of affirmation and encouragement to their own kids when they dreamed big dreams of serving God.

Other leaders, though, began ministry with huge emotional and relational deficits. They've had difficulty in relationships in every area of life because affection and wisdom weren't imprinted on them when they were young. Without a secure foundation, they entered the ministry trying to pour out something that had never been poured into them. It's confusing and exhausting.

In an online article, Bob Buford recounted the story of Jim Collins, author of outstanding books like *Good to Great* and *Built to Last*. When he was twenty-five, Collins realized he hadn't received many intangibles a father should pass on to a son. Instead of remaining passive, he built a board of directors for his personal life. He selected people who were willing to invest in him like a loving dad would gladly invest in his son. These people provided what Collins had missed.

> Often we have no time for our friends but all the time in the world for our enemies.
>
> —Leon Uris

When Bob shared Collins's strategy with church leaders, he received some powerful feedback. One commented that he, like Collins, needed God to insert a "father key-card to be fully released into our greatest human capability" because they lacked "the effecting fathering relationship that would release the potential." This man actively pursued relationships with wise men who were older than him—father figures—to be "right-for-the-time mentors whose contribution . . . was measured not in raw hours but in invaluable insights."[2]

Some of us began with relational deficits, and others have been drained dry in our roles as spiritual leaders, but none of us has to remain empty.

Known and Loved

An *accurate perception* and *genuine love* can't be separated. When someone looks behind our masks and sees our shadow side, but we don't feel loved, we feel terribly threatened by the exposure. When someone expresses sentiments of love but doesn't really know us, we easily discount the display of affection as superficial. But it's incredibly powerful—life changing—to be in a relationship where we can be totally vulnerable without fear, when the person knows the worst about us and still accepts us.

Ultimately, this kind of love is found only in the gospel of grace, but we can at least taste it in a few human connections—people who impart God's grace to us. These are the friendships that give life meaning and hope.

We may find professional counselors and executive coaches we pay to know us and believe in us, and these relationships are tremendously significant. But true friends are invaluable. We don't find this level of perception and acceptance in an instant. We cultivate them slowly, carefully, and intentionally. We take small steps of risk to share our hearts one layer deeper than before, and then we see how the person handles it. And the other person takes the same risk with us. If no one says, "Oh, my God! I can't believe you thought that [or said that or did that]!" or ran away or laughed derisively, another block in a foundation of trust has been laid. And the next time and the next, more truth is risked and perhaps more trust is built. As long as both are willing to take these risks, to be honest on one side and to patiently listen on the other, the relationship can deepen and grow.

Of course, we're thoroughly human. We have bad days. We react poorly and need to heal the wound inflicted by careless words, or we neglect the friend and need to resolve the offense before we can move on. It's amazing, though, that two people who love and trust each other can pick up a relationship after months apart like they had shared their hearts only yesterday.

The greatest sweetener of human life is friendship.
To raise this to the highest pitch of enjoyment is a
secret which but few discover.

—Joseph Addison

Selecting Well

A leader confided, "I have a friend who has been with me through thick and thin. We've been with each other through all the ups and downs of life and ministry, but recently I realized something. When I'm with him, I'm not a better person. I'm not more positive, more joyful, or more faithful. I don't know if it's been this way all these years, but this has been true in the past months." He sighed deeply and reflected, "I may need to find a better friend."

When a multitude of catastrophes struck Job, his friends came to see him. Eliphaz began well, affirming that Job had been a source of strength to other people, but he immediately blamed Job for his problems (Job 4:3–8). Bildad joined the chorus of certainty that death and destruction couldn't have touched Job unless he was at fault (Job 8:20). Zophar didn't want to be left out. He assumed the cause of the calamity was Job's secret sin, and he urged him to repent and be restored (Job 11:14–17). Elihu (Job 32:1–22) was angry at Job—and the other three guys! Job's wife was crushed by the loss. She gave up on God and any hope for the future. Her advice was, "Curse God and die!" (Job 2:9).

The long discourses between Job and his friends are painful to read, and undoubtedly it was excruciating for Job to endure. We get a glimpse of God's perspective of these friends in the last chapters when God speaks from heaven, not to answer Job's "why" question, but to assert his ultimate rule over all creation and to put Job's faulty friends in their place. In a twist of irony, God tells Job to pray for the men who should have been praying and listening to their friend all along.

Not all of our friends are pain partners. We need to be selective. After having his last meal with his disciples, Jesus went to the Garden of Gethsemane to pray. At the entrance of the garden, he told the group to stay, but he invited three—Peter, James, and John—to come with him as he faced the horror of the coming hell he would experience. They were his pain partners. It was, they undoubtedly realized later, one of the greatest honors of their lives, but they fell asleep as Jesus prayed, begged for another path, yet accepted the Father's will for him. In his grace, Jesus gave them only a mild rebuke. He understood they were going to face a lot of pain, too, only hours later.

Sometimes those who have betrayed us can become our most valued partners. It takes grace—in them and in us. Paul was angry when John Mark deserted him on one of his dangerous missionary journeys (Acts 13:13; 15:38). In fact, Paul was so upset that the dispute caused a split between him and his close friend Barnabas. For years of Paul's ministry we don't hear anything more about John Mark, but as Paul awaited death in a Roman prison, he wrote to Timothy, "Only Luke is with me. Get Mark and bring him with you, because he is helpful to me in my ministry" (2 Timothy 4:11). A person who had inflicted pain now was helping to relieve pain.

The people we are closest to—our spouse, brother, sister, parents, children, or staff member—may not be the right partner for us in our pain. Why? Because they may not be able to be objective as we pour out our hearts to them. Our pain threatens their security, so they may feel uncomfortable with our distress. They want us to feel happy and get over it quickly, so they give us simplistic answers. Or these people may be a major source of our pain, and they don't make good candidates for a confidant. Or they may have power over our income, so they have more power (and an agenda) than we'd like in a pain partner.

Different pains, then, call for different partners. Choose wisely, but choose.

Building Friendships

It is a dictum of human relationships that if you want a friend, you need to be a friend. The problem, of course, is that we need a friend when we're stressed out, angry, evasive, and consumed with protecting ourselves instead of feeling comfortable reaching out to help others. Here are a few clear, profound principles about building and keeping friends. Most will read these and sigh, "I already knew that," but we may need to be reminded to actually *do* them. British author Samuel Johnson observed, "People need to be reminded more often than they need to be instructed."

Listening

The first and arguably the most important principle in connecting with others is to listen . . . *really* listen . . . to their hearts, not just their words. Too often we're so focused on our hurts and hopes that we completely miss the people sitting in front of us (or in the bed, the boardroom, or on the other phone). In his insightful book *Just Listen*, Mark Goulston observes the barriers to others' listening to us, which are also reasons we may not listen to them:

> People have their own needs, desires, and agendas. They have secrets they're hiding from you. And they're stressed, busy, and often feeling like they're in over their heads. To cope with their stress and insecurity, they throw up mental barricades that make it difficult to reach them even if they share your goals, and nearly impossible if they're hostile. Approach these people armed solely with reason and facts, or resort to arguing or encouraging or pleading, and you'll expect to get through—but often you won't. Instead, you'll get smacked down, and you'll never have a clue why. . . . The good news is that you can get through, simply by changing your approach.[3]

Goulston's approach is to learn the art of listening. Among the commonsense but seldom-practiced arts of listening is empathy, that is, mirroring people's feelings so they feel felt, and being more interested in the other person than in yourself. There are many different ways of making people feel valuable, but simplistic statements like "You're great!" don't cut it. Authentic relationships drown in a sea of empty jargon. (Goulston's principles of listening apply in every relationship. I recommend his book to strengthen marriages and staff teams too.)

Revealing

A second characteristic that helps us build real friendships is self-disclosure. Some people give TMI—too much information—too quickly and too often. They assume their courage to be open necessarily leads to a deeper relationship, but perceptive people realize those who are too open aren't really safe. Instead, relationships deepen gradually through a slow dance of self-disclosure—a little at a time, not too much or too little—so that both people feel comfortable, understood, and trusted.

> Intimate attachments to other human beings are the hub around which a person's life revolves.
>
> —John Bowlby

Finding Common Ground

Of course, real friendships seldom happen when people don't have anything in common. Romances may be the attraction of opposites, but friends generally congeal around a common bond: a team to cheer for (or cry over), kids, hobbies, or something else that's important to both. In *The Four Loves*,

Lasting friendships are built on these three pillars: listening, revealing, and finding common ground.

Keeping Friends

Some people make friends slowly and keep them forever; others have tons of friends, but they change with the wind. For busy, stressed-out leaders, keeping good friends is as essential as finding a few friends. When relationships are damaged, we can't always mend them, but we can try. Here are four concepts that can help.

Honesty

I've never known a strained relationship that mended without someone having the courage to say, "Something between us is broken. Can we try to fix it?" Time certainly does *not* heal all wounds. Time usually only hardens the perception that "I'm right and the other person is wrong." Repairing a broken relationship may require only a single honest conversation, or it may need a complete teardown and rebuild. Count the cost to determine if it's worth it. Often you won't know until you've taken the first few steps to uncover the extent of the real damage. (Before then, your negative assumptions may have been exaggerated, or the problem may be much worse than you imagined.)

Begin the conversation with gentle, inviting words. You may feel hurt and compelled to attack, but the other person may feel just as wounded and defensive. Defuse the beginning by expressing sadness over the breach in the relationship and your desire to repair it. Then offer an invitation for dialogue—and listen, really listen, without defending, explaining, or giving advice. Instead, ask open-ended questions. Later, when the vat of suspicion and anger is drained dry, it's time to say, "Thank you for being honest with me. Let's see where we can go from here." Be willing to say, "I was wrong."

Forgiveness

Forgiveness goes against human nature. When we've been hurt, we want either distance or revenge (or *both*). As much as we can and as soon as we can, we need to express forgiveness to those who have hurt us, and we need to ask for forgiveness for anything—and I mean anything—we've said or done to hurt others. Forgiveness is the only thing that salves the pain in our lives and mends a broken relationship. Pastor and philosopher Lewis Smedes commented, "Vengeance is having a videotape planted in your soul that cannot be turned off. It plays the painful scene over and over again inside your mind. . . . And each time it plays you feel the clap of pain again. . . . Forgiving turns off the videotape of pained memory. Forgiving sets you free."[4]

You've probably heard it before, but refusing to forgive is like drinking poison and expecting the other person to die.

Bearing with Others

Stressed-out people are fragile, brittle, and prickly. They aren't usually the most patient people, but keeping friends requires the trait of bearing with people when they are annoying, difficult, and defensive—people just like us! We need wisdom to know when to call a friend on his foolishness and when to let it slide. If it's a recurring problem or one that can cause irreparable harm, we need to step in and speak up and then bear with our friend while he processes what we've said. But more often we need to let mildly offensive words evaporate in the warmth of our love and understanding. If God nicked us for every foolish, selfish, or offensive thing we thought or said, we'd never have a minute to think about anything else. God bears with us all day, every day. His Spirit very carefully picks the moments to convict us. We should do the same with our friends. A lot of the time, we just need to shut up and be supportive. That's bearing with those who are hurt, brittle, or annoying.

Investing in the Relationship

We need to invest our hearts and our time in rebuilding a relationship that has been broken. And if we're friends long enough, misunderstanding and conflict are inevitable. Healing doesn't just happen. In the human body, red blood cells constantly carry nutrients to every part of the body, and when there's a sickness or a wound, the white cells rush the body's healing properties to the site. We invest in the friendship by focusing now on what's good and admirable about our friend—instead of clobbering him in our hearts as we did before we started the healing process. Remember what brought laughter and meaning before the break. Camp out there again, and see if the fires are rekindled.

When we're in pain, the last thing we may want to do is pick up the phone and call someone to ask for help. Everything in us screams, "Hide! Don't be vulnerable! Protect yourself at all costs!" That voice sounds reasonable, but it leads to further isolation, misery, and despair.

When you're in trouble, don't wait. Pick up the phone. Call someone and ask for help. It's essential for your mental and emotional health, and it's necessary for you to be the leader, spouse, and parent you want to be.

Know This

I've never known any leaders who *thrived*—in their roles, in their families, or in their lives—without at least a few trusted friends.

Do This

Do a quick study of your history with friends. Who are the best friends you've ever known? What did they (or do they) mean to you? What would your life be like without them?

Think About This

1. What's wrong—emotionally, relationally, and theologically— with the statement: "All I need is God. God and me, that's plenty"?
2. Why is it crucial for rich relationships to include both being known *and* being loved? What happens when either one is missing? Have you experienced relationships when one or the other was absent? How did it affect you?
3. What are the criteria for selecting a pain partner? What advice would Job, Jesus, and Paul give for selecting one?
4. Are you a good listener? How would your wife, staff, and best friends answer that question about you?
5. Which of the principles of building friendships do you need to apply? How will you do it?

6. Which of the principles of keeping (and rebuilding) friendship do you need to work on? What difference will it make?

   And remember: *you'll grow only to the threshold of your
pain.*

11

IT'S YOUR MOVE

You will never truly know yourself, or the strength of your relationships, until both have been tested by adversity.
—J. K. ROWLING

Sheryl Brady, Sheryl Brady Ministries, Plano, Texas

One of the most life-altering moves my husband and I made occurred when we went to Nashville to plant a church. We had been doing itinerant ministry based in Detroit where my husband's father was pastoring a church. We were both very young and full of life! Things initially started out very well, but Nashville became a kind of Gethsemane for me.

I moved there with all kinds of hope, vision, and expectation. We were building a church and expecting it to be just wonderful. Many successful churches inspired us with ideas we were sure we could implement in Nashville. I was the worship leader. One of my greatest joys was helping the people to prepare their hearts for the word of the Lord that my husband would so powerfully bring. I loved our church. I loved the people. The longer I was there, the more involved I became in their lives. It just felt right. Part of my purpose was to help them find their purpose in life. I wore many hats in this ministry. I was the nanny/delivery service/secretary or whatever I was needed to be. I loved these people, and if they had a problem, I just wanted it fixed. If I could help them get where they were going by becoming a bridge, that's what I wanted to do. At different times, I had needed a bridge, and now I was ready to be one! I just wanted God to bless our church.

Our new church had no financial base outside tithes and offerings, and we were always challenged with financial issues. Many times we had to choose between buying groceries and buying gas to get us back and forth to the services. Times were very hard for us. We pawned everything valuable we had to keep the lights on, the doors open, and food on our table. We were in some of the darkest nights and tightest places we had ever experienced. All I could do was hope and pray that this season of our lives had an expiration date attached to it. It took all the faith I had each day to get out of bed and show up for the fight.

"What fight?" you might ask. The fight to survive! I often read the words of the apostle Paul: "There hath no temptation taken you such as is common to man: but God is faithful, who will not suffer you to be tempted above that ye are able; but will with the temptation also, make a way to escape, that ye may be able to bear it" (1 Corinthians 10:13). I've heard preachers quote this verse for years. Most of the time they were referring to temptation as something strictly related to sin and lust, but these are not the only temptations we face. What about the temptation to quit? To walk away? To lose the faith and throw in the towel? What about the temptation to give yourself the permission to wave your flag of surrender as you are crumbling under the weight of concerns? I was *there*! I was borrowing from Peter to pay Paul. Pouring water in the milk to stretch it. Swimming upstream, trying to hold it all together. Smiling on the outside, but dying on the inside. Preaching faith yet living in fear. Laying hands on the sick yet going home sick myself. Trying to juggle the things I could see, all the while bracing for the things I couldn't see. Trying to navigate and work my way through the land mines of my life. Things that came out of nowhere. Things that knocked the breath out of me. Burdens that blindsided me. Contrary winds that blew in bills, betrayals, and broken dreams in the middle of the night. My home, my family, my mind, my marriage, my ministry—everything about me was hurting, and I wanted to quit! I wanted to give up and become a victim of my circumstances!

If it shocks you to hear me say this, I'm sorry. I know it doesn't sound very spiritual, but it's very human. I don't care how spiritual we are, we all have human reactions to life! I didn't know it then, but what I was feeling wasn't that unusual. My emotions and reactions were "common to man." My husband and I kept thinking that the tide was about to turn, that things were going to get better, all because we knew we were where God wanted us to be. In hindsight, it's almost comical how many things went so wrong, one after another. But often these are the most crucial times for us to let go of our expectations. If we ever want to discover the greatness that God has planted inside us, we have to be willing to rely on Him unconditionally—and not just when it feels good or when we're so desperate that there's no other option. God wants our attention focused on Him so that we'll go wherever He leads us without talking back. In the midst of those moments, it usually feels like the hardest thing we've ever done. But greatness always requires sacrifice to activate it. We should take comfort in realizing that what we sacrifice now is nothing compared to what we're about to gain.

After about a year and a half into the church we had birthed, we began to realize it wasn't going to make it. It was like carrying a child for nine months, preparing for its arrival, setting up the nursery, buying all the baby clothes, blankets, and diapers, giving birth to it, and after all of that, it dies in your arms, under your watchful eye, while being cradled in your tender care. I asked God, "Why? Why did you let me have it if you knew it wasn't going to live? What was the point? What was the purpose? Why did you let me love it? Why the birth pains? Why did it die? How do you expect me to keep on living?"

When my husband and I were working so hard to make our lives and ministry work in Nashville, I remember someone asking, "What are you going to do if this doesn't work out?"

I replied, "Doesn't work out? It *has* to work out! We're here for the duration. We'll be here the rest of our lives as far as we know." We were going for broke, and broke is exactly what we got. Our bank account was broken. Our confidence was broken. Our spirits were broken. Our pride was broken. Our vision was broken. My heart was broken. My body was broken, and I couldn't even afford to go anywhere to get it fixed. I didn't know what was going on anymore. We were doing everything we knew to do. I mean, if we had known a better way, we would've done it. I don't have any real answers as to why the church dwindled and died except perhaps God allowed it to dry up like Elijah's brook, forcing us to move on to the next assignment He had planned for us. Nashville became a grain of wheat that fell to the ground and died, thus becoming the seed that produced the harvest that I am bringing in today.

Later, we realized that we were passing through a training season. At the time I told God, "You brought us here to build a successful church." Later I realized He was saying, "No, I brought you here to build a successful leader." He was teaching me through all those experiences how to be—and how not to be—a pastor. Ironically, He was teaching me how to lead in a place where I would never be given an opportunity to lead. I thought my painful position would destroy me, but it was really just a place for my personal preparation. It was never meant to work there because it was simply a training ground. I fasted there, but it wasn't for there. I served there, but it wasn't for there. I prayed there, but it wasn't for there. And no matter how much I tried to get it to work, it simply would not work there. My husband and I used every ounce of faith we had to make it work, but it clearly wasn't destined to be.

We knew it was time to leave when there was no sign of life in our church. It was over. It was time to pronounce the benediction on that season in my life so I could move on. I walked away from Nashville just as you would walk away from a gravesite. I thought I was through with ministry. I wanted nothing else to do with it. I loved God, but I was just going to be a good member at someone else's church. For a long time I wouldn't even talk about it. I was numb. I felt like a failure. We couldn't even talk about it between ourselves. Sometimes you don't realize how hard you've pushed until it's over. I didn't understand it until God came to me and said, "Sheryl, you have to forgive the process." Never once did I believe I had to forgive God. He does all things well. However, the pain that I went through, the depression, the regret, the mistakes that caused me to make choices that left me feeling like a failure: those things were all wrapped up in the word *process*. I needed to be able to say, "Process, you lied to me, but it's okay. You left the church, but it's okay. You weren't there for me when I needed you most, but I forgive you."

Forgiving the process is a very important step because when we forgive these types of things, God then works it all together for our good. He reveals, "I was just getting you ready for where I needed to take you eventually." I couldn't see where all the pain would lead, but He could. I didn't think I had the strength to endure, but God knew it was there. He knew what was inside me and was cultivating it for when it would be needed most. The whole process and experience were preparation for a future role.

There is a promise over our lives that God wants to bring to pass, but He often has to take us through a repositioning phase first. It's confusing and heart wrenching because you know you're following Him and His will for your life, but your expectations have been dashed on the rocks of hard times. This is when you must keep going, step by step, day by day. This is when your hungry heart must follow the daily bread crumbs God always gives and accept that you have enough hope for today. These morsels take many forms, from a sense of God's presence during the day to an unexpected kindness from a complete stranger. You recognize them by paying attention and asking God to show you. You may not have enough for tomorrow or ten years from now, but you have enough for today. Eventually you can thank God for giving you the grace to come through the fire without being burned. Sometimes you have to walk with Him for a while to realize just how good He is. Sometimes you have to let some time go by before you can see His purpose in a painful situation. And then, nobody has to tell you to give Him thanks. It's just natural because you know what He has done in your life. Giving thanks to the Lord for all he's brought you through is a wonderful thing. I often find myself simply saying, "Thank you, Lord. Thank you, Jesus."

Thank God for all the "training sessions" you've endured and all the lessons you've learned. Thank Him for the hard ways that the treasure inside you has been uncovered so that you are now fulfilling your divine destiny, becoming all you were meant to be. Thank Him for knowing what you needed even when you didn't know it yourself!

If you're in the midst of a "training session" right now, be encouraged that this season will not destroy you. It will prepare you. As painful as all the blows may feel, cling to God and trust Him to bring you through it. Praise Him for where He's leading you and how well equipped you'll be once you arrive.

Exerpt from *You Have It in You*, Chapter 10,
"Hope for the Hungry Heart," Sheryl Brady.

Pain is inevitable.

Pain incubates.

Pain is indifferent.

The way we interpret and respond to pain throws us into a gear that propels us forward or backward. While pain itself is indifferent, it never has an indifferent effect. Pain will shift you one way or the other. We all have a default mode of dealing with pain: fight, flight, or freeze. It's the way we've dealt with conflicts, threats, fears, and loss all our lives, but our default mode may not be a productive, healthy way to handle pain any longer. Now it's time to change.

Change only happens when our level of desire (or actually desperation) rises above the level of our fears. Pain is a watershed: it can cause us to shrink back into a hole and hope it goes away, or it can galvanize new hopes, new plans, and new passions to learn the lessons it can teach us.

Facing pain may require more courage than we've ever had in our lives. At many different points—maybe even today—I can guarantee that you will reach the threshold of your pain and think, *I've had it! That's all I can take. Get me out of here!* But it's not over. You've simply turned the next page in your life's story of excellent leadership. You're at this moment because you have successfully navigated many types of hurt, loss, grief, betrayal, and complexity. You've raised your pain threshold many times in the past. It's time to raise it again.

Blessings sometimes come through brokenness that could never come in any other way. In reflecting on my own life, I have to conclude that grace has come through me more powerfully sometimes when I have been very dysfunctional and maladjusted.

—Gerald G. May
The Awakened Heart

Common to Us All

The pain you experience isn't unique. Countless leaders in churches, nonprofit organizations, and businesses have suffered the same kinds of hurts and confusion. The answer isn't to try to construct a life that is pain free. That won't happen in this life. Only dead people—and resurrected people—feel no pain.

Leadership necessarily involves pain. The higher you push your pain threshold, the more pain you'll experience. It's true in every field. Look at the photos of U.S. presidents on the day they took office and the day they left. The strains and pains of leading the free world turn their hair gray and put bags under their eyes. The problem isn't poverty. They live pampered lives. They have on-site medical care, the best nutrition, their own plane, and outstanding staff to perform every assigned task. But the pain takes a toll. We may complain that the weight of the world is on our shoulders, but it is literally on theirs.

> We either make ourselves miserable, or we make ourselves strong. The amount of work is the same.
>
> —Carlos Castaneda

Hopefully, the principles and perceptions in this book have helped you to understand the power of pain to destroy and build up, but even more, I hope you've gotten some insights about your responses to different types of pain. You have choices. And all choices are consequential. At some point, you'll stop seeing pain as the enemy and make peace with it. Like Paul, you'll see pain as a surprising source of strength. God's power, Paul learned, "is made perfect in weakness" (2 Corinthians 12:9).

Paul was under no illusions about the difficulties believers face. Just as Christ suffered, his people are called to suffer too. In a letter to the Corinthians, Paul gave a glimpse of God's purposes for our past, present, and future. We are "unadorned clay pots" containing "God's incomparable power" in us. With this brutal realism and steadfast hope, we can find God's heart even in the deepest darkness. Paul explained,

> We've been surrounded and battered by troubles, but we're not demoralized; we're not sure what to do, but we know that God knows what to do; we've been spiritually terrorized, but God hasn't left our side; we've been thrown down, but we haven't broken. What they did to Jesus, they do to us—trial and torture, mockery and murder; what Jesus did among them, he does in us—he lives! Our lives are at constant risk for Jesus' sake, which makes Jesus' life all the more evident in us. While we're going through the worst, you're getting in on the best! (2 Corinthians 4:7–12, MSG)

When we experience the goodness and greatness of God in our most painful moments, people around us—family and friends, believers and unbelievers, strangers and enemies—notice and are amazed at the presence of Christ in us!

But that's not all. Paul doesn't just look at the painful past or the purposeful present; he also points to a glorious future. No matter how much heartache we endure, we have hope that God will make sense of it all. He concluded:

> So we're not giving up. How could we! Even though on the outside it often looks like things are falling apart on us, on the inside, where God is making new life, not a day goes by without his unfolding grace. These hard times are small potatoes compared to the coming good times, the lavish celebration prepared for us. There's far more here than meets the eye. The things we see now are here today, gone tomorrow. But the things we can't see now will last forever. (2 Corinthians 4:16–18, MSG)

When we believe this—not just in our words but in the depths of our hearts—we'll be able to withstand far more pain. Our threshold will rise, and we'll be far better leaders.

Expect Even More

Do you want to be strong in God's grace and power? Make peace with the pain God sends your way. Recognize it as a springboard for growth and a platform for greater effectiveness. You'll need it. God has much more in store for you.

In sports, when teams get to the play-offs, the games that really matter, many players are suffering the greatest pains of the season. In every sport—the NBA, the NFL, the World Cup, MLB, and in all sports at all levels of competition—players are battered at the end of the regular season. But now they stand on the precipice of a championship. They've played hard for months, and they're nicked, bruised, strained, and even broken—but they've dreamed and worked hard to make the play-offs. They wouldn't miss it for the world! Even in the play-offs, they may not be in bad shape for the first game, but each game multiplies their injuries. By the time they get to the championship game, many of them can barely walk. But they keep playing, refusing to be taken out. They lay it all on the line for the goal of winning a trophy.

In one of the most amazing feats in sports history, Chicago Bulls star Michael Jordan woke up in the middle of the night before a crucial play-off game. He had the flu. He excused himself from the morning practice. As game time approached, he was dehydrated and weak. He had lost several pounds. He dragged himself out of bed. His teammate Scottie Pippen later said, "The way he looked, there's no way I thought he could even put on his uniform. I'd never seen him like that. He looked bad—I mean really bad."

Jordan sat in a dark room near the locker room. He visualized himself playing the game: running, shooting, and passing. He staggered to the locker room, put on his uniform, and told his coach, "I can play."

During a first-quarter time-out, Jordan bent over, closed his eyes, and almost fell to the floor. A few minutes later he slumped into a chair on the sideline. Somehow Jordan kept playing, and somehow he scored. Incredibly, he put up thirty-eight points that night, including the game-winning shot with seconds to go.

After the game, Jordan explained, "That was probably the most difficult thing I've ever done. I almost played myself into passing out just to win a basketball game. If we had lost, I would have been devastated."

His coach said, "Because of the circumstances, with this being a critical game in the finals, I'd have to say this is the greatest game I've seen Michael play. Just standing up was nauseating for him and caused him dizzy spells. This was a heroic effort, one to add to the collection of efforts that make up his legend."

Pippen added, "He's the greatest, and everyone saw why tonight."[1]

Are we playing for anything less? Paul compared our willingness to endure the pain of following Christ to the pain of athletic discipline: "Do you not know that in a race all the runners run, but only one gets the prize? Run in such a way as to get the prize. Everyone who competes in the games goes into strict training. They do it to get a crown that will not last, but we do it to get a crown that will last forever" (1 Corinthians 9:24–25).

This perspective doesn't minimize the pain we endure as leaders. It puts it in context. Paul sometimes went into elaborate detail to describe how he had suffered, and Luke tells us much more about the beatings, torture, and opposition he witnessed as he followed Paul on his journeys. The pain is intense. There's no denying that. But another layer of meaning is added: God is using it, even if it makes no sense at the time, for a greater purpose.

> We should be astonished at the goodness of God, stunned that He should bother to call us by name, our mouths wide open at His love, bewildered that at this very moment we are standing on holy ground.
>
> —Brennan Manning

The Crucible of Humility

This leadership journey can often be lonely, so we need to make sure we find at least a pain partner or two to help us carry the load. When we feel burdened and alone, we become either pitiful or furious—and some of us can be both in the same hour. We need someone to remind us that pain is inevitable, incubates, and is indifferent and that God is raising our pain threshold so we can be even more effective.

Self-pity isn't humility. It's the opposite of humility. It screams for people to look at us and notice how much we've suffered. Humility is the bedrock security that doesn't demand or expect applause or recognition. The essence of genuine humility isn't thinking less of ourselves but thinking of ourselves less. Pain has the power to crush us, but what's left in the bottom of the crucible? Is it someone who is angry, resentful, and self-absorbed, or is it someone who has met Christ there, experienced his grace in a new way, and been transformed and freed by the encounter with pain?

When we think of powerful leaders, perhaps the last character quality we imagine is humility. History is punctuated by leaders at the helm of military conquests, political revolutions, and industrial advances who changed nations and the world. Machiavelli's famous quote is, "It's better to be feared than loved." Raw power, though, has its limitations, especially for those who aspire to be spiritual leaders.

For leaders the choice isn't between being powerful or weak; the choice is between using your talents to exploit people for your own ends or to use them for the greater good. Leaders who are both powerful and humble are rare, but they have a profound impact on everyone in their organization. They value each person from the lowest cleaning staff to the executive suite. This is the kind of leader people love to follow. This is the kind of leader they believe in even when times are tough. This is the kind of leader who marshals the efforts of everyone to accomplish more than anyone dreamed possible. This kind of leadership begins with humility.

Paying It Forward

Those around you are sponges soaking up your attitudes about life. Your spouse and children, your friends, your team, your church members, your neighbors, and your community are eager to see how you handle the many pains life and leadership throw at you. For them, you are a sentinel of hope—not of perfection but of the genuine hope that a mere mortal can suffer terribly and come out on the other side with more joy, love, and purpose than ever before. We desperately need people with this kind of hope. The path through the storms may be dark and confusing, but we can trust that God is with us, holding our hands even when we don't sense his presence.

> God wants us to choose to love him freely, even when that choice involves pain, because we are committed to him, not to our own good feelings and rewards. He wants us to cleave to him, as Job did, even when we have every reason to deny him hotly.
>
> —Philip Yancey, *Where Is God When It Hurts?*

A few years ago Philip Yancey was driving home on a slippery winter highway. He lost control of his car and crashed. When emergency personnel arrived, they discovered he had a broken neck. They told him that a piece of bone could at any moment pierce an artery and kill him. He realized he might have only minutes to live. He lay strapped to the backboard for seven hours before doctors told him he was out of danger. Yancey said that during those hours of pain and fear, he incessantly pondered three questions:

- Who do I love?
- What have I done with my life?
- Am I ready for whatever is next?

He reflected, "I should have been living in light of those ultimate questions all along, of course. It took that concentration of pain to bring them into focus. Pain is inevitable, yet it can be useful and even redemptive."[2]

Don't run from your pain. Don't deny it exists. It's the most effective leadership development tool the world has ever known. You'll grow only to the threshold of your pain, so raise it!

Know This

You're at this moment because you have successfully navigated many types of hurt, loss, grief, betrayal, and complexity. You've raised your pain threshold many times in the past. It's time to raise it again.

Do This

Describe the differences between self-pity and true humility.

Think About This

1. Why does the temptation to crawl in a hole not work as a strategy to deal with pain?
2. What would it mean for you to make peace with your pain?
3. Describe a Level 5 leader. Who do you know who is like this (or close to it)? What would it take for you to become this kind of leader?
4. How would you answer Philip Yancey's three questions?
5. What are the most important insights you've gained from this book? What are your plans to implement them (if you haven't already)?

And remember: *you'll grow only to the threshold of your pain.*

NOTES

Chapter 1

1. Elisabeth Kübler-Ross, *On Death and Dying* (New York: Scribner, 1969), 37–132.
2. Paul Brand and Philip Yancey, *The Gift of Pain* (Grand Rapids: Zondervan, 1997), 3–5. Used by permission of Zondervan. www.zondervan.com.
3. Dorothy Clarke Wilson, *Ten Fingers for God: The Life and Work of Dr. Paul Brand* (1966, reprint, Seattle: Paul Brand Publishing, 1996), 142–45.
4. David Brooks, "What Suffering Does," *New York Times*, April 7, 2014.
5. Paul Devlin, "Shelton SportsBeat: NFL, Concussions and Death," Patch.com, May 9, 2012, http://patch.com/connecticut/shelton/shelton-sportsbeat -nfl-concussions-and-death.
6. N. T. Wright, *When God Became King* (New York: HarperCollins, 2012), 198–99.
7. Philip Yancey, *Reaching for the Invisible God* (Grand Rapids: Zondervan, 2000), 69.
8. Among many outstanding books, I recommend *The Healing Path* by Dan Allender, *Leading with a Limp* by Dan Allender, *Where Is God When It Hurts?* by Philip Yancey, *Disappointment with God* by Philip Yancey, *Walking with God through Pain and Suffering* by Tim Keller, *Leading on Empty* by Wayne Cordiero, and *Glorious Ruin* by Tullian Tchividjian.

9. Now Beulah Heights University, www.beulah.edu.
10. Dan Allender, *The Healing Path* (Colorado Springs: WaterBrook, 1999), 5–6.

Chapter 2

1. Fuller Institute, George Barna, and Pastoral Care Inc., "Why Pastors Leave the Ministry," July 21, 2009, http://freebelievers.com/article/why -pastors-leave-the-ministry.
2. Richard J. Krejcir, "Statistics on Pastors," Francis A. Schaeffer Institute of Church Leadership Development, 2007, cited at Archive, Into Thy Word, 2007, www.intothyword.org/apps/articles/?articleid=36562.
3. Dan Allender, *Leading with a Limp: Turning Your Struggles into Strengths* (Colorado Springs: WaterBrook, 2006), 98.
4. Adapted from "Eight Reasons Why Pastors Fail," by Joseph Mattera, May 6, 2010, cited at barryboucher.typepad.com/ministers_matter/2010/05 /eight-reasons-why-pastors-fail-joseph-mattera.html.
5. See, for example, Rebecca Barnes and Lindy Lowry, "7 Startling Facts: An Up Close Look at Church Attendance in America," *Church Leaders*, 2014, www.churchleaders.com/pastors/pastor-articles/139575-7-startling-facts -an-up-close-look-at-church-attendance-in-america.html.
6. Ross Douthat, *Bad Religion: How We Became a Nation of Heretics* (New York: Free Press, 2013), 55–82.
7. Krejcir, "Statistics on Pastors," Archive, Into Thy Word, 2007, http://www .intothyword.org/apps/articles/?articleid=36562.

Chapter 3

1. Richard Swenson, *Margin: Restoring Emotional, Physical, Financial, and Time Reserves to Overloaded Lives* (Colorado Springs: Navpress, 1992).
2. Patrick A. Means, *Men's Secret Wars* (Grand Rapids: Revell, 1996), cited in Bo Lane, "How Many Pastors Are Addicted to Porn? The Stats Are Surprising," Expastors, March 25, 2014, www.expastors.com/how-many -pastors-are-addicted-to-porn-the-stats-are-surprising/.
3. Fuller Institute, George Barna, and Pastoral Care Inc., "Why Pastors Leave the Ministry," July 21, 2009, http://freebelievers.com/article/why -pastors-leave-the-ministry.
4. Richard J. Krejcir, "Statistics on Pastors," Francis A. Schaeffer Institute of Church Leadership Development, 2007, cited at www.intothyword.org /apps/articles/?articleid=36562.
5. Excerpted from *Can You Drink the Cup?* By Henri J. M. Nouwen. Copyright

©1996, 2006 by Ave Maria Press®, Inc., P.O. Box 428, Notre Dame, IN 46556, www.avemariapress.com. Used with permission of the publisher.

6. Cited in Stephen E. Ambrose, *Band of Brothers: E Company, 506t Regiment, 101st Airborne from Normandy to Hitler's Eagle's Nest* (1992, reprint, New York: Simon & Schuster, 2001), 203.

7. Mae Mills Link and Hubert A. Coleman, *Medical Support of the Army Air Forces in World War II* (Washington DC: Office of the Surgeon General, Department of the Air Force, 1955), 851.

8. Ivan Maisel, "Archie Manning faces family history," ESPN.com, September 24, 2013, http://espn.go.com/college-football/story/_/id/9716260 /spurred-book-manning-archie-manning-reluctantly-embraces-legacy.

9. Jon Saraceno, "Through aches and pains, Minnesota Vikings QB Brett Favre still driven by dad," *USA Today*, December 17, 2009, http://archive .greenbaypressgazette.com/article/20091217/PKR01/91217175/Through -aches-pains-Minnesota-Vikings-QB-Brett-Favre-still-driven-by-dad.

10. J. I. Packer, *Knowing God* (Downers Grove, IL: InterVarsity, 1973), 221–23.

11. Mayo Clinic Staff, "Diseases and Conditions: Dysthymia," www.mayo clinic.org/diseases-conditions/dysthymia/basics/definition/con-20033879.

12. "Silent Suffering: Pastors and Depression," Church Leaders, www.church leaders.com/?news=144651.

13. Packer, *Knowing God*, 227.

14. Gary L. McIntosh and Samuel D. Rima Sr., *Overcoming the Dark Side of Leadership: The Paradox of Personal Dysfunction* (Grand Rapids: Baker, 1997).

15. Sam Ranier, "What Happens When Leaders Go Numb," *Church Leaders*, www.churchleaders.com/pastors/pastor-articles/172466-sam-rainer -happens-when-leaders-go-numb.html.

16. Quoted by Chris Huff, "The Key Is the Key," March 25, 2014, http://chrishuff .net/2014/03/25/the-key-is-the-key/.

Chapter 4

1. James MacDonald, "The Cross of Leadership," *Church Leaders*, www.church leaders.com/pastors/pastor-articles/151532-james-macdonald-the-cross-of -leadership.html.

2. Carl F. George, *How to Break Growth Barriers: Capturing Overlooked Opportunities for Church Growth* (Grand Rapids: Baker, 1993).

3. Nelson Searcy, "Growing Pains," *Church Leaders*, www.churchleaders.com /pastors/pastor-articles/138767-growing-pains.html.

4. Searcy, "Growing Pains."

5. Eugene H. Peterson, *The Jesus Way: A Conversation on the Ways That Jesus Is the Way* (Grand Rapids: Eerdmans, 2007), 22.

6. For more about Scott's efforts, see *Ready, Set, Grow: Three Conversations That Will Bring Lasting Growth to Your Church* (Springfield, MO: My Healthy Church, 2013).

7. Branimir Schubert, "Organizational Pain," *Christianity Today*, ©2007 Christianity Today International. Used by permission of *Leadership Journal*. www.leadershipjournal.net.

8. Joseph Mattera, "Why Pain Comes Before Promotion," August 1, 2013, www.coalitionofapostles.com/why-pain-comes-before-promotion.

Chapter 5

1. Drew Hendricks, "8 Signs You're an Entrepreneur," *Forbes*, November 29, 2013, www.forbes.com/sites/drewhendricks/2013/11/29/8-signs-youre-an -entrepreneur/2.

2. John Ortberg, *Overcoming Your Shadow Mission* (Grand Rapids: Zondervan, 2008), 35. Used by permission of Zondervan. www.zondervan.com.

3. Ortberg, *Overcoming Your Shadow Mission*, 36.

4. Mark Love, "These Are Your Pastor's Secrets: Read Slowly," *Church Leaders*, www.churchleaders.com/worship/worship-articles/169791-mark -love-your-pastors-secrets-read-slowly.html.

5. Henri Nouwen, *Bread for the Journey: A Daybook of Wisdom and Faith* (San Francisco: Harper SanFrancisco, 1997), April 3.

6. A. W. Tozer, *The Root of the Righteous* (Harrisburg, PA: Christian Publications, 1955), 47.

Chapter 6

1. Neal E. Boudette, "GM CEO to Testify Before House Panel," *Wall Street Journal*, June 17, 2014, cited at online.wsj.com/articles/gm-ceo-to-testify -before-congressional-subcommittee-wednesday-1403021529.

2. Ibid.

3. Adapted from Samuel R. Chand, *Cracking Your Church's Culture Code: Seven Keys to Unleashing Vision and Inspiration* (San Francisco: Jossey-Bass, 2011), 144–145.

4. Eric T. Wagner, "Five Reasons 8 out of 10 Businesses Fail," *Forbes*, September 12, 2013, www.forbes.com/sites/ericwagner/2013/09/12/five-reasons-8-out -of-10-businesses-fail.

5. Sandra Sanger, "The Illusion of Control," World of Psychology, psychcentral .com/blog/archives/2011/10/03/the-illusion-of-control.

6. Timothy Keller, *Walking with God Through Pain and Suffering* (New York: Dutton, 2013), 163.

Chapter 7

1. Katie Arnold, "Drafting Dean: Interview Outtakes," *Outdoor*, December 8, 2006, www.outsideonline.com/outdoor-adventure/running/Drafting -Dean--Interview-Outtakes.html.
2. Michael Hyatt, "Why Discomfort Is Good for You," Intentional Leadership, December 19, 2011, michaelhyatt.com/why-discomfort-is-good-for-you.html.
3. Robert I. Sutton, "How Bad Apples Infect the Tree," *New York Times*, November 28, 2010, http://www.nytimes.com/2010/11/28/jobs/28pre.html ?_r=0.
4. From Samuel R. Chand, *Cracking Your Church's Culture Code: Seven Keys to Unleashing Vision and Inspiration* (San Francisco: Jossey-Bass, 2011), 5–6.
5. Craig Groeschel, "You're an Idiot!" February 22, 2011, cited at http:// tonymorganlive.com/2007/02/22/c3-craig-groeschel.
6. John Newton, "I Asked the Lord That I Might Grow," Olney Hymns (London: W. Oliver, 1779), cyberhymnal.org/htm/i/a/iaskedtl.htm.

Chapter 8

1. Larry Crabb, *Finding God* (Grand Rapids: Zondervan, 1993), 18. Used by permission of Zondervan. www.zondervan.com.
2. Craig Groeschel, "Creating a Culture of Self-Awareness," willfjohnston .com/2012/11/15/craig-groeschel-creating-a-culture-of-self-awareness -catalyst-one-day.

Chapter 9

1. Fuller Institute, George Barna, and Pastoral Care Inc., "Why Pastors Leave the Ministry," July 21, 2009, http://freebelievers.com/article/why -pastors-leave-the-ministry.
2. See J. D. Greear, "Why You Should Pray for Your Pastor, and President Obama," Archives for Leadership, www.jdgreear.com/my_weblog/category /leadership/page/10.
3. Jeff Z. Klein and Stu Hackel, "Slap Shot: Playing When It Hurts Till a Playoff Run Ends," *New York Times*, May 29, 2011, query.nytimes.com /gst/fullpage.html?res=9B06E1DF163DF93AA15756C0A9679D8B63.
4. Gina Kolata, "How to Push Past the Pain, as the Champions Do," *New York Times*, October 18, 2010, www.nytimes.com/2010/10/19/health /nutrition/19best.html?pagewanted=all&_r=0.
5. Ibid.
6. Ibid.
7. Ibid.

8. Associated Press, "Former Rep. Jesse Jackson, Jr. sentenced to 30 months in prison," August 14, 2013, www.foxnews.com/politics/2013/08/14 /former-rep-jesse-jackson-jr-to-be-sentenced/.

9. Associated Press, "Son's Woes weigh heavily on the Rev. Jesse Jackson," *USA Today*, December 1, 2012, www.usatoday.com/story/news /politics/2012/12/01/jesse-jackson-jr-jesse-jackson/1738899/.

10. Seth Barnes, "Where Is God When I'm in Pain?" *Church Leader*, www .churchleaders.com/pastors/pastor-articles/175028-seth-barnes-god -when-im-in-pain.html. Used by permission.

11. Bob Gass, "Resilient People," www.convergingzone.com/ricciardelli/resilient -people-by-bob-gass/.

12. Wayne Cordiero with Frances Chan and Larry Osborne, *Sifted: Pursuing Growth Through Trials, Challenges, and Disappointments* (Grand Rapids: Zondervan, 2012), 10. Used by permission of Zondervan. www.zondervan.com.

13. Cordiero, *Sifted*, 31–32.

14. J. R. Briggs, "Transforming Failure," *Leadership Journal*, Spring 2014, 21–24.

15. Paraphrased by Tim Keller, "Arguing About the Afterlife" (sermon), July 1, 2001.

Chapter 10

1. Anugrah Kumar, "Nearly 3 in 4 Pastors Regularly Consider Leaving due to Stress, Study Finds," *Christian Post*, June 21, 2014, www.christianpost. com/news/nearly-3-in-4-pastors-regularly-consider-leaving-due-to-stress -study-finds-121973.

2. Bob Buford, "The Cuts Make the Key—The Power of Metaphors," October 8, 2013, leadnet.org/my_next_book_year_9_chapter_11_the _cuts_make_the_key_the_power_of_meta/.

3. Mark Goulston, *Just Listen: Discover the Secret of Getting Through to Absolutely Anyone* (New York: American Management Association, 2010), 7–8.

4. Lewis Smedes, "Forgiveness: The Power to Change the Past" *Christianity Today*, ©1983 Christianity Today International. Used by permission of *Leadership Journal*. www.leadershipjournal.net.

Chapter 11

1. Rick Weinberg, "79: Jordan battles flu, makes Jazz sick," ESPN.com, sports.espn.go.com/espn/espn25/story?page=moments/79.

2. Quoted in Jonathan Merritt, "Bestselling author Philip Yancey on how to find God in tragedy," Religious News Service, February 17, 2014, jonathan merritt.religionnews.com/2014/02/17/bestselling-author-philip-yancey -find-god-tragedy.

ABOUT THE AUTHOR

As a Dream Releaser Dr. Sam Chand serves Pastors, ministries, and businesses as a Leadership Architect and Change Strategist. Dr. Chand has served as senior Pastor, college President, Chancellor and President Emeritus.

He personally consults, mentors and coaches some of the country's largest church Pastors, speaks regularly at leadership conferences, churches, corporations, Leadership Roundtables, Ministers Conferences, seminars, and other leadership development opportunities. He was named in the top thirty global leadership Gurus list.

His singular vision for his life is to Help Others Succeed. Dr. Chand develops leaders through Leadership Consultations, Leadership Resources—books/CDs, and Leadership Speaking. Leaders are using Dr. Chand's books as handbooks worldwide in leadership development.

Being raised in a pastor's home in India has uniquely equipped Dr. Chand to share his passion—mentoring, developing, and inspiring leaders to break all limits—in ministry and the marketplace.

SamChand.com

ABOUT DR. SAM CHAND

Who would have thought, when in 1973 "student" Dr. Sam Chand was serving Beulah Heights Bible College as janitor, cook and dishwasher, that he would return in 1989 as "President" of the same college! Under his leadership it became the country's largest predominantly African-American Bible College.

Dr. Sam Chand is a former Pastor, college President, Chancellor and now serves as President Emeritus of Beulah Heights University.

In this season of his life, Dr. Sam Chand does one thing--Leadership. His singular vision for his life is Helping Others Succeed.

Dr. Sam Chand Develops Leaders Through:

- Leadership Consultations
- Leadership Resources--Books, CDs, DVDs
- Leadership Speaking
- Dream Releaser Coaching
- Dream Releaser Publishing

As a Dream Releaser he serves Pastors, ministries and businesses as a Leadership Architect and Change Strategist. Dr. Sam Chand speaks regularly at leadership conferences, churches, corporations, ministerial conferences, seminars and other leadership development opportunities.

Dr. Sam Chand...

- Consults with large churches and businesses on leadership and capacity enhancing issues
- Named in the top-30 global Leadership Gurus list
- Founder & President of Dream Releaser Coaching and Dream Releaser Publishing
- Conducts nationwide Leadership Conferences
- Serves on the board of Beulah Heights University
- Serves on the board of Advisors of EQUIP (Dr. John Maxwell's ministry), equipping 5 million leaders world-wide

www.samchand.com

CONSULTATION

"IT'S NEVER TOO LATE TO BE WHAT YOU MIGHT HAVE BEEN."
- GEORGE ELIOT

Are you at the intersection of
"Where you want to be?" and **"Where you want to go?"**

YOU NEED A DREAM RELEASER
A DREAM RELEASER is what I was built to be.

DISCOVERIES AS A DREAM RELEASER:
- After a certain level, you are finding fewer people who can understand you and your needs.
- After a certain level, you are finding it difficult to identify credible, and trusted counsel.
- After a certain level, your own dreams scare you!

I will be your DREAM RELEASER by serving you in two primary roles:

1. LEADERSHIP ARCHITECT
This is where I hear your dream, understand your vision and context and provide you with a customized blueprint to release your dreams.

2. CHANGE STRATEGIST
All dream releasing entails different levels and consequences of change. I provide you with a detailed step-by-step change strategy.

So, what do I BRING to you?

As A DREAM RELEASER I Develop Leaders Who Reproduce More Leaders

DEVELOPING: Training focuses on the task and is single-focused, whereas development focuses on the person and is multi-dimensional.

LEADERS: People who can see it (KNOW) pursue it on their own (GROW) and help others see it (SHOW).

REPRODUCING MORE LEADERS: A leadership culture with an action bias that makes leadership reproduction a natural process.

www.samchand.com

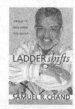